A CURIOUS CALLING

A CURIOUS CALLING

Unconscious Motivations for Practicing Psychotherapy

Michael B. Sussman, Psy.D.

JASON ARONSON INC.
Northvale, New Jersey
London

Production Editors: Bernard F. Horan and Leslie Block
Editorial Director: Muriel Jorgensen

This book was set in 10 point Highland by Alpha Graphics of Pittsfield, New Hampshire. It was printed and bound by Haddon Craftsmen of Scranton, Pennsylvania.

Library of Congress Cataloging-in-Publication Data

Sussman, Michael B.
    A curious calling : unconscious motivations for practicing
psychotherapy / Michael B. Sussman.
        p. cm.
    Includes bibliographical references and index.
    ISBN 0-87668-516-5
    1. Psychotherapists—Psychology. 2. Psychotherapist and patient.
I. Title. II. Title: Unconscious motivations for practicing
psychotherapy.
    [DNLM: 1. Career Choice. 2. Professional-Patient Relations.
3. Psychotherapy. WM 62 S964c]
RC480.5.S83 1992
616.89'14—dc20
DNLM/DLC
for Library of Congress   91-25913

Manufactured in the United States of America. Jason Aronson Inc. offers books and cassettes. For information and catalog write to Jason Aronson Inc., 230 Livingston Street, Northvale, New Jersey 07647.

To my family:
Raquel, Maurice, Paul, and Daniel

CONTENTS

FOREWORD

Psychotherapeutic theory has been open to the revision or casting out of many venerated theoretical ancestors. Certain lingering clinical specters, however, still haunt us. Prime among these are neutrality and the relative indifference accorded to the impact of the therapist's personality. The original therapeutic frame suggested a laboratory-bound, scientific therapist who was sufficiently neutral to fit all types, ages, and conditions and both sexes. Clinical experience has taught us otherwise: contemporary sensitive accounts of transference include the countertransference. Yet there has remained a vast ignorance of the personality of those who attempt the impossible profession of healing minds. It is important to describe this missing link in the interaction of therapy in order to gauge its influence.

The value of this book lies not only in the satisfaction of questions answered, but also in those questions it raises. Consideration of the topics reviewed in this volume will convince the reader of their complexity. Undoubtedly, many further years of research are required to achieve adequate perspective on such complex issues as the optimal combination of the therapeutic pair according to gender, ethnicity, personality, sexual preference, and so on. I suspect that this book will encourage many to pursue this daunting subject of self-study.

A unique and outstanding feature of this volume is found in the chapter containing character sketches (disguised) of psychotherapists. The therapists who have stepped forward and offered us a piece of their lives have provided our profession with a precious gift. With tactful questioning and dignified revelation, Dr. Sussman leads the reader through the privileged portal of understanding. Character is action. Through the example of these psychotherapists, self-analysis is graciously and enduringly etched into our professional image.

Sheldon Roth, M.D.
Newton, MA

ACKNOWLEDGMENT

A major impetus for this study comes from my own experiences as a psychotherapy patient. When I first consulted a therapist, in my late teens, I was entering unfamiliar territory. Like most novices, I felt a strange mixture of excitement and dread. There seemed to be no structure or guidelines, no way of knowing how to proceed or what to expect of the therapist. This unusual state of affairs brought with it a sense of freedom, but also left me wondering: "Just who is this person sitting across from me? Why has he chosen this odd sort of work, and what exactly does he get out of it?"

I imagine that such musings are fairly typical of psychotherapy clients. In my case, however, they were not fleeting thoughts but developed into deep and lasting concerns as I encountered a succession of therapists who by ill chance were particularly idiosyncratic. It was years later, during my clinical training, that I came to understand from a theoretical perspective what I had suspected all along: much of what these therapists did met their own needs rather than mine. Even more disturbing was the realization that this aspect of my therapeutic relationships had remained totally unacknowledged and unexplored. Thus, the difficulties that I confronted in attempting to come to terms with my own problems eventually spawned my interest in the underlying motives of psychotherapists. While I regret having chosen to work with certain practitioners, ultimately I must acknowledge them, for without their blunders and peculiarities I would have never written this book.

My thinking regarding clinical matters has been influenced by the many supervisors from whom I have learned. I would like to thank Stephen Farina, Leonard Horowitz, Sydney Smith, Patrick Dattore, David Beale, David Bellows-Blakely, Vincent Leoni, Frank Schwoeri, William Annitto, Fred Gross, Deena Adler, Ilda Ficher, Herb Walker, Talia Eisenstein, Judith Coché, Naomi Rosenberg, Leslie Poul Melman, Robert Gordon, Anita Bell, Frances Hovey, Andrew Saykin, and Steven Stelzer.

This volume is an outgrowth of my doctoral dissertation, completed at Hahnemann University in 1987. I would like to acknowledge my gratitude to the members of the thesis committee, Pat Bricklin, Jules Abrams, and Ed Volkman, all of whom are currently associated with Widener University's Institute for Graduate Clinical Psychology. I am especially indebted to Dr. Abrams, who encouraged me to return to the topic after dropping it in near despair and switching to one that did not touch so close to home.

Special thanks are due to Melanie Wilson, who played an integral part in writing the dissertation, and to Angel Eberhardt, whose warmth and sense of humor were much appreciated during my years at Hahnemann. During my fellowship at the Menninger Foundation, I received helpful comments and suggestions from Glen Gabbard, Jon Allen, Sydney Smith, and Mary Ann Clifft. Were it not for Dr. Gabbard's urging, I may never have sought to publish this work. I would like to express my appreciation to Sanford Gifford of the Boston Psychoanalytic Institute for allowing me to make use of the library facilities, and to Ann Menashi, the Institute's wonderful librarian. Thanks also to Bernie Horan, Muriel Jorgensen, Leslie Block, and Anne Patota for help in preparing the final manuscript, and to Norma Pomerantz for her enthusiasm and support.

I would also like to thank Sheldon Roth, who has been instrumental in bringing this work to fruition. Unsure of myself, I suggested a collaboration, but he insisted, "No, Michael, this is your book." Although I was paralyzed by the notion that it must be an earth-shaking achievement, he tempered my grandiosity by declaring, "You may yet achieve something earth-shaking in your lifetime, but this won't be it! It will be, however, a *useful* book." Reframed in this manner, a tenacious case of writer's block was swiftly overcome. Both he and Jason Aronson have provided me with a good deal of support and encouragement, as have Jane Fagnant, Jay Smith (who also supplied creative consultation), Marcella Bohn, Ronnie Solomon, Kelly Blight, the clinical and clerical staff at Stoney Brook Counseling Center (especially Judith Schwartz, who was mysteriously linked to a number of fortuitous events), my sister-in-law Jane Sussman, my cousin Karen Sivin, and my brothers, Daniel and Paul. I am deeply grateful to my parents, Maurice and Raquel, for their encouragement throughout my years of training and for instilling within me a fierce curiosity and love of knowledge.

Finally, I would like to express my appreciation to the therapists who participated in my study and who graciously agreed to be profiled in Chapter 7. There appears to be a stigma within the profession against therapist self-disclosure, not only in relation to clients, with whom such a prohibition can often be justified, but also in relation to students and colleagues, with whom it usually cannot. I admire these therapists who were willing to share material of such a personal and intimate nature in order to further our profession's understanding of an important topic. It is my hope that this volume may contribute to the rejection of such a stigma and add momentum to the trend toward greater openness regarding the therapist's contribution to the therapeutic process.

1

THE FASCINATION
OF PSYCHOTHERAPY

T he road to becoming a professional psychotherapist is typically long and arduous. Having arrived, the practitioner of psychotherapy is often emotionally taxed; the process is frequently characterized by a good deal of anxiety, ambiguity, and doubt. The therapeutic outcome, moreover, is always uncertain, and when progress is made it is often painfully slow to manifest. Given this rather forbidding scenario, it seems remarkable that anyone ever enters what Freud (1937) deemed one of "those 'impossible' professions in which one can be sure beforehand of achieving unsatisfying results" (p. 248). With each generation, however, there emerges a ready supply of individuals who are willing and eager to pursue this curious calling. What, one wonders, are the underlying motivations that provide the impetus for such an undertaking? This is the complex and intriguing question to which this book is addressed.

The picture that has just been sketched is admittedly one-sided, overlooking the many satisfactions that this work may entail. Moreover, students may initially have a limited idea of what they are getting into when they decide to become therapists. Nevertheless, one must conclude that, for certain people, the practice of psychotherapy holds a fascination and appeal that remains somewhat difficult to fathom.

A NEGLECTED TOPIC

In a 1929 paper entitled "The Psychology of the Psychotherapist," Edward Glover comments as follows:

> A cursory glance at the syllabus of any representative body of psychologists is sufficient to remind us how rarely psychotherapists inflict on themselves the discipline of self-examination. Papers on the subject-matter of clinical investigation are as plentiful as blackberries, but only once in a while is the instrument of investigation, the psychotherapist himself, subjected to purposive scrutiny. [p. 1]

Today, more than 60 years later, it cannot be stated that this situation has been fully remedied. The influence of the therapist's personality and motivations on the therapeutic process remains a relatively neglected area of inquiry.

Perhaps the most basic tenet of the psychoanalytic approach to personality is that unconscious motivations play a major role in human functioning and are largely responsible for the suffering that brings many individuals into psychotherapeutic treatment. From the psychoanalytic perspective, any therapeutic approach that neglects such hidden strivings must remain relatively superficial and focus on symptomatic relief rather than fundamental character change. Given the emphasis placed on the importance of unconscious motivations in understanding human behavior, the attention that has been paid in the psychoanalytic literature to the unconscious motivations of the *analyst* seems rather meager.

It is difficult to attribute this state of affairs to any failing on the part of the founder of psychoanalysis. With his publication of *The Interpretation of Dreams*, Freud (1900) set an example that few have lived up to. Freud subjected himself to intense self-scrutiny, courageously disclosing the workings of his own unconscious thought processes as well as his pathological tendencies. Refusing to set himself above those distressed individuals who sought his help, Freud applied the same model of neurosis to studying his own psyche as he did to those of his patients.

It was Freud's honest self-appraisal that enabled him to balance his concept of transference with the complementary notion of countertransference. Although he introduced the term as early as 1910, the concept of countertransference remained relatively neglected until the latter part of this century. Indeed, Racker (1953a) went so far as to liken the status of the concept to that of "a child of whom the parents are ashamed" (p. 314).

Since the mid-1980s the field has witnessed a burgeoning interest in the personal lives of psychotherapists (Goldberg 1986, Guy 1987, Kottler 1986). While such studies may still not be as plentiful as blackberries, there does appear to be a growing acknowledgment of the importance of the therapist's subjective experience. This trend may be related to the fact that the research literature has yet to find strong support for the differential effectiveness of particular schools or techniques of psychotherapy (Dryden and Spurling 1989).

WHY BOTHER?

Perhaps therapists' motivations have been neglected for good reason. Do they really matter? One could certainly argue, for instance, that automobile mechanics do not need to know why they chose to fix cars for a living in order to perform adequately. Why should psychotherapists be any different? Well, to begin, humans are far more complex than cars, and human interactions can be exceedingly complicated and multifaceted. Secondly, introspection is unlikely to provide mechanics with greater understanding of motor vehicles, but it may very well aid clinicians in understanding their fellow humans. A third distinction is that the therapist generally uses no mechanical instruments, no technology. It is the *person* of the therapist that constitutes his or her primary tool. Therefore, the psychological makeup of the individual psychotherapist must determine, to a large extent, the effectiveness of the treatment.

Despite his emphasis on intellectual insight, Freud (1905b) believed that the therapist's personality is a crucial factor in the therapeutic process. He notes: "It is not a modern dictum but an old saying of physicians that these diseases are not cured by the drug but by the physician, that is, by the personality of the physician, inasmuch as through it he exerts a mental influence" (p. 259). Jung (1934) wrote that "the personality and attitude of the doctor are of supreme importance" (p. 160). Based on his research findings, Strupp (1958, 1959) concluded that a therapist's personal influence outweighs the effects of particular techniques on treatment outcome. He found support for the notion that therapists' unconscious attitudes subtly bias their "technical" approach to therapy cases, including diagnostic formulations, prognostic estimates, treatment plans and goals, and the nature of their interventions. Strupp (1959) reached the conclusion that "in the absence of a favorable emotional matrix, no amount of expert technique could shift the psychodynamic balance in the direction of therapeutic growth" (p. 349).

Therapists' backgrounds and experiences can also shape their theories of personality, their views of psychopathology, and their interests in particular patient populations. Using a psychobiographical model, Stolorow and Atwood (1979) describe the influence of life experiences on the theories of Freud, Jung, Reich, and Rank. They propose, for instance, that Jung's personal concerns with feelings of isolation and self-dissolution led to his conception of the collective unconscious. Adler, who grew up in the shadow of an older brother, built his personality theory around the concepts of sibling rivalry and the inferiority complex. Further examples are cited by Kottler (1986), such as the therapist who in childhood lost her mother from cancer and came to view all psychopathology in terms of maternal deprivation, or the social worker who had difficulties dealing with authority figures and was drawn to working with rebellious adolescents.

Late in life, Freud addressed the issue of the personality and psychopathology of the analyst as it relates to the analytic process. In "Analysis Terminable and Interminable" (1937), he points out that no one claims that a physician with lung or heart trouble is incapable of properly treating internal diseases in others. Even so, Freud concedes that the situation is not entirely analogous to the treatment of psychological disorders: "The analyst, on the other hand, because of the peculiar conditions of his work, is really prevented by his own defects from discerning his patient's situation correctly and reacting to it in a manner conducive to cure" (p. 401). One such "defect," it can be argued, is a motivation of which the practitioner is unaware for entering the profession.

Even if the importance of the topic is granted, it might still be asserted that the matter is best left unexamined. The following argument can be made: Is it not enough that there exist individuals willing to learn and practice such a difficult and demanding profession without having to question their deepest and darkest motives? And if all sorts of unsavory dynamics should emerge, might this not produce disenchantment, disappointment, and even cynicism?

But how can psychotherapists purport to dispel the illusions of their clients while protecting and maintaining their own? Furthermore, a therapist's belief in and commitment to the therapeutic process ought not to be based on naive idealism, but rather on realistic appraisal. Psychoanalysis has had a good deal to say about the general question of the role of unconscious factors in the choice of occupation. Whether sculpting is viewed as a sublimation of the wish to play with feces, or surgery as a constructive channeling of sadistic impulses, it is generally assumed that even the most intellectual and sublime activities are powered, at least in part, by primitive instinctual strivings. Is the activity of the therapist or analyst[1] the exception to the rule? Shall we accept at face value the proposition that they are motivated purely by the altruistic desire to understand and to help others? This investigation begins and proceeds on the assumption that such a stance is ultimately antitherapeutic, and that it is only when the practitioner's unconscious motivations are discovered and understood that their destructive potential can be held in check.

A final note is provided by the Jungian analyst, Guggenbuhl-Craig (1971), who comments that no person acts out of exclusively "pure" motives:

---

[1]The terms *therapist* and *analyst* will be used, for the most part, interchangeably.

Even the noblest deeds are based on pure and impure, light and dark motivations. Because of this, many people and their actions are unjustly ridiculed or compromised. A generous philanthropist is almost always motivated, among other things, by the desire to be respected and honored for his generosity. His philanthropy is in no way less valuable for that. Similarly, a social worker strongly prompted by power motives may nevertheless make decisions helpful to his client. But there is a great danger that the more the case worker pretends to himself that he is operating only from selfless motives, the more influential his power shadow will become until it finally betrays him into making some very questionable decisions. [pp. 10–11]

TRANSFERENCE
AND COUNTERTRANSFERENCE

Faced with a succession of analytic patients who became enamored of him, Freud refused to believe that this pattern was merely a reflection of his personal charm. Instead, he was ultimately able to discover the phenomenon of transference, which soon became a central pillar of psychoanalytic theory and clinical practice. Freud (1905a) wrote:

What are transferences? They are new editions or facsimiles of the impulses and phantasies which are aroused and made conscious during the progress of the analysis; but they have this peculiarity, which is characteristic for their species, that they replace an earlier person by the person of the physician. To put it another way: a whole series of psychological experiences are revived, not as belonging to the past, but as applying to the person of the physician at the present moment. [p. 116]

Thus, transference refers to the patient's tendency to displace childhood feelings and attitudes onto the current relationship with the analyst.

Unlike the concept of transference, there is little consensus regarding the meaning of the term *countertransference*. The *classical* definition is the narrowest, referring only to the analyst's transferences to the patient. These responses are outside of awareness, and represent distortions that derive from the analyst's own unconscious conflicts and attitudes. Heimann (1950) introduced the *totalistic* approach, a broader conception of countertransference as consisting of all of the analyst's emotional responses to the patient, both conscious and unconscious. Other authors have distinguished between *subjective* and *objective* countertransference reactions. The former refers to atypical responses to the patient that are attributable to the analyst's own idiosyncrasies and unresolved conflicts. The latter, in contrast, refers to feelings that are realistically induced by the patient's personality, behavior, and transference attitudes. All responses are thought to comprise an admixture of both objective and subjective elements. Some theorists, however, insist that appropriate and realistic responses to the patient should be called *noncountertransference reactions*.

There have also been divergent opinions regarding the clinical value of countertransference. The classical approach views countertransference as a hindrance to treatment; it is rooted in the analyst's neurotic conflicts and interferes with the unfolding of the patient's transference. As with transference, manifestations of countertransference are regarded as an indication that further analysis—on the part of the *analyst*—is needed. Contemporary approaches view countertransference as an inevitable product of the therapeutic interaction, which can provide an important means of understanding the patient. A few writers, such as Maroda (1991), advocate the judicious use of countertransference disclosure, especially during a treatment impasse.

TWO-PERSON PSYCHOLOGY

The therapeutic situation involves an interaction between two complex and multidetermined individuals. Investigation and discussion, however, have focused mostly upon the dynamics and motivations of just one of the collaborators in the therapeutic process, the patient. If the therapist is viewed solely as a detached scientist-observer, then the importance of his or her personality and motives appears to be minimized—although, even so, they might be found to influence which aspects of the patient's material are attended and responded to. To the extent, however, that the therapist is regarded as a participant in a communicative field, and as engaged in an affective relationship with the patient—to this extent the therapist's traits and strivings must be considered crucial.

Few analysts today advocate the degree of anonymity and reserve implied in Freud's analogy of the analyst functioning as a mirror or blank screen, receiving and reflecting back the projections of the patient. (And from all indications, Freud, too, departed considerably from this ideal in actual practice.) In recent decades there has been a clear trend in the psychoanalytic literature away from a patient-centered focus and toward viewing the analytic situation increasingly as a *two-person* situation, involving significant input from both participants (McLaughlin 1981, Stone 1961, Wolstein 1959). The increased focus on the interpersonal aspects and bilateral nature of the analytic process is reflected in the attention given to such concepts as the *therapeutic alliance* (Zetzel 1956), the *working alliance* (Greenson 1967), in the increased emphasis on transference interpretation (Gill 1982), as well as on the importance of the analyst's countertransferences.

In this intersubjective approach, the analyst is no longer the detached observer, but rather a coparticipant whose behavior and personality shape the transference paradigm. Transference and countertransference, in fact, are viewed as reciprocally generating and interpenetrating each other (Greenberg and Mitchell 1983). Such a perspective brings into sharp relief the impact of the therapist's motivations on the treatment process. An interaction between two individuals can only be understood within the context of the aims and intentions of both participants. The patient enters the clinical setting for symptomatic relief and resolution of various presenting problems. The complementary context for the practitioner can be conceived of as his or her motives for entering the profession (Sussman 1987). These are what have brought the therapist into the relationship with the patient, and they will inevitably shape all subsequent interventions.

This contemporary approach to the therapeutic process is more in line with twentieth-century scientific concepts, such as relativity theory and the principle of indeterminacy. Strupp (1959) refers to an increased realization that in psychotherapy, perhaps more than in most areas of scientific investigation, the participant observer becomes subject to the principle of indeterminacy, since it is impossible to make observations in the interpersonal field without altering that field in potentially important ways. To the extent that the therapist is clearly aware of the alterations he introduces, he may adjust and correct for his biases; to the extent that he is unaware of the ways in which he influences the interpersonal process, he is at the mercy of unknown forces and may merely observe and record events which his very operations have brought about. [p. 350]

SELECTION OF TRAINEES

In a discussion of the selection of psychoanalytic candidates, Namnum (1980) points to the issue of applicants' motivations to enter the field as greatly complicating the selection process, and as constituting the single most vital consideration in their evaluation. Similarly, Greenson (1962) views an individual's skills, personality traits, and motivations for entering the profession as the three crucial factors in determining how an analyst works with patients.

Consider, for example, the act of interpretation. Central to psychoanalytic technique, interpretation is the means through which the analyst attempts to bring to light the unconscious significance of the patient's associations, to remove resistances, and to foster insight and self-mastery. Although this is the intended effect, it is clear that the analyst may unwittingly use the act of interpretation for his or her own unconscious ends. An interpretation may fulfill sadistic aims when it is given prematurely or expressed in a way that causes the patient unnecessary pain (Horney, cited in Azorin 1957). It may also serve narcissistic aims, fulfilling the analyst's need to appear wise and omniscient (Marks 1978). Alternatively, it may be used to create greater distance between patient and analyst, functioning for the latter as a defense against intimacy. Yet another of countless possibilities, the act of interpreting can serve to project the analyst's own psychopathology onto the patient (Searles 1959). Certainly any interpretation, no matter how tactfully put, may be experienced by the patient as a threat, in that it involves the possibility of having to change. But whether an interpretation is ultimately helpful or harmful to the patient will to some degree depend on the intentions, conscious and unconscious, of the individual doing the interpreting.

The dangers entailed when therapists are insufficiently aware of their motivations are all too real and have been documented by numerous authors. For instance, in their paper entitled "The Psychiatrist as Wounded Physician," Groesbeck and Taylor (1977) write:

> Only in an approach to the practice of psychiatry that includes the personal equation of potential and actual illness, wounds, or vulnerabilities of the healer himself can one hope to adequately deal with the dangers of this vocation—dangers that accrue to both patients and psychiatric physician. That is, if this personal equation is *not* accounted for, the chances that the patient may not be healed or that the psychiatrist will "catch the illness," or at least have his own wounds aggravated, is greatly increased. [p. 131]

Similarly, Lindner (1978) emphasizes the importance of personal psychotherapy for the therapist "to reduce the danger that unresolved unconscious motivations might overwhelm the therapist and compel him toward choices [of therapeutic orientation and technique] that are less in the interests of his patient" (p. 407). English (1977) also warns that a tragic outcome for a single patient offers only temporary relief to the therapist with unconscious sadistic or masochistic trends, and that, left unexamined, the compulsory need to act them out with another patient recurs after a brief respite.

To cite but one more example, Hammer (1972) discusses the importance of trust and security in the therapeutic relationship. He states that patients can only allow themselves to be vulnerable if they sense that their therapists are free from any major psychopathology, and free of any need to use their patients as objects for achieving their own gratification or for elevating their own self-esteem. Hammer continues:

> Quite often students choose psychotherapy as a career precisely for these reasons. If the student is to really be an effective therapist it

might be well for him to honestly explore his basic motivations for becoming a psychotherapist and thereby be in a position to prevent his inappropriate needs from having a deleterious effect in therapy. [p. 21]

CONSCIOUS MOTIVATIONS

Little attention will be devoted, in the pages to follow, to psychotherapists' *conscious* reasons for entering their profession. Certainly this too is a topic worthy of investigation. It may well be that in order to practice effective psychotherapy certain conscious motivations are preferable to others. Both Sachs (1947) and Sharpe (1947), for instance, warn selection committees not to accept applicants who view a career as psychoanalyst primarily as a way of making a living, insisting that the work demands total dedication. Nevertheless, compared to unconscious needs, it appears that therapists' conscious motives constitute less of a potential danger and also hold less promise in terms of advancing our understanding of the therapeutic interaction. They present less of a risk because, by definition, they do not function outside of awareness. And they explain less because, in general, they conceal more than they reveal.

Take, for instance, the desire to help people. This has been cited as the primary motivation of a large percentage of individuals who practice psychotherapy (Henry et al. 1971). At first glance, this aspiration appears to be an important—perhaps indispensable—attribute of the psychotherapist. Upon further reflection, however, it becomes clear that this is a generalization that tells us little. There are a multitude of reasons why certain persons might wish to help others. For some it may be an expression of compassion, or moral duty, or perhaps even guilt. Others may do it for the sheer pleasure involved, some deriving a sense of power, others fulfilling a wish to feel needed, and still others vicariously enjoying the prospect of receiving aid and comfort. This list is hardly comprehensive, and additional motivations are addressed in the chapters to come. For no two individuals, however, are the needs identical. For each person with a "need to help" there probably exists a unique constellation of underlying motives and aims.

Moreover, the question remains as to why one particular means of helping is chosen over all others. Many individuals become nurses, physicians, chiropractors, social workers, or ministers in order to help people. Why psychotherapy? To answer this, it is necessary to look more closely at the actual interventions or procedures engaged in by the person attempting to proffer assistance. The surgeon helps by making incisions into, and at times by removing, parts of the body. The acupuncturist attempts to aid by sticking needles in the client, the massage therapist by rubbing and stroking the body. Each of these means, whatever their respective merits, can be seen to involve distinct interactions giving rise to specific gratifications for the practitioner. Clearly the choice of the particular avenue of helping must be determined to a great extent by deeper motives underlying the wish to help. Hence the necessity of ascertaining what needs might be gratified by the procedures and interactions that comprise the work of the psychotherapist.

To reiterate, because they tend to be acceptable and therefore conscious, the more "positive" and "creative" motives for practicing psychotherapy are beyond the scope of this review. Nevertheless, it is important to acknowledge that one may overpathologize the urge to help.

SOURCES OF DATA

The major portion of this volume consists of a review of the literature relevant to the topic under consideration, followed by a discussion of the results of a series of in-depth interviews conducted with psychotherapists and trainees. The literature has been gleaned from diverse sources. Various authors, most of them psychoanalytically oriented, address issues that are directly or indirectly related to therapists' motivations and satisfactions. There has also been a handful of empirical studies focusing on the choice of psychotherapy as a profession, as well as the factors involved in medical students' choice of psychiatry as their specialty. Relevant discussions also appear in works that focus on the training and supervision of therapists as well as on the selection of candidates. Finally, there are biographical works that address the issue. While much of the material to be presented is admittedly of a speculative nature, it ought to be kept in mind that the authors arrived at their formulations on the basis of a wide range of data, including personal psychotherapy, experiences with colleagues, and the supervision and treatment of trainees.

FEMALE THERAPISTS

In most of the literature to be reviewed there is a glaring absence of material that focuses specifically on female psychotherapists. This deficiency ought to be considered intolerable, especially in view of the large and growing number of women clinicians in practice. When male authors discuss countertransference issues they rarely touch on gender-related aspects or speculate on the psychodynamics of female therapists. Perhaps even more disturbing is the fact that, with few exceptions, female authors have largely neglected this area as well.

There is a similar dearth of relevant literature that deals with social workers. Formerly referred to as the "handmaiden of professions," social work has trailed the other mental health disciplines in regard to status, esteem, and remuneration that is accorded its practitioners. In an article entitled "Giving Up Martyrdom," Ephross (1983) notes that surprisingly little has been written about the careers or the inner experiences of social workers, and that biographies and autobiographies of prominent figures in the field are rare. It is probable that a major reason for this paucity is that the profession is overwhelmingly composed of women, who are more likely than men to be socialized into a role of "selfless giver." Ephross also attributes it to the profession's self-devaluation, and to a typical pattern of submerging individual identity in order to advance the work of the employing agency or institution. Whatever the sources of this phenomenon, studies by and about social workers—and female clinicians in general—are regrettably underrepresented in the pages to follow.

THE "FIFTH PROFESSION"

A final consideration involves the selection of the group to be studied. Why has the generic category of psychotherapists been chosen rather than a possibly more homogeneous one, such as clinical psychologists or psychoanalysts? The answer is twofold. First, any such narrowing of focus would have greatly limited the selection of appropriate literature. Second, there is now ample evidence that, whatever professional route is initially taken, those who engage primarily in the work of psychotherapy share a great deal in common. Holt (1971), for example, points to, and argues in favor of, the emergence of psychotherapy as an autonomous profession in which elements of psychiatry, psychoanalysis, clinical psychology, and social work shall be fused. In what appears to be the largest and most comprehensive study of psychotherapists to date, Henry and colleagues (1971, 1973) attempted to determine whether psychiatrists, psychoanalysts, clinical psychologists, and psychiatric social workers are indeed similar enough to constitute a fifth profession—that of psychotherapist. Their research, using both questionnaires and intensive interviews, revealed striking commonalities among therapists of all four specialties with regard to personality development, family background, cultural origin, social class, religious background, and political leanings, as well as the influences on their choice of profession. Based on their findings the authors concluded that a fifth profession does, in fact, exist, despite four distinct training routes, and they question the need for maintaining four different training systems that arrive at essentially the same profession. Given this apparent overlap, it appears unnecessary to limit arbitrarily the focus of this inquiry to one particular discipline.

2

THE ATTEMPT TO MASTER ONE'S OWN CONFLICTS

In their pioneering study of the personality patterns of psychiatric residents, Holt and Luborsky (1958a) state that "psychiatry attracts people who are in the process of mastering personal problems. It may be from this source that one develops an interest in treating people" (p. 66). This notion, echoed throughout the relevant literature, in a sense encompasses the entire array of motivations to be discussed in the ensuing chapters. The basic formulation is that behind the wish to practice psychotherapy lies the need to cure one's own inner wounds and unresolved conflicts.

A reasonable point of departure in investigating this hypothesis is to determine whether those individuals who are drawn to the practice of psychotherapy do in fact exhibit significant psychopathology of their own. If they do not, then such a formulation must be rejected outright. If they do, however, then the notion that personal problems are a determining factor in the decision to become a therapist receives support.

Several drawbacks to this approach soon become apparent. Any emotional difficulties exhibited by therapists may have resulted from the hardships of practicing their profession rather than reflect some factor predisposing them to that career choice. This difficulty can be overcome by studying therapists-in-training rather than established practitioners. Better yet, one may look at *applicants* to training programs, thereby eliminating as an intervening factor the various stressors associated with training itself.

Another difficulty stems from the multiplicity of disciplines represented within the field of psychotherapy. The literature dealing with the psychological makeup of clinical psychology students, psychiatric residents, and psychoanalytic candidates is reviewed in this chapter. Comparable studies concerning those individuals who become social workers, marriage and family counselors, or psychiatric nurses are not available. Moreover, many who enter the fields of clinical psychology and psychiatry do not ultimately become psychotherapists.

It must be noted that the reliability and validity of many of the relevant studies remain in doubt. Most of the findings are derived from self-reports and surveys as well as from clinical and supervisory experience. The self-selection of subjects is common, and the use of control groups is exceedingly rare. Given the various methodological problems, it is best to view results with caution. Nevertheless, the great majority of available reports appear to point in a common direction.

MENTAL HEALTH PROFESSIONALS

Elvin Semrad is reported by Shapiro (1982–1983) to have defined individual psychotherapy as "an encounter between a big mess— and a bigger mess" (p. 24). There is certainly a strong suspicion among the general public that many therapists, and especially "shrinks," are mentally unbalanced. Is there any truth to this impression, or is it mere prejudice born of fear and mystery?

Several studies have suggested that there may be a high incidence of mental illness among psychotherapists. Looney and colleagues (1980) surveyed 263 psychiatrists nationwide and reported that 73 percent had experienced moderate to incapacitating anxiety during their early years of professional practice, while 58 percent experienced serious depression. Bermak (1977) also surveyed psychiatrists and found that more than 90 percent reported that they and their colleagues experienced a wide variety of mental illness. A Swiss study introduced a clever approach by examining the military conscription records of people who later entered various medical specialties. When compared to those individuals who became surgeons and internists, significantly more of the eventual psychiatrists were found to have been declared unfit for military service due to psychiatric disorders (Willi 1983). Deutsch (1985) surveyed 264 psychotherapists representing various disciplines, and found that a majority of them had experienced significant personal problems, including relationship difficulties (82 percent), depression (57 percent), substance abuse (11 percent), and suicide attempts (2 percent).

It is widely believed that therapists commit suicide at a rate that exceeds that of the general population (Guy and Liaboe 1985). The most startling figure is that reported by Moore (1982). In her sample, female psychiatrists committed suicide at a rate forty-seven times that of the general population. Following the publication of various conflicting and methodologically flawed studies on the incidence of suicide among psychiatrists, the Task Force on Suicide Prevention of The American Psychiatric Association initiated its own study of the matter (Rich and Pitts 1980). Investigators calculated the suicide rate for each of the medical specialties during the five-year period from 1967 to 1972. The data indicate that when compared to other specialties, psychiatrists kill themselves at nearly twice the rate expected. When they looked at the statistics for all diplomates of The American Specialty Boards, the frequency for psychiatrists was found to be over twice that expected, whereas no other group of certified specialists was found to have committed suicide at greater than the expected frequency. Applying a method of determining the morbid risk of primary affective disorder in a particular population from the suicide rate, these investigators calculated that nearly one in three psychiatrists should exhibit evidence of affective disorder when a systematic interview is administered. This represents a morbid risk figure, they note, that is approximately three times that of the general population.

There are few reports regarding the suicide rates of nonmedical psychotherapists. Steppacher and Mausner (1973) reported the incidence of suicide among members of the American Psychological

Association between 1960 and 1970. Although male psychologists killed themselves at a slightly lower rate than that of males in the general population, the rate of suicide among female psychologists was nearly three times that of nonpsychologist females.

CLINICAL PSYCHOLOGY STUDENTS

In a collection of autobiographical accounts by contemporary psychotherapists, Ellis (1972) describes his surprise at having discovered that nearly all of his fellow graduate students in clinical psychology had entered the field because of their own emotional disturbances. He recounts:

> They had suffered from anxiety and depression for many years (not a few were practically psychotic), had gone for some kind of psychoanalysis, had decided while being analyzed that they might enjoy doing this type of work themselves, and had picked clinical psychology as the easiest of the respectable ways to get into the field. [p. 108]

There appear to be few empirical studies of the emotional status of clinical psychology students. Kelly and Fiske (1950) carried out an extensive study of clinical psychology interns in the Veterans Administration program. Based on their scores on the Minnesota Multiphasic Personality Inventory (MMPI), male trainees were found to be slightly more subject to depression, far more hysterical, and extremely feminine when compared to the normal male population. In regard to the latter finding, Roe (1956) suggests that this is because they exhibit traits that are usually considered to be feminine in our culture, such as a deep interest in people and a high degree of verbalization. Hafner and Fakouri (1984a) compared the manifest contents of ninety college seniors majoring in accounting, secondary education, and psychology. Students were asked to visualize the earliest incident they could recall, and these memories were then classified according to themes. Psychology students exhibited themes relating to fear- or anxiety-provoking situations significantly more than did the other two groups. In a related study, the same investigators (1984b) compared the early recollec-tions of ninety male university or professional school students in clinical psychology, dentistry, and law. The earliest memories of the psychology students involved significantly more negative af-fect and threatening situations than did those of the other two groups. From these two studies one might infer that students who are drawn to the study of psychology associate greater emotional stress with their early childhood than do students in a variety of other professional fields.

On the other hand, Greenwald (1976) found no significant dif-ferences in the degree of current emotional disturbance between psychology and nonpsychology graduate students and applicants. All of her subjects, she notes, were female.

Emotional difficulties do appear to interfere seriously with the capacity of some graduate students to function effectively in a clini-cal setting. Boxley and colleagues (1986) surveyed APA-accredited psychology internship programs and found an average annual trai-nee-impairment rate of 4.6 percent. Among the most frequently reported factors associated with impairment were personality dis-orders (35 percent), depression (31 percent), and "emotional prob-lems" (31 percent).

Although the great majority of clinical psychology students would not be classified as "impaired," certain authors suggest that a high level of emotional adjustment and stability is far from the norm. In a study concerning the difficulties of being in training and treatment simultaneously, Kaslow and Friedman (1984) inter-viewed clinical psychology graduate students as well as therapists with extensive experience in treating them. Based on these inter-views, the authors conclude that clinical psychology students tend to exhibit significant emotional pathology. They state:

The unusually high standards of achievement by which clinical admissions committees rate their applicants . . . has led to the even-tual acceptance into the field of a high percentage of students whose superior cognitive development is just the visible flag for what one therapist in our sample termed the "superb" false self constructions (Winnicott, 1965) of many clinical students. Some therapists further stated that not only do trainees tend, as a rule, to have more "primi-

tive" internal structures than people in the general population, but
they also tend to be psychologically less intact than most professional therapists who are seen in treatment. [p. 45]

The latter finding was presumed to be due to the advanced age and
greater years in personal therapy of established therapists. In responding to questions regarding career choice, many of the graduate students were found to worry that they were "too crazy" or not
sufficiently bright, and to have developed concerns about the
neurotic nature of their choice.

Finally, in a discussion of the development of psychological-
mindedness in psychotherapists, Farber (1985) makes the following
remarks:

Applicants to clinical psychology programs invariably note that they
have, since childhood, felt acutely aware of the "hidden meanings"
of others' messages and that they have also experienced themselves
as highly introspective, self-probing, sensitive to hurt, and often self-
critical. Many remember feeling lonely and even "different" as a
result of having a perspective that others could not share. [p. 171]

PSYCHIATRIC RESIDENTS

Research focusing on the emotional status of psychiatric residents
has rather consistently demonstrated the existence of significant
personal difficulties among a considerable portion of trainees. In
what appears to be the largest of such studies, the residency training directors of all the active psychiatric residency programs in the
United States and Puerto Rico were surveyed by questionnaire
(Russell et al. 1975). The final sample represented 91.5 percent of
the first- through third-year residents in training for the 1971-1972
academic year. The authors report that greater than 8 percent
"either did not complete their training because of emotional problems or remained in training despite marginal performance, and/or
severe emotional illness" (p. 266). Four of the residents that year
killed themselves, representing a suicide rate of 106 per 100,000—
far higher than the highest rate recorded for any other medical

specialty. The investigators conclude that the problem of the emotionally disturbed and failing psychiatric resident is indeed great.

Two smaller studies reported even higher rates of emotional disturbance among psychiatric residents. Garfinkel and Waring (1981) studied one hundred psychiatric residents at two Ontario universities over a three-year period. They found that 9 percent of the sample displayed emotional disturbances shortly after beginning training. Psychological testing revealed abnormally high scores on the neuroticism scale of the Eysenck Personality Inventory and on the depression, schizophrenia, social isolation, psychasthenia, and hypochondriasis subscales of the MMPI. A longitudinal study of graduates over a twenty-five-year period at one residency found that 13 percent had been psychotic, severely neurotic, or addictive personalities (Garetz et al. 1976).

A number of authors specifically cite the presence of psychological conflict as a central motivating factor in the decision to pursue psychiatric training. In a review of the literature, Eagle and Marcos (1980) found that a number of personality factors appear to predispose medical students to choose psychiatry as a specialty. Included in their list are the following: higher levels of anxiety, greater fear of death, and lower self-esteem. In an attempt to discover whether psychiatrists might be recruited in medical school, Levine and colleagues (1983) conducted an intensive study of thirty medical students. Summarizing their results, they suggest that students with a predilection for psychiatry can be identified at admission, based upon a single discriminating factor: the perception of personal or family problems of a psychological nature.

Finally, Ford (1963) reports on a study in which he collected autobiographical accounts submitted by psychiatry residents over a three-year period. Of twenty-five male residents, twenty-four indicated that they entered the profession in response to an awareness of their own inner needs and conflicts. Based on fifteen years of experience in training residents, Ford concludes that most individuals who choose careers as psychiatrists exhibit underlying emotional conflict that is "often severe but not necessarily of clinical neurotic quality" (p. 476). He sums up the predominant theme in the career choice as "the search for an answer to strong inner drives demanding resolution of conflict about life's goals and purposes" (p. 475).

PSYCHOANALYTIC CANDIDATES

A relatively small percentage of psychiatrists enter years of additional training in order to become psychoanalysts. Those who complete psychoanalytic training could be considered the most highly trained mental health professionals. The considerable amount of time and money required to become an analyst suggests that these are individuals with especially strong needs to advance within their chosen profession. Given that these are among the most highly motivated individuals in the field, and proceeding with the hypothesis that such motivation derives in part from personal difficulties of an emotional nature, it may be particularly illuminating to determine the psychological status of those who enter into psychoanalytic training.

Sachs (1947) was one of the first to dispel the notion that analytic candidates are particularly free of neuroses, asserting that those individuals most attracted to psychiatry and psychoanalysis are the ones with considerable neurotic problems of their own. He writes:

> I must say that I have found the difference between the analyses of training candidates and of neurotic patients negligible. . . . Psychoneurotic trends in our present state of civilization are so universal that a person who is practically free of them or their equivalents is a rare exception, still less likely to be found among those who want to become analysts because the vivid interest in the psychoneuroses, their etiology and therapy, is regularly motivated by one's own neurotic problems, past or present, and more often the latter. [p. 158]

Included in the largest and most comprehensive study of mental health professionals to date (Henry et al. 1971) were 638 psychoanalysts who responded to a questionnaire, and fifty-seven who were interviewed in depth. The results of the study suggest that the wish to resolve personal problems is an important, although initially unconscious, motivation for seeking analytic training. The authors state:

> Many psychoanalysts (and, indeed, many members of the other mental health professions) who, at the time they began their own

analyses, thought they were doing so for professional reasons only report "discovering" later that personal reasons also dictated this decision. Most likely this is also true for psychoanalysts' decisions to begin analytic training. [p. 134]

Khan (1974), who also insists that the wish for self-cure is of primary importance, goes so far as to suggest that "[individuals who] are content to be helped with their problems seek treatment; those who seek a cure demand training" (p. 117).

The same conclusion is put forward by Keller and Schneider (1976), reporting the results of a longitudinal study conducted by the Dusseldorf Research Institute for Psychoanalysis to investigate the psychodynamics of the initial phase of analytic training. All candidates participated in a series of interviews regarding motivations for seeking training. Based on the interview results the hypothesis was formulated that behind the conscious motivation to become a psychoanalyst, "a deep identity crisis can be found together with the (more or less) conscious wish for therapeutic help" (p. 36). The authors assert that this hypothesis was subsequently verified on the basis of psychological testing, dream analysis, and the observations of training analysts. They conclude that the wish to become an analyst represents a repeated effort to overcome one's own pathology, in the sense of a deficient ego and identity development.

Additional support for this position may be drawn from a study on the effectiveness of the training analysis, the personal analysis that every candidate must undergo. Shapiro (1976) had self-assessment questionnaires filled out anonymously by 121 graduates of the Columbia University Psychoanalytic Center for Training and Research. He notes that since the study excluded candidates whose training was incomplete, the results refer to a highly select population—those already deemed "successful" according to the standards of the institute. Shapiro found that the most frequently cited difficulties in training analyses were the candidates' own characterological problems. Nearly half (44 percent) of the graduates reported that problems arising from their own personal limitations or psychological makeup posed "severe" or "major" difficulties. Shapiro states:

Considering the special motivations of persons attracted to psychoanalysis as a life work, the relatively high percentage of personal
pathology acknowledged by this group reflects the degree to which
pain, suffering, conflict, and the wish to understand and master
them can prompt a sustained, even life-long, interest in introspection, understanding, and resolution of conflict. [p. 20]

Shapiro's results were also consistent with Klein's (1965) finding
that two-fifths of the graduates of the same analytic institute presented with severe initial pathology.

FAMILY BACKGROUND

Menninger (1957a) writes that, as children, therapists commonly
experienced emotional rejection, often resulting in a self-image that
was intolerably painful. Repression and subsequent projection of
such feelings, he suggests, can produce an enduring identification
and interest in lonely, conflicted, and unloved people. Based on his
analysis of autobiographical accounts written by prominent clinicians, Burton (1972) concurs with Menninger that professional
functioning serves to compensate for therapists' interpersonal conflicts derived from their families of origin. He views their early
family experiences as sensitizing therapists to emotional pain, as
well as providing motivation for vocational choice.

Several studies provide support for the notion that individuals
who enter the mental health professions tend to have experienced
a high level of emotional and interpersonal stress within their
families of origin. Two such studies focused on how the subjects
perceived their parents during childhood. Frank and Paris (1987)
report that psychiatrists, when compared with nonpsychiatrist
physicians, rate themselves as having been significantly more
disappointed in their parents. Harris (1976) interviewed a small
sample of child psychotherapists and found that they tended to
perceive their parents in negative terms, as having been largely
unaware or unresponsive to their emotional needs as children.

The remainder of these studies looked at various characteristics
of the families of origin. Henry (1966) conducted intensive inter-

views with psychiatrists, clinical psychologists, and psychiatric social workers. Citing such factors as parental death and divorce, maternal illness, lack of contact with peers, and social marginality, he concludes that mental health professionals exhibit personal histories that result in a "special sense of isolation" and "a heightened awareness of inner events" (p. 49). In a survey of psychoanalysts and psychoanalytic psychotherapists, Burton (1970) also found that a high degree of emotional distress in early life was commonly reported. The majority of his sample of forty practitioners came from families with significant problems, most often involving emotional pathology such as psychotic depression, schizophrenia, and severe character disorders. Marsh (1988) found that alcoholism was twice as common in the families of college students interested in social work than in the families of business majors. Finally, in regard to interviews he conducted with the children of psychotherapists, Maeder (1989) writes:

> In conversations, it is truly astounding how many children of psychotherapists spontaneously bring up the subject of their therapist parent's horrendous early life and subsequent difficulties in coping with the family, something they credit with being the critical determinant in their parent's choice of profession. . . . They paint portraits of their therapist parents as exceptionally lonely and unhappy, socially ostracized at school and abused at home, either psychologically or, sometimes, physically. They were people who had been ill at ease with themselves and with others, who sought through association with the world of adults and a retreat into the world of the intellect, and ultimately through the field of psychotherapy to understand and manage their misery and to protect themselves and, later, their families. [pp. 19, 75]

Not every author concurs with such findings. Henry and colleagues (1971, 1973) surveyed all mental health professionals in New York, Chicago, and Los Angeles by questionnaire and conducted in-depth interviews with nearly one hundred from each city. With regard to early family experiences, the authors claim they found nothing that differed significantly from the norm and that could account for the choice of mental health work. This statement is surprising in view of the research findings, and, indeed, others have disagreed with their interpretation of the data. Racusin and colleagues (1981), for example, point to such evidence as the high rate of severe physical illnesses, difficulties in emotional expression, and intense adolescent struggles over independence, suggesting that these results confirm the stressfulness of therapists' family relationships. A major difficulty here, as in most of the literature reviewed, is the absence of comparable data on members of other professions. Lacking such comparison groups, it is not possible to make any confident statements regarding the influence of early background on the choice of psychotherapy as a profession.

HANDICAP OR ASSET?

The presence of significant emotional conflict in those individuals who choose to become psychotherapists raises the ironic possibility that this may be a necessary prerequisite for succeeding in the field. In a discussion of the personalities of psychotherapists, Burton (1972) suggests that many therapists have gone through periods of psychological disorganization and that this may contribute not only to the desire, but also to the *ability*, to cure others. He states:

> The lives of therapists, from Freud and Jung and Sullivan onward, convince me that most therapists experience themselves as closer to the shoals of psychosis than do other people. Their reality is somewhat different than the ordinary; conscious, preconscious, and unconscious fuse for them into a greater integral harmony. Therapists who have psychotic episodes invariably come out of them with greater ego strength than they had before and then develop more intense rapport with their clients. [p. 20]

The image of the *wounded healer* has a venerable history. Anthropological studies of primitive cultures reveal that before becoming a healer or shaman, an individual must undergo a period of intense distress and illness (Eliade 1964, Lommel 1967). Only by weathering such a crisis of physical and psychological suffering can the prospective shaman gain the power to cure others:

Infringements of taboo bring misfortune, sickness, and death upon men and it seems that an unfortunate, sick man has a greater ability to rectify such infringements of the law than an ordinary healthy man. In any case, there are frequent references to the fact that the shaman must have overcome inhibition and illnesses, that he was or is a sick man, a man in every way underprivileged, a man who began his life with a false start. [Lommel 1967, p. 32]

Lommel's accounts of Siberian shamans contain some intriguing elements. An informant notes that shamans are born in the far north, "at the source of the terrible sicknesses" (p. 55). The future shaman is believed to be cut into pieces and then eaten by the spirits that cause misfortune and affliction. He will later be able to treat only those ailments caused by the spirits who partake of his flesh. During this procedure, the shaman lies in a deep swoon for several days and undergoes a psychological experience of death and rebirth. His suffering is thought to be so profound as to influence his loved ones as well, and in many accounts one or more of the shaman's blood relatives must die for him to come into his full powers. If the individual himself does not achieve psychic rebirth through overcoming this mental sickness, the result is insanity or death.

The image of the wounded healer appears to transcend time and place. Meier (1967) points to a tradition stemming from ancient Greece in which doctors were considered able to heal precisely because of their own illnesses. The Greeks regarded the divine physician as both the sickness and the cure. Meier explains: "Because he was the sickness, he himself was afflicted (wounded or persecuted like Aesculapius or Trophonius) and because he was the divine patient he also knew the way to healing" (p. 5). The healer is able to obtain the knowledge of life and death, yet is unable to use it to heal his own incurable wound.

In a similar vein, Guggenbuhl-Craig (1971) traces the archetype of the wounded healer to Greece and beyond:

Chiron, the Centaur who taught Aesculapius the healing arts, himself suffered from incurable wounds. In Babylon there was a dog-goddess with two names: as Gusa she was death and as Labartu, healing.

In India Kali is the goddess of pox and at the same time its cure. . . .
Jesus Christ was wounded and bore the sins of man. He came to heal
the world of sin and death yet he bore all sins and had to die. [pp. 91,
100]

Jung (1946) appears to follow in this tradition when he suggests
that the therapist needs to be vulnerable to the patient's illness in
order to be of help. By voluntarily involving themselves with their
patients' psychic suffering, Jung indicates, therapists expose themselves to the overpowering contents of their patients' unconscious
thought processes. Jung views this as an "unconscious infection"
(p. 176), which brings with it the real possibility that the illness is
transferred to the therapist by activating his or her own latent
conflicts. He remarks:

> The more one sees of human fate and the more one examines its
> secret springs of actions, the more one is impressed by the strength
> of the unconscious motives and by the limitations of free choice. The
> doctor knows—or should know—that he did not choose his career
> by chance; and the psychotherapist in particular should clearly un-
> derstand that psychic infections, however superfluous they seem to
> him, are in fact the predestined concomitants of his work, and thus
> fully in accord with the instinctive disposition of his own life. [p. 72]

Jung goes on to suggest that by coming to this realization, the
therapist approaches the patient as someone who holds personal
meaning to him, thereby creating the optimal conditions for treatment.

More recently, research on child psychotherapists by Poal and
Weisz (1989) supported their hypothesis that therapists who faced
numerous problems in childhood were especially effective in empathizing with and assisting their clients. It is of interest that this
enhanced therapeutic efficacy did not depend on a match between
the specific problems of client and therapist. The authors conclude:
"This pattern of findings suggests that it may be broad, general
experience in having confronted and coped with childhood problems that enhances therapist effectiveness, not experience linked to
some specific type of problem" (p. 205).

This question of the therapist's personal pathology takes on practical significance in the literature dealing with the selection of candidates for analytic training. Two early authorities on this subject, Sharpe and Sachs, indicate somewhat tentatively that the presence of neurotic difficulties in an applicant does not necessarily constitute a handicap. Sharpe (1947) states that she does not view an unstable personality as automatically disqualifying an individual from the ranks of psychoanalysts. She suggests, in fact, that such disequilibrium may allow for a perspective unavailable to those who are more stable. She writes: "As with many a painter, poet, or great scientist, his very brilliance is inseparable from his deep malaise, his insight coming from depths of the personality inaccessible to the more robust or protected psyche" (p. 115).

While stopping short of recommending that candidates be required to have neurotic difficulties, Sachs (1947) does suggest that when present they may allow for greater intuitive understanding and empathy for the mentally disturbed. Sachs asserts that it comes down to a question of degree, rather than an either/or choice. He proposes that candidates ought to have neither too great nor too limited a degree of psychopathology. On the one hand, the suitable applicant ought to have an intact ego, with no sign of psychotic or antisocial tendencies, nor any significant addictions or perversions. On the other hand, Sachs suggests that certain individuals are paradoxically unfit to function as analysts because they are too well adapted to reality and lack neurotic symptoms. This is the result, he states, of massive repression of psychic conflicts, leaving the individual without access to or understanding of her or his unconscious. Sachs further rules out such candidates by adding that to analyze and break through their resistance amounts to a "superhuman task," and that any attempt to teach them the language of the unconscious "is like discussing color schemes with the blind" (p. 161).

In the ensuing years, this position was reiterated and augmented. Nielson (1954) describes as the general consensus that institutes should not accept candidates who do not feel the need for personal analysis—that is, that the candidate "must have some sort of neurosis and know it" (p. 247). He concurs that it is difficult or impossible to analyze very stable and well-adapted individuals because the impetus for analysis is personal suffering. Stone (1961) also claims that a genuine analysis can only be motivated by the suffering and need for help of the patient, and can never be primarily investigative, exploratory, or educational. This criterion would appear to rule out a proper training analysis for those largely free of neurotic suffering.

Holt and Luborsky (1958b) solicited the opinions of a nationwide sample of analysts involved in selection. According to the respondents, among the qualities to be sought in applicants is a history that includes such experiences as childhood traumas, early childhood illness of self or sibling, a severe illness of the mother during latency, and a stormy, rebellious adolescence.

Based on ten years' experience of serving on the admissions committee of the New York Psychoanalytic Institute, Eisendorfer (1959) asserts that a prime consideration in determining the suitability of applicants involves the degree of perception of inner conflicts, as well as the awareness that their need to treat others stems from a personal need for self-therapy. He emphasizes that an inability to dispense with a "facade of normality" indicates a lack of sensitivity, a deficient emotional awareness, and often, a coverup of chronic pathology.

In a survey of psychoanalytic education in the United States, Lewin and Ross (1960) conclude that a certain amount of neurosis is inevitable, is not a deterrent, and, if mastered through the personal analysis, may be an asset. And in a critical review of the literature on the selection of candidates, Greenacre (1961) also concludes that the majority opinion is that neurosis, as long as it is analyzable, is not a handicap. Rather, she suggests, it "might furnish effective motivation and add to psychoanalytic sensitivity" (p. 53).

In conclusion, there appears to be a broad consensus that, regardless of primary discipline, a major determinant for becoming a therapist involves the conscious and/or unconscious wish to resolve one's own emotional conflicts. Those who choose to enter the profession typically manifest significant psychopathology of their own, which, if sufficiently understood and mastered, may actually enhance their ability to understand and help their clients. From this perspective, personal suffering is a prerequisite for the development of the empathy and compassion that characterize competent therapists. Yalom (1989) writes:

Patienthood is ubiquitous; the assumption of the label is largely arbitrary and often more dependent on cultural, educational, and economic factors than on the severity of pathology. Since therapists, no less than patients, must confront these givens of existence, the professional posture of disinterested objectivity, so necessary to scientific method, is inappropriate. We psychotherapists simply cannot cluck with sympathy and exhort patients to struggle resolutely with their problems. Instead, we must speak of us and our problems, because our life, our existence, will always be riveted to death, love to loss, freedom to fear, and growth to separation. We are, all of us, in this together. [p. 14]

3

SATISFACTIONS AND PSYCHOLOGICAL BENEFITS DERIVED FROM THE PRACTICE OF PSYCHOTHERAPY

One way to assess an individual's motivations for undertaking a particular activity is to determine what that person derives from performing it. For example, we may initially be perplexed by someone who willingly jumps from an airplane at 15,000 feet. Our bewilderment is considerably reduced, if not eliminated, upon learning that this person is a parachutist and experiences intense excitement and exhilaration from engaging in this hair-raising sport. Most of what is written about the therapeutic process focuses solely on what the therapist gives and the client receives. After all, it is the client who solicits help and the therapist who is paid to provide it. When it comes to understanding the motivations of the therapist, however, it becomes necessary to turn the tables and ask: What is provided by the client and gained by the therapist?

At first glance, the answer may seem obvious. Rogow (1970) notes that the most common satisfactions anticipated by individuals entering the field of psychiatry include helping people, feeling socially useful, and gaining financial security. But this tells us very little about the gratifications that are unique to the psychotherapeutic setting. Burton (1975) addresses the widespread avoidance of discussion regarding the treatment needs of the psychotherapist, characterizing it as "almost a silent conspiracy" (p. 115). He takes the position that the therapist's satisfactions, largely ignored in the literature, are equally, if not more, important than those of the client, "for the simple reason that the unconscious takes over in extreme therapist dissatisfaction and punishes or even eliminates the client" (1972, p. 2).

Szasz (1956) also points to resistance on the part of clinicians to the recognition of satisfactions derived from their work. He likens the situation to the conventional conception of the parent–child relationship in which the child is generally viewed as the receiver and the parent as the giver, the one who makes the sacrifices. Szasz suggests that both therapists and clients tend to idealize the role of the therapist as the "wished-for parent who labors for his children with no regard for his own satisfactions" (p. 215). Szasz asserts that this conception of both parent and therapist is inaccurate and represents a distortion of the true nature of human interactions. Bypassing the complexities of what is "exchanged" in such dyadic relationships, this approach reduces them to a simplistic formula, according to which A does something for B, or vice versa. Szasz elaborates:

> Further, since it is often difficult to be clear about what B "gets," insistence that A "gives"—and "receives" *nothing*—makes for apparent clarity. Abandoning this simplification exposes us to the anxiety of being much less certain about the nature of the "gains" and "losses" in human relationships than we have been heretofore. [p. 217]

Szasz describes three stages in the development of an individual's conception of giving and taking. The first stage is that of the small child who believes the parent exists only to cater to his or her own needs. In the second stage, the older child now views the parent as entirely selfish and feels that his needs are completely subordinate to those of the parent. The third stage refers to the arrival of a mature notion of mutuality. Turning to the psychoanalytic conception of the therapeutic situation, Szasz submits that an emphasis on transference corresponds to his first stage, whereas an emphasis on countertransference, or the personality and behavior of the therapist, corresponds to his second stage. In sum, Szasz advocates viewing the therapeutic process from a third, more fully evolved, point of view—that of mutuality. And a crucial step in that direction is the acknowledgment of the therapist's psychological satisfactions.

A similar neglect of the gratifications of the physician can also be discerned. McLaughlin (1961) states that the sick individual, suffering from illness as well as wounded narcissism, has a powerful need to idealize the doctor and to project onto him those qualities a child hungers for in a parent. This contributes to the great disillusionment and rage with which society reacts whenever it appears that a physician is practicing primarily for personal gain. McLaughlin adds:

> In our era a more subtle form of society's frowning upon personal gratification for the physician is indicated in the unspoken judgement that the only good doctor is the one busy to the point of exhaustion, and in the expectation that he not readily admit gratification from his work excepting in the guise of joy of healing others. [p. 116]

Singer (1971) points to a consistent theme in the psychoanalytic literature that analysts derive little personal gratification from their work other than financial compensation and the sense of a job well done. All other satisfactions, claims Singer, have generally been suspected of involving countertransference tendencies stemming from the analyst's own unresolved conflicts. While this assessment may be somewhat of an exaggeration, it does not appear to be far off the mark.

It is in her paper entitled "The Psychoanalyst," published posthumously in 1947, that Sharpe attempts to give a full account of the nature of analytic work and the gratifications that it affords. Among those mentioned are the following: a fundamental pleasure in listening, gratification of sublimated sexual curiosity, pleasure obtained from making sense out of what is at first confusing, mastery of the dreads of one's own childhood, and enrichment of the ego by contact with a rich variety of personalities and life experiences.

In a discussion of what he terms the "irreducible and unavoidable satisfactions" (p. 199) of the analyst, Szasz (1956) adds to Sharpe's list. He begins with the pleasure derived from doing useful work and from being needed by others, which is not specific for analytic work. The satisfaction that is unique to such work is the "pleasure derived from the *mastery of conflicts in human relationships* through verbalization and mutual understanding" (p. 207). He likens this activity to the process of "working through" in the patient, and further delineates it as "re-creating situations of interpersonal stress and disharmony and then solving them by virtue of the most 'progressive' forces at our command (i.e., by thinking and understanding rather than by persuasion or force)" (p. 208). Finally, Szasz points to the pleasure obtained from nonspecific human contact, which may serve as a protection from loneliness. He suggests that this satisfaction differs from the others in that it is more avoidable, and also possibly undesirable.

Greben (1975) writes that each individual comes to the profession of psychoanalysis with his or her own expectations. While some expectations are realistic and can be gratified, others are fantasy-based and will be frustrated. Greben mentions the following realistic gratifications: the pleasure of uncovering a mystery and of using one's intellect to solve a complex problem, the gratification of knowing deeply another person, and the satisfaction of aiding in the process of human growth and of releasing imprisoned energies. Among the fantasy-based, and therefore neurotic, satisfactions he includes voyeuristic indulgence, the pleasure of controlling others, and the narcissistic gratification of maintaining an illusion of omnipotence. Greben emphasizes the importance of becoming aware of the forces in oneself and in therapeutic work that threaten to expand the neurotic aspects and to diminish the more realistic and creative ones.

The role of therapist can provide certain benefits in terms of one's social adjustment, involvement, and status. Becoming a therapist can bring an individual recognition and prestige. Kafka (1989) suggests that practicing psychotherapy satisfies generative and altruistic aims, enabling one to express prosocial instincts to aid others and thereby promote the survival of the species. For those who assumed during childhood the stance of "rebel" or "outsider," working as a therapist can represent a constructive application of their prototypical role, and eventually lead to greater social integration (Schechter 1978). A dysfunctional variation of this theme is presented by Guy (1987), who terms it "vicarious rebellion" (p. 18). The therapist is in a position to attack authority and tradition covertly by encouraging patients to disregard societal norms and conventions. As Guy notes, the therapist's vicarious enjoyment of the patient's defiance may not be in the latter's best interest.

A number of authors have indicated ways in which therapists receive something very directly from contact with their patients. Groddeck, a contemporary of Freud's, wrote as early as 1928 that each patient has something new to teach the therapist—regarding both the proper conduct of psychotherapy and the bringing to light of new and hidden aspects of the therapist's personality. He states: "The patient helps the doctor make his unconscious conscious. This is why I believe that the doctor should be grateful to his patient. The patient is the doctor's teacher. Only from the patient will the doctor be able to learn psychotherapy" (p. 221).

Issacharoff (1983) suggests that analysts commonly have a depressive predisposition, and that contact with certain patients can be liberating. He writes: "When our work is stimulating, the depressive core recedes and we are alive in relation to the patient" (p. 41).

A far less charitable view of this process is provided by Guggenbuhl-Craig (1971). He describes the gratifying aspects of "vicarious living" (p. 55) in which patients are expected to make up for the therapist's loss of intimate contact and meaningful life experience:

> The analyst no longer has his own friends; his patients' friendships and enmities are as his own. The analyst's sex life may be stunted; his patients' sexual problems provide a substitute. Having chosen such a demanding profession, he is barred from attaining a powerful political position; his investment of energy is all the greater in the power struggles of a politician-patient. In this way the analyst gradually ceases to lead a vital life of his own and contents himself with the lives of his patients. [p. 56]

Possibly one of the most bald statements of what a therapist receives, and may even seek out, from patients is provided by

Robertiello, a psychoanalyst. In an autobiographical account (1986), he describes how he found himself receiving more referrals than he could handle and began to enjoy the luxury of choosing which patients he wished to treat. He writes:

> I ask myself during the first session, "Do I wish to spend a part of my life with this person? Is he (or she) interesting enough for me to make an emotional commitment to? Will I consistently look forward to seeing him with anticipation and pleasure? Can I relate easily to the needy child in him, so that I will not be seriously put off by whatever facade he may present? Do I enjoy the facade as well? . . . This ability to choose, which neither I nor any other analysts have at the beginning of their careers, makes my present work a pleasure. I see myself as sitting in a comfortable office and having a group of interesting, bright, talented people come visit me every day. [pp. 101-102]

Other authors suggest that the practice of psychotherapy can at times serve a defensive function in the psychic economy of the practitioner. Menninger (1957b), for example, asserts that for many psychiatrists professional functioning serves to refute early fears and fantasies regarding mental illness (e.g., that it is due to excessive masturbation, a curse of nature, or a punishment of God). Greenson (1967) also points to a common counterphobic attitude in which one masters the fear of disease by treating, and thereby confronting, the illnesses of others. Similarly, through contact with their patients, therapists may gain reassurance that their own experiences are not beyond the boundaries of what is human, "that we are not alone in our strangeness or nastiness" (Issacharoff and Hunt 1983, p. 166).

Practicing psychotherapy may also be, in part, a way of denying one's own problems by becoming involved in those of others. Rather than assume the role of the troubled patient, one may decide to become the therapist, the one with all the answers. Gilberg (1977) comments on the defensive aspect of the wish to enter into psychoanalytic training, noting that it rationalizes the need for a personal analysis while denying the concept of not being well. Moreover, individuals who achieve such defensive aims through practicing psychotherapy may need to keep their patients from getting well. Searles (1979) warns that, to the extent that the patient's illness serves to protect the therapist from confronting his or her own conflicts, the therapist will unconsciously seek to maintain the status quo and preserve the patient's immature level of ego functioning.

This emphasis on the defensive functions of psychotherapeutic practice, however, can obscure the more positive, maturational aspects of the work. After all, the attempt to overcome personal fears and anxieties cannot simply be reduced to counterphobic maneuvers. The role of therapist provides an individual with opportunities to confront and master the unknown. As expressed by Kafka (1989): "Through our willingness to go into the patient's dark places, we transcend our own fears. Holding patients' hands, we explore unfamiliar regions of being, ours as well as theirs" (p. 291).

Numerous writers in the field have indicated that the psychotherapeutic situation offers the potential for personal growth to both participants. Mullan and Sangiuliano (1964), for example, assert that psychotherapy ought to result in mutual self-affirmation, and Burton (1972) claims that what therapists do is "to share our self with another self for the purpose of finding a higher level of fulfillment for both" (p. 196).

Whitaker and Malone (1953) discuss at length the opportunities that psychotherapy presents for expanding the limits of the therapist's growth and maturity, likening the process to the notion that parents grow up by raising their children. They state:

> The continued challenge of the patient's demand for greater integration on the part of the therapist, for his deeper participation in their own suffering, for help in their struggle with their world and with themselves, inevitably produces personal growth in the therapist. [p. 149]

The authors suggest that this fuller integration of the therapist's personality is achieved by a process of projecting disowned "selves" onto the patient and eventually reintegrating them. This idea is shared by Issacharoff and Hunt (1983) who propose that, for many therapists, professional functioning enables them to "enjoy the mastery of integrating scattered, disparate and conflicted parts of the self" (p. 104).

In psychoanalytic treatment, the patient's emotional conflicts are said to crystallize in the *transference neurosis*, the resolution of which is viewed as the key to recovery. Certain authors have indicated that a reciprocal process occurs in the analyst, and that this constitutes an important part of the treatment. Tower (1956), for example, states that this *countertransference neurosis* becomes the vehicle through which the analyst can fully comprehend the patient's transference neurosis. She remarks:

> I doubt that there is any thorough working through of a deep transference neurosis, in the strictest sense, which does not involve some form of emotional upheaval in which *both* a transference neurosis and a corresponding countertransference "neurosis" (no matter how small and temporary) are analyzed in the treatment situation, with eventual feelings of a substantially new orientation on the part of both persons toward each other. [p. 232]

Wolstein (1959) also addresses the interdependence of the transference neurosis and the countertransference neurosis, explaining that "the resolution of the transference becomes a mutual experience in which the neurosis that has crystallized out of the meeting of this particular analyst and this particular patient has to be resolved from both sides" (p. 167). Clearly this is a far cry from a "blank screen" approach to treatment. Wolstein insists that the analyst's emotional involvement is crucial to the progress of the analysis. He writes:

> Once an interlocking of transference and countertransference sets in, the analyst may be said to need his patient's recovery because, in a sense, his own is actually involved. . . . Both the analyst and his patient have now to find their way to a new level of relatedness and integration that will be richer and more meaningful than the one they are capable of at that point. [p. 169]

Finally, it has been suggested that therapists' own needs and personality dynamics may play an important role in their choice of patients, as well as their choice of theoretical orientation. Burton

(1972) comments that many therapists appear to be on the lookout for that "ideal client" who might perfectly fulfill their own needs. Whitaker and Malone (1953) imply that certain clinicians may be internally impelled to work with a more severely disturbed population. They suggest that "the enthusiasm and elation felt when contemplating the possibility that schizophrenic patients may be amenable to psychotherapy may reflect a perception that some residual needs can perhaps be answered only in therapeutic experiences with the schizophrenic" (p. 101). In this regard, it is of interest to note that a study by Yulis and Kiesler (1968) found that therapists tend to either over- or underemphasize in their patients those areas of conflict that resemble their own.

Lindner (1978) proposes that therapists choose an orientation and a way of practicing that reduces their own psychic tensions. Those who desire power, for instance, may be drawn to therapeutic modes that furnish them with positions as authority figures. Likewise, those individuals struggling with inner anger tend to find ways of believing and practicing that permit, at least indirectly, the expression of aggression and hostility. In essence, Lindner maintains that, under the guise of choosing the most effective therapeutic orientation, many psychotherapists derive personal benefits that satisfy their own intrapsychic needs.

From this entire discussion there arises an essential question: To what extent is it legitimate for the therapist to obtain psychological benefits from the therapeutic process? While this question cannot be dealt with here in depth, the two major positions regarding it shall be presented briefly.

There exists a general consensus that therapists do inevitably derive psychological benefits from working with their clients. The disagreement concerns whether or not this process should be minimized. Some view it as potentially antitherapeutic for the client and therefore seek to guard against it. Others, however, downplay the dangers and view it as an essential component of the treatment process.

In the recent literature, these two positions are best illustrated by Schafer and Langs. In his book *The Analytic Attitude*, Schafer (1983) portrays any use of the therapeutic situation for the therapist's own ends as an exploitation of the patient. He writes:

One way or another, the analyst's temptation is to use the analytic work to get otherwise unavailable gratifications, support faltering defenses, enhance grandiose fantasies, and, in the end, to *use* the analysand rather than to *work for* him or her. How much the analysand's sense of danger within the analysis depends on the frequency and extent of the analyst's nonneutral violations in this respect! [p. 25]

In a discussion on countertransference, Langs (1983) suggests that the resolution of restricted aspects of the therapist's own psychopathology is a valid function of the therapeutic interaction as long as it remains secondary to the task of curing the patient. He indicates that this is a difficult notion for many to accept because it is misinterpreted as exploitation of the patient. Instead, Langs views it as a fundamental part of the therapeutic process that actually renders the therapist far more effective in treating the patient.

Stierlin (1972) presents what could be viewed as a rapprochement of these two stands. He recommends that therapists ought to steer a path between the Scylla of needing their patients too much and the Charybdis of needing them too little. Those therapists who need their patients too much for their own self-actualization, reasons Stierlin, exploit their patients in that they will tend to keep them dependent and needy. Conversely, those therapists who require too little from their patients, in terms of their own psychological needs, will lack the motivation to invest deeply in them and will tend to be insufficiently empathic. This latter point appears to corroborate the conclusion of the previous chapter, that the need to master one's own emotional conflicts is a common, and perhaps indispensable, motivation of the psychotherapist.

As the introduction to this chapter suggests, there is a strong connection between a person's motivations for engaging in a particular activity and the satisfactions derived. It should be no surprise, therefore, that many of the satisfactions surveyed here correspond to one or more of the common unconscious motivations to be discussed. Indeed, one might infer from this correspondence that only those individuals who consciously or unconsciously seek out these particular satisfactions are initially drawn to, or ultimately able to tolerate, the work of the psychotherapist.

4

MOTIVES RELATED TO INSTINCTUAL AIMS

Classical Freudian theory postulates that human behavior and psychological activity are rooted in the instincts. Freud (1938) defines the instincts as follows: "The forces which we assume to exist behind the tensions caused by the needs of the id are called *instincts*. They represent the somatic demands upon mental life" (p. 148). Freud (1920) postulates that there exist two primary instincts, Eros and Thanatos. Eros, the sexual instinct, gives rise to the erotic component of mental activities, while Thanatos, the death instinct, gives rise to the destructive component.

Although the terms Eros and Thanatos are no longer widely used, modern psychoanalytic theory continues to distinguish between two drives: the sexual or erotic, and the aggressive or destructive. The psychic energy associated with the sexual drive is termed *libido*, while the psychic energy associated with the aggressive drive is referred to simply as *aggressive energy* or *aggression*.

In *Civilization and Its Discontents* (1930), Freud emphasizes the instinctual basis of human work:

Work is no less valuable for the opportunity it and the human relations connected with it provide for a very considerable discharge

, of libidinal component impulses, narcissistic, aggressive and even erotic, than because it is indispensable for subsistence and justifies existence in a society. The daily work of earning a livelihood affords particular satisfaction when it has been selected by free choice, i.e., when through sublimation it enables use to be made of existing inclinations, of instinctual impulses that have retained their strength, or are more intense than usual for constitutional reasons. [pp. 33–34]

Thus, in Freud's view, vocational choice provides a channel for the sublimated expression of fixated drives, in accordance with societal and reality constraints.

The relation of instinctual fixations to career choice is also evident in Simmel's (1926) analysis of the selection of medical specialties. In essence, Simmel suggests that physicians tend to have unresolved libidinal impulses bound to the particular erotogenic zones in which they decide to specialize. A number of more recent studies have furnished support for the notion that a major determinant of career choice involves the opportunities for instinctual expression afforded by the particular vocation (Galinsky 1962, Morse and Young 1973, Nachmann 1960, Segal 1961).

This chapter focuses on those motives for becoming a psychotherapist that involve instinctual gratification or conflict. For the sake of clarity, motives related to the libidinal instinct will be considered separately from those related to the aggressive instinct. One ought to keep in mind, however, that these primary instincts are abstractions; reality is not so clear-cut. In Brenner's words: "In all of the instinctual manifestations which we can *observe*, whether normal or pathological, *both* the sexual and the aggressive drives participate. To use Freud's terminology, the two drives are regularly 'fused' though not necessarily in equal amounts" (1974, p. 20).

INDIRECT SEXUAL GRATIFICATION

In its broadest sense, libido refers to all forms of love and pleasure. Using this extended definition, a complete accounting of the libidinal strivings underlying the decision to become a psychotherapist would have to include most of the satisfactions surveyed in the previous chapter: the pleasure of listening, the pleasure of solving problems and mastering conflicts, the pleasure of being needed and of aiding growth in others, and so on. The role of therapist provides a unique opportunity to share a form of intimacy with both males and females, young and old, people of every ethnic and socioeconomic background. Motives related to this wider meaning of libido as pleasurable human contact will be addressed more fully in Chapter 6. Here we will focus on the narrower sense of libido as sexuality.

In the preface to his discussion of the case of Dora, Freud (1901) makes the following remarks to justify his having addressed sexual matters with his young female client:

> Am I, then, to defend myself on this score as well? I will simply claim for myself the rights of the gynaecologist—or rather, much more modest ones—and add that it would be the mark of a singular and perverse prurience to suppose that conversations of this kind are a good means of exciting or of gratifying sexual desires. [p. 9]

One can appreciate the social and professional constraints with which Freud had to contend and still observe that he appears to protest too vigorously on this account.

In a discussion of the common unconscious motivations for becoming a psychiatrist, Menninger (1959) states that many people assume that unconscious voyeurism plays a large role in the desire to practice psychiatry, as mediated by the interest in the sexual behavior of others. Nevertheless, Menninger downplays this motive, noting that "the essence of Freud's discovery was that psychiatrists did *not* investigate these areas as they should" (p. 493). He fails to consider, however, that this alleged neglect of sexual issues by Freud's colleagues may have been a function of the social mores or of defense mechanisms, rather than of a limited interest in the topic.[1]

---

[1]In an earlier article, dealing with the unconscious motivations for becoming a physician, Menninger (1957b) appears once again to avoid acknowledging a sexual component. He analyzes in detail the unconscious appeal of the various medical specialties, and yet mentions gynecology only in passing, as involving "psychoanalytic speculations rather complicated for simple generalization" (p. 100).

Menninger is clearly in the minority on this point. Numerous sources concur that the practice of psychotherapy can provide sexual pleasure derived from looking, or the vicarious satisfaction of being privy to the sexual life of others (Eisendorfer 1959, Fisher 1969, Gitelson 1952, Greenson 1967, Hammer 1972, Marston 1984, Schafer 1954, Searles 1979, Sharpe 1947, Templer 1971). In a discussion of the motivations of psychoanalytic candidates, Eisendorfer (1959) notes with regret that "few are the candidates whose scoptophilic impulses are subordinate to a zealous desire to explore and understand the nature of the unconscious" (p. 376). Fisher (1969) takes a more benevolent view of the issue, insisting that "a keen taste for vicarious experience is essential in the therapist. We are all voyeurs though, to be sure, our desire to look is not limited to sex" (p. 89). Referring to the difficulty with which many therapists confront this quality in themselves, Marston (1984) comments that "jokes are made about voyeurism in order to maintain some distance from guilt about it; yet most would agree that the more fascinating the lives of patients, the more rewarding the therapist's work" (p. 458). Discomfort with sexual impulses may also help to explain why so few clinicians appear to be interested in working with sexual offenders.

Templer (1971) notes that few therapists discourage their patients from discussing sexual matters, and that prevalent attitudes range from permission, to encouragement, to extraction of material from the patient. He maintains that the therapist whose own sex life is unsatisfactory may obtain vicarious satisfactions from listening to patients' narrations. Similarly, Hammer (1972) contends that certain therapists are especially prone to using the therapeutic relationship as a way of peeking into the private lives of others. They may be particularly interested in sexual matters, although any kind of secret can hold erotic excitement. Such therapists, Hammer asserts, are constantly attempting to expose their patients' secrets; they ask prying questions, often of an erotic or perverse nature. The use of "penetrating interpretations" may also provide a form of libidinal gratification.

Voyeurism is generally attributed to the wish to view tabooed scenes from which one had been excluded as a child. Perhaps one of the most unabashed descriptions of the part played by voyeuristic tendencies is given by the analyst called Aaron Green, in Janet Malcolm's *The Impossible Profession* (1981). Malcolm quotes him as follows:

> Everyone's analysis unearths a central fantasy, and mine is that of an outsider looking into the bedroom: feeling excited and scared, getting aroused, trying to figure out what is going on, but not having to get involved, not having to risk anything. There are many ways of playing out this fantasy. I could have become a Peeping Tom, for one extreme possibility, but I became a scientist instead—a psychoanalyst, a person who gets to know another person very intimately but doesn't have to get involved with him. [p. 61]

This theme is also taken up by Greenson (1967), who notes that many analysts appear uncomfortable with the initial interviews in which they must sit face-to-face with the patient, preferring the safety and comfort of their position behind the couch. Greenson states that his experience with training-analyses suggests that this stems from "a form of stage fright which covers repressed exhibitionistic impulses and a generalized aggressivation and sexualization of looking and being seen. The position behind the couch offers them the opportunity to look without being seen" (p. 400).

Schafer (1954) views voyeurism in the psychologist in a similar light. He addresses a number of subjective factors involved in doing psychological testing that he considers to be present regardless of what brings an individual to the professional role of tester. Most of what Schafer writes about the psychological tester is equally applicable to the role of therapist, as he himself notes. Describing the voyeuristic aspect, Schafer states: "He peeps into the interiors of many individuals and never once commits himself, as would be required under normal social conditions, to a relationship. . . . All is observed from the safety of psychological distance and transiency of relationship" (p. 21). Although the therapist generally engages in more of a relationship with the client than does the tester, the same sort of psychological distance is typically maintained. In this sense, voyeuristic gratifications appear to be associated with conflicts over intimacy, a factor that will be discussed in Chapter 6.

In his extensive discussion of therapists' unconscious motivations, Roth (1987) suggests that psychotherapists are also "entendeurs" (p. 5), that is, they take great pleasure in listening to others. Notwithstanding the well-known quip in regard to the strain of listening to patients all day long ("so who listens?"), those individuals who do not obtain a deep sense of satisfaction from listening are not likely to fare well as therapists. As with voyeurism, Roth indicates that such tendencies may derive from the experience of having been denied access to parental conversations, and the "sounds of closed rooms filled with secret happenings within the early family life" (p. 5).

What is regarded by many as crucial is the degree to which the practitioner's voyeurism is sublimated. Holt and Luborsky (1958b) warn that curiosity, like helpfulness, can be closely bound up with defense mechanisms or with acting out in the service of relatively direct instinctual gratification, and therefore not in the best interests of therapeutic work. For this reason, they suggest that clinical indications of relatively unsublimated voyeurism be considered a negative finding in an analytic candidate. Similarly, Sharpe (1947) views sexual curiosity as a common motive among analytic candidates, but states that it must be "purged of its infantile characteristics" (p. 121) if it is to become useful and beneficial. When adequately sublimated, voyeuristic tendencies can furnish an insatiable curiosity about human behavior and emotional functioning. Such inquisitiveness may prove essential to the psychotherapist in solving the diagnostic puzzle presented by each patient. Thus, it appears that this curious calling is also a calling for the curious.

Interestingly, there is little to be found in the psychoanalytic literature regarding the therapist's exhibitionistic impulses. Perhaps those clinicians who are more at home with their exhibitionism gravitate toward the fields of family or group therapy! It has been suggested that exhibitionistic tendencies could account for the common occurrence of therapists' boasting about the accomplishments, notoriety, or special qualities of their patients (Epstein and Simon 1990). Such trends may also contribute to inappropriate self-disclosure during therapy sessions.

Conversely, individuals who are heavily defended against their exhibitionistic impulses may be drawn to the concealment provided by the role of therapist. In his novel *The Doctor of Desire*, Wheelis (1987) portrays an analyst who comes to this realization while immersed in the pleasure of giving a lecture to colleagues:

> I should have been an actor, he thought, or a musician or a dancer, should be doing something like this all the time. He had chosen the opposite extreme, lived behind a couch, could not be seen at all. He didn't talk, he listened. As far from performing as one could get. As a young man he had been most afraid of what he most wanted; and, as fear was stronger than desire, his vocation had been chosen by fear. Only now, he thinks, when it's too late, have I overcome the fear and come to know how much I enjoy showing off, being on stage. (p. 47)

DIRECT SEXUAL GRATIFICATION

Voyeuristic tendencies appear to be optimally gratified when therapists assume a distant, uninvolved stance. In contrast, conscious or unconscious strivings for direct sexual gratification can lead therapists to trespass the necessary boundaries that separate them from their patients. As we have seen, the therapist's voyeuristic tendencies can provide an important source of interest in clinical work. Direct attempts at sexual gratification, on the other hand, can only serve to damage the therapeutic process. When the therapist approaches the patient as a real love object, he rends the "therapeutic barrier" (Tarachow 1962, p. 379) that provides the basis for interpretation and change.

The prohibition against sexual involvement with patients is included in the 2,500-year-old Hippocratic Oath, as well as an even earlier code of the Nigerian healing arts (Brodsky 1989). Until recent years, however, the professional literature had largely shunned the topic, taking a "hear no evil, see no evil, speak no evil" approach. During the 1960s and 1970s, some professionals collected data on the incidence of therapist–patient sex, but feared publishing or even presenting the results (Brodsky 1989). Pope (1990) cites sources indicating that active suppression of such studies has existed for some time, and remains especially strong among social work organizations.

Both cultural changes and shifts in therapeutic theory and practice have contributed to create an atmosphere in which sexual contact with patients has become considerably more thinkable than was formerly the case.[2] The so-called sexual revolution has made sexual expression, in general, more open and acceptable. The trend toward distrust and debunking of authority figures has placed therapist and patient on a more equal footing. In addition, humanistic and interpersonal approaches to psychotherapy have attempted to remove any artificial distance between the participants in therapy, and have shifted the emphasis from the patient's internal psyche to that of the interactional process.

The 1960s and 1970s brought a profusion of therapeutic modalities involving physical contact, including encounter and marathon groups, nudist group therapy, psychodrama, awareness-expansion exercises, bioenergetics, and Rolfing, among others. According to Mintz (1969), touching is used in such therapies to facilitate the lowering of unconscious resistances and to foster regression to various phases of childhood development. Although sexual interactions are generally excluded, nonerotic touching is promoted in an attempt to deepen the level of intimacy, to improve the therapeutic relationship, and to provide a corrective emotional experience. The influence of such physical contact modalities has combined with that of the behavioral approaches, including sex therapy, to alter profoundly the relationship between therapist and patient. No longer subject to traditional constraints, the therapist's role has become highly flexible, and even improvisational. In many approaches to psychotherapy, the emphasis has shifted from interpretation and insight to empathy, warmth, closeness, and the mutual expression of feelings. It is not surprising that, in the process, the boundary separating professional from personal involvement has become increasingly blurred (Serban 1981).

During the late 1960s and early 1970s two psychiatrists went so far as to advocate sexual intimacy with clients. In his paper entitled

---

[2]We have no way of knowing the incidence of therapist–patient sex during the early years of psychoanalysis. Although Freud (1915) insisted that the analyst should never attempt to gratify the patient's erotic longings, a number of his followers went on to marry their analysands.

"Overt Transference," McCartney (1966) suggested that certain patients cannot get well merely by talking with the therapist, but may need to caress, fondle, and examine his body and, in some cases, to engage in intercourse. McCartney obtained consent from patients and their families in order to administer this "treatment" to some 1,500 women. Shepard (1971) also published accounts of therapy cases in which he claimed that sex between therapist and patient had resulted in beneficial effects. Indeed, in a 1973 survey of physicians (Kardener et al.), 13 percent of the respondents offered explanations for the usefulness of erotic practices in therapy, including such statements as:

> "demonstrates doctor's effectiveness to his patient," "stimulating the clitoris helps a patient relax," "improves sexual maladjustments," "helps patients' recognition of their sexual status," "for teaching sexual anatomy," "disclosing areas of sexual blocking," "to demonstrate there is no physical cause for absence of libido," "to relieve frustration in a widow or divorcee who hasn't yet reengaged in dating," and "in healthy patients by mutual consent, making the therapy go faster, deeper, and increases dreams." [p. 1079]

The diversity and inventiveness of such rationalizations are certainly impressive. What remains to be addressed, as Pope and colleagues (1979) wryly remark, is why such an effective treatment seems to require an older male for administration and is contraindicated for all patients who are not young and attractive females.

In their 1970 publication, *Human Sexual Inadequacy*, Masters and Johnson noted that a large number of their patients reported having had sex with prior therapists. In the same year, Dahlberg (1970) reported on eight such patients encountered in his practice. These reports constituted the first indications that the phenomenon was not so rare as was previously supposed. Another shift that occurred at that time concerned the question of the locus of responsibility. Previously, sexual acting out was generally viewed as a manifestation of the patient's illness. Marmor (1972), who introduced the concept of *countertransference sexual acting out* (p. 3), was one of the first to suggest that the therapist could also be seductive.

The actual prevalence of therapist–patient sexual contact has been difficult to establish reliably. Many of the surveys have involved small or geographically restricted samples, and return rates are often low. Because these studies rely on self-reports, it is generally assumed that the results represent conservative estimates of the true incidence. Using a random sample of male physicians in the Los Angeles area, Kardener and colleagues (1973) found that 10 percent of 114 psychiatrists reported erotic contact with clients, with half of these specifying sexual intercourse. In a nationwide survey of over fourteen hundred psychiatrists, 7 percent of the male and 3 percent of the female respondents admitted to sexual contact with their patients (Gartrell et al. 1986).

Similar rates have been reported for psychologists. Holroyd and Brodsky (1977) surveyed some 666 licensed doctoral-level psychologists, and found that nearly 11 percent of the males and 2 percent of the females acknowledged erotic contact with opposite-sex patients. (Erotic contact with same-sex patients was far less common and was mostly limited to kissing and holding.) About half of these therapists—5.5 percent of the males, and 0.6 percent of the females—had engaged in intercourse during treatment. An additional 2.6 percent of the men and 0.3 percent of the women reported sexual involvement with patients within three months of termination. Pope and colleagues (1979) found that 7 percent of the Psychotherapy Division membership of the American Psychological Association reported engaging in sexual contact with their clients, and a 1986 mail survey of psychologists in private practice resulted in a similar figure of 6.5 percent (Pope et al. 1986).

The first national study of sexual contact between social workers and their clients was not completed until 1985 and was never granted acceptance by the leading social work journals (Gechtman 1989). In a survey of 500 male and 500 female social workers, Gechtman and Bouhoutsos (1985) found that 2.6 percent of the male respondents were involved sexually with their clients during the course of therapy, and another 1.2 percent after termination. None of the female respondents acknowledged sexual contact with clients. Unlike the fields of psychology and psychiatry, the great majority of social workers are female. Given that therapists who become sexually involved with clients are usually male, the incidence of therapist–patient sex for the social work profession as a whole is considerably lower than the survey figures suggest. Gechtman (1989) attributes this lower incidence to several possible factors: Through a self-selection process, men who are drawn to social work possess more of the traditionally female characteristics (e.g., nurturance, responsibility, sensitivity to others' needs), which may be incompatible with sexual exploitation of clients; social workers are more likely to work in institutional settings, offering less privacy, clearer therapist–patient boundaries, and greater accountability; and finally, social workers may be less likely to admit to sexual activities because such behaviors could be perceived to be too dissonant with such dominant social work values as moral integrity, compassion, and maternal concern.

The most recent data available suggests a significant decline in self-reported incidents of therapist–patient sexual involvement. The two latest studies (Borys and Pope 1989, Pope et al. 1987) reported figures of 0.9–3.6 percent for male therapists and 0.2–0.5 percent for female therapists. Although this trend is certainly encouraging, the reasons for it remain obscure. Increased efforts at education and prevention, highly publicized malpractice awards, and recent legislative successes in criminalizing the act may have influenced the behavior of exploitive psychotherapists, or may have merely decreased their willingness to admit to engaging in sex with clients. Random sampling error or bias in return rate could also account for the apparent discrepancy (Pope et al. 1987).

Numerous studies have provided convincing evidence that patients who are sexually victimized by their therapists sustain serious psychological harm (Bouhoutsos et al. 1983, Butler and Zelen 1977, D'Addario 1977, Feldman-Summers and Jones 1984, Sonne et al. 1985). Based on his review of the literature, Pope (1989) identified the "therapist–patient sex syndrome" (p. 40) and described ten major areas of damage: (1) intense ambivalence toward the exploitative therapist, (2) chronic guilt feelings, (3) a sense of emptiness and isolation, (4) sexual confusion, (5) impaired ability to trust, (6) boundary disturbance and identity diffusion, (7) emotional lability, (8) suppressed rage, (9) increased suicide risk, and (10) cognitive dysfunction, often involving impaired attention and concentration, flashbacks, intrusive thoughts, and nightmares. Apfel and Simon

(1986) also note the frequent occurrence of a questioning of reality and sanity, constricted intimacy with men, and a desire for revenge.

The issue of patient risk factors has generated a good deal of controversy. Serban (1981) described a personality profile involving emotional instability, hysterical traits, seductiveness, impulsivity, and a need for attention. Other authors (Smith 1984, Stone 1976) have suggested that a history of incest predisposes patients to later sexual abuse by therapists, and Brodsky (1989) includes all patients who were physically or sexually abused as children. Gutheil (1989) has argued that patients with borderline personality disorder are particularly likely to evoke boundary violations, including sexual acting out. As of yet, none of these notions appears to have been backed up by reliable research.

While the identification of patient risk factors is clearly of value, taking such an approach to the issue of therapist–patient sex brings with it the danger of blaming the victim. Therapists may point to pathologically seductive behavior on the part of patients as an explanation or justification of their sexual involvement. In the extreme, it is the *therapist* who claims to be victimized by the patient-rapist. An example, so blatant that it appears comical, is provided by Walker and Young in *The Killing Cure* (1986). An analyst who has been accused of sexual exploitation is cross-examined during the malpractice trial:

> "In order to engage in this oral copulation, you took your pants off, didn't you?"
> "She took them off."
> "Did you fight her?"
> "Sometimes."
> "Did you struggle?"
> "Sometimes I held her away."
> "And was it difficult? Would you say she raped you?"
> "I never said she raped me."
> "Yes, but you were struggling to keep your pants on, and she was pulling your pants off. Is that what you are saying?"
> "She would try and take my pants off. I would try and stop her, and she would say, 'You have to let me. You have to let me love you.'"
> "Did you ever voluntarily take your pants off?"
> "I don't believe so."

"Doctor, then did you ever remove any of her articles of clothing?"
"No."
"Doctor, at times you were the one that was the aggressor; that is, you were the one who put your mouth on her vagina, isn't that right, and kissed her?"
"She insisted that I do."
"Well, did she take your head and forcibly put it there?"
"Several times."
"Did you fight to get away?"
"I tried to talk to her."
"Did this irritate you, that she was doing this with your head?"
"Yes."
"You weren't enjoying it?"
"Sometimes I did, but I still—I still was irritated by it." [p. 295]

As noted by Wohlberg (1990), the absurdity of the blame-the-patient position is clearly exposed when one substitutes masochistic for seductive behaviors. In other words, could a therapist ever justify complying with a patient's wish to be beaten? Moreover, many of the sexually abusing therapists acknowledge involvement with multiple patients, reducing the likelihood that particular patient characteristics are a key contributing factor. Gutheil (1989) also notes in passing that borderline patients may be at greater risk simply by "diagnostic default" (p. 598). That is, because psychotic patients are not generally perceived as attractive, and neurotics are well enough to know better than to become sexually involved. In sum, the issue of patient risk factors clearly requires further study. At the present time, as Bates and Brodsky (1989) conclude in a recent review of the literature, "the best single predictor of exploitation in therapy is a therapist who has exploited another patient in the past" (p. 141).

How, then, are we to understand the involvement of a sizable minority of therapists in activities that are clearly antitherapeutic and that entail such high legal, professional, and ethical risks? A wide variety of explanations and predisposing personality characteristics have been proposed. So wide, in fact, that to review them is to anticipate most of the motivations surveyed in this volume. I believe that this is because the phenomenon of sexually abusive therapists is highly complex and overdetermined. There are certainly cases in which the conscious intention involves malicious exploitation of patients, and whatever the therapist's intentions may be, the behavior can never be justified in any way. Nevertheless, in analyzing the dynamics of abusive therapists it seems that we can also observe the entire spectrum of therapeutic strivings gone awry.

In attempting to understand the phenomenon of therapist-patient sex, several authors delineate a typology of psychotherapists who sexually abuse patients. The most frequently mentioned is the middle-aged male therapist who is overtly or covertly depressed, due to a recent separation, divorce, or unsatisfying marriage. Work frustrations and doubts regarding professional competence are also cited as contributing factors. Exploitation of a positive transference enables such a therapist to gain affection, nurturance, and ultimately sexual gratification, typically from much younger, female clients. These therapists tend to report having been "in love" with the client, and to have viewed the relationship as more than sexual in nature (Apfel and Simon 1986, Averill et al. 1989, Butler and Zelen 1977, Collins 1989, Dahlberg 1970, Stone 1984). Apfel and Simon (1986) also suggest that some alienated and impaired clinicians may engage in sexual intimacy with clients as a cry for help—an appeal to the community to take notice.

A second type of clinician prone to sexual misconduct is the antisocial or psychopathic therapist (Gabbard 1991, Marmor 1976, Stone 1984, Twemlow and Gabbard 1989). His sexual involvement with patients can be viewed as just one aspect of a personality style characterized by poor impulse control, a defective superego, and blatant manipulation and exploitation of others. Gabbard (1990) surmises that such therapists constitute a relatively small percentage of boundary-violation cases, and describes their psychodynamics as follows:

> In these individuals there is a profound impairment of internalization during childhood development. The absence of a mature moral sense in these therapists makes it difficult for them to experience other people as separate individuals with feelings of their own. Hence, patients who come to them for help are seen merely as objects to be used for their own sexual gratification. No empathy for

the victim or concern for the harm that might come to the patient is present. [p. 6]

Gabbard notes that antisocial therapists frequently reveal early histories of profound abuse or neglect, and that their cruel exploitation of patients involves an identification with the aggressor, or of turning-passive-into-active.

Another type of abuser is the psychotherapist with the *Don Juan syndrome*, one whose chronic doubts concerning sexual adequacy and sexual identity (e.g., fear of homosexuality) may result in a persistent need to seduce and dominate female clients (Marmor 1976).[3] Stone (1984) cites the sexually "liberated" therapist whose idea of sexual liberation includes having sex with patients. He also points to psychotherapists who act out a perverse sexual fixation with patients, including those who have sex with patients they have rendered unconscious. The therapist's sexual involvement can be regarded as perverse in every case in which his excitement is enhanced by the sense of sinning or risk-taking, and when the sexual involvement does not end in lasting intimacy (Twemlow and Gabbard 1989).

Many authors look to the Oedipus complex for factors predisposing therapists to boundary violations. Saul (1962) suggests that the therapist may engage in sexual contact in a benevolent attempt to gratify the patient's eroticized wish for a parent. Similarly, the patient can unconsciously represent the incestuous parental object for the therapist. Sexual involvement with this forbidden lover constitutes an acting out of the therapist's oedipal wishes. The therapist may believe that he is saving his female client from an unhappy fate or marriage. Thus, by turning her sexuality toward himself, the therapist symbolically rescues the suffering mother from the wicked father (Apfel and Simon 1986, Gabbard 1991, Kardener 1974, Smith 1989).

Lester (1990) proposes that in some instances a female patient's preoedipal wishes for nurturance and merger may be misinter-

---

[3]It is of interest that seductive male therapists tend to have poor track records as lovers, suffering frequently from impotence and premature ejaculation (Belote 1974, Dahlberg 1970).

preted by the male therapist as erotic oedipal wishes. She suggests that the therapist's fears of symbiotic merger can contribute to sexual acting out, which, ironically, may allow for defensive distancing from the patient. Lester writes:

> In two cases of sexual abuse by a male analyst in which I was a consultant to the Ethics Committee, the sexual acting out occurred at a time when the female patient, in a state of severe regression, made what appeared to the analyst a desperate demand for "love." The sexual acting out permitted the analyst to gratify the patient's demands while maintaining affective separateness from her. On her part, the patient accepted satisfaction at this pseudo-genital level since it provided her with the physical contact she craved for, basically a craving for maternal care and nurturance. [pp. 438–439]

Although some have likened therapist–patient sex to rape (Dahlberg 1970), Smith (1984) suggests that the closer resemblance is to incest. He found that out of eighteen patients who had engaged in sex with prior therapists, seventeen reported having been sexually abused by their fathers, while the remaining patient had been abused by her mother. Smith compares the psychological state of the abused patient to that of the molested child. Both feel helpless, tend to place the blame on themselves, and are afraid to reveal their experiences. The abusing therapist, like the molester, makes a pact of secrecy with the patient, telling her that to reveal their secret would destroy the relationship. In turn, the patient over-idealizes the therapist, as she had her father, wishing to believe that he can do no wrong. This interpretation is also consistent with that of Sharpe (1947), who states that the analyst's unconscious striving for sexual satisfaction derives from unanalyzed infantile incestuous wishes toward one or both parents.

Twemlow and Gabbard (1989) estimate that approximately one-half of the reported cases of therapist–patient sexual relations involve a "lovesick therapist" (p. 71), who genuinely believes he is hopelessly in love with his patient. Based on their work with both therapists and patients, they conclude that primitive preoedipal issues are at least as important as oedipal dynamics in understanding the lovesick therapist:

The hallmark of the Oedipus complex is ambivalent, triangular object relations, characterized by jealousy, rivalry, and the capacity for whole-object relatedness. In the state of lovesickness, on the other hand, object ties are intensely dyadic rather than triangular. Moreover, whereas ambivalent oedipal relations are fused with negative feelings, the object relations of lovesickness are so idealized that they are completely free from contamination by any negative feelings whatsoever. "Badness" in oneself and in one's lover is denied, so neurotic guilt is absent. In the lovesick state no one exists outside the intense passionate dyad, so rivalry is peripheral or absent. Finally, all the foregoing relates to the fact that fully rounded, ambivalently held, whole-object relations are not present in pathological lovesickness. The relationship is a part-self-representation connected with a part-object-representation—only the idealized aspects of self and object exist. [p. 78]

What sorts of preoedipal dynamics are most likely to be found in therapists who engage in sexual misconduct? It appears that the two predominant areas are those involving dependency needs and narcissistic needs, issues that will be more fully addressed in subsequent chapters. Twemlow and Gabbard (1989) suggest that many abusive therapists remain guilt-free because they are convinced that they are healing their patients by providing the care and nurturance that was previously absent. This misguided notion of "love feeding" (p. 79), ubiquitous within the field of psychotherapy, can lead some practitioners to resort to sexual ministrations as a despairing final effort (see also Searles 1979).[4] An extreme example, involving a psychotic therapist, is presented by Twemlow and Gabbard:

A clinical psychologist working on a girls' adolescent unit of a state mental hospital became convinced that God was speaking to him.

---

[4]Freud's disciple, Ferenczi, experimented with hugging and kissing his female patients, in an attempt to make up for their early emotional deprivation. When Freud learned of this innovation, he issued a warning that other practitioners would rationalize further intimacies in a similar fashion, until "God the father Ferenczi, gazing at the lively scene he [had] created [would] perhaps say to himself, 'Maybe, after all, I should have halted in my technique of motherly affection *before* the kiss'" (Jones 1957, p. 164).

He maintained that God had told him that his semen would confer eternal salvation on his patients, so he systematically set out to seduce every adolescent patient on his unit before finally being hospitalized himself. [pp. 72–73]

These authors suggest that "love feeding" represents the therapist's vicarious attempt to fulfill his own denied yearnings for dependency and love. Thus, the psychotherapist who becomes enamored of his patient may unconsciously be seeking to supply love to a part of himself identified with the needy patient (Gabbard 1991).

Narcissistic problems may also predispose therapists to engage in sexual involvement with clients. Marmor (1953) refers to a sense of superiority and grandiosity that results from years of admiration and idealization by patients. Such attitudes may lead therapists to feel that they can practice unfettered by professional and ethical guidelines. The narcissistic gratifications provided by the role of psychotherapist may, in part, explain why many individuals with a narcissistic disturbance appear to be drawn to the field (Claman 1987, Finell 1985, Miller 1981, Sharaf and Levinson 1964). During periods of pronounced stress and depletion, such individuals may turn to their patients to bolster a deflated sense of self. As will be elaborated in Chapter 5, therapists may repeatedly "fall in love" with clients who gratify their unfulfilled longings for mirroring and idealization.

Investigators of therapist–patient sex repeatedly emphasize that no explanation or understanding of the phenomenon can ever serve to justify this unacceptable behavior on the part of practitioners. Nevertheless, some of the proposed psychodynamics may at times be heard as excuses or rationalizations. As in the case of rape, one may ask, are not hostile impulses more central than libidinal ones? Even the therapist who believes he is in love with his client must on some level be aware that he is acting destructively.

A number of authors address destructive wishes underlying sexual involvement with patients. Marmor (1976) refers to "an unconscious hostility toward women with a sadistic need to exploit, humiliate and ultimately reject them" (p. 322). Holroyd and Brodsky (1977, 1980) assert that deep-seated attitudes regarding power, status, and sex roles influence the abusive therapist's behavior.

Since the typical dyad involves a male therapist and female patient, they concur that therapist–patient sex often stems from feelings of contempt and a sense of superiority on the part of the male toward the female. Twemlow and Gabbard (1989) also share this view, noting that "the sadistic wish to destroy is the perverse core of the lovesick therapist's relationship with his patient . . . [and the] key feature that allows for differentiation from normal varieties of lovesickness" (p. 84). Gabbard (1991) adds that sexual acting out can also express the therapist's resentment and hostility toward his place of employment. By bringing disgrace upon himself, he may unconsciously seek to embarrass the hospital, clinic, or analytic institute in which he practices, thereby hoping to achieve some measure of revenge.

Smith (1984) reports on his therapeutic work with a therapist who had engaged in intercourse with a patient. The treatment of this therapist revealed that the sexual intimacy had not developed out of loving feelings, but out of escalating rage and the desire for power over the patient. Smith came to view the therapist's sexual transgression as a form of eroticized hatred: the motive was not love, and certainly not therapy, but rather hostility and vindictiveness. In a later paper, Smith (1989) elaborates on this type of erotic practitioner:

The sadistic therapist blames the patient for whatever goes wrong. The patient is reviled by the therapist on every front: she is told that she is ugly, that her wish for some kind of fulfillment is not merited, that her illness is an expression of her own badness, and that her sexuality is not exciting, and only out of her sexual neediness does the doctor have contact with her at all. [p. 64]

Frequently, the patient must put up with this abuse or face abandonment.

Having completed this review of the various motives attributed to therapists who become sexually involved with clients, it becomes necessary to place this phenomenon within a wider context. Although clearly more common than was once believed, therapist–patient sex must still be viewed as an extreme consequence of therapists' libidinal strivings. Nevertheless, it may be an error to discount it as totally unrelated to the unconscious motives of the majority of practitioners. How many therapists have never felt sexual attraction toward a client, experienced gratification from a client's idealization and positive transference, made an intervention that served one's own needs more than the client's, enjoyed some degree of emotional union and relaxation of boundaries, or struggled with feelings of anger and hostility toward a client? With the exception of cases involving sociopathy, it appears that most sexual misconduct on the part of therapists results from familiar libidinal and aggressive strivings that have returned to an unmodulated, desublimated form (Searles 1979).

Sexual transgressions, of course, are not the only form of exploitation that therapists can engage in. Milder forms of boundary violations, including excessive familiarity, seductiveness, nonclinical business dealings, and breaches of confidentiality, are far more prevalent than overt sexual activity (Borys and Pope 1989, Epstein and Simon 1990). As noted earlier, many humanistic therapists advocate the use of nonerotic touching. Moreover, it appears that sexual violations do not emerge out of the blue, but usually occur after a prodromal period involving lesser forms of exploitive behavior (Simon 1989). In their description of an "exploitation index," Epstein and Simon (1990) assert that any trespassing of treatment boundaries constitutes exploitation, "because it violates a treatment contract based on both overt and implied agreement that the therapist's sole purpose is to treat the patient's disorder in return for monetary compensation" (p. 456). Under the heading of generalized boundary violations they include social contact with clients, inappropriate self-disclosure, therapist and client addressing each other by first name, accepting mediums of exchange other than money, and accepting referrals from relatives, friends, or previous clients. Gutheil (1989) argues that even minor irregularities or exceptions to the usual treatment procedure should raise a red flag of caution in the therapist's mind. Clearly, one must conclude, mental health professionals cannot afford to view sexual misconduct as an utterly foreign matter that only concerns fringe groups of practitioners.

We are still faced with the fact, however, that exceedingly few female therapists report sexual involvements with clients. Survey results suggest that between 85 and 96 percent of all self-reported instances of therapist–patient sexual intimacies involve a male psychotherapist (Bouhoutsos et al. 1983, Gartrell et al. 1986, Holroyd and Brodsky 1977). Why do female therapists appear to be relatively immune from such practices? Lester (1990) notes that strong erotic oedipal transferences are most common in the male therapist–female patient dyad, suggesting that female therapists may not typically be exposed to the same intensity of libidinal stirrings in the treatment setting. She also proposes that female therapists are more comfortable with their patients' preoedipal wishes for nurturance and merger, and therefore are less likely than their male counterparts to misread patients' demands as oedipal or erotic. Do these observations fully explain the statistical discrepancies, or are other factors involved? Do women possess greater control of their sexual and aggressive impulses? Does the conventional power differential between the two sexes come into play? Or are women, as a group, simply more likely to behave in ethical, nonexploitive ways? This is clearly an area requiring further study. What is apparent is that the issue of therapist–patient sex, like other forms of abuse in which the perpetrator is typically male and the victim female, has yet to be adequately confronted by the mental health professions. The important issue of prevention will be addressed in the final chapter.

AGGRESSIVE STRIVINGS

The origin of human aggression has been an enduring topic of debate. Does it spring from instinctual sources, or is it produced by the social environment? Is it part of our genetic heritage, or an unfortunate byproduct of civilization?[5] Berger (1974) summarizes evidence from historical, anthropological, and clinical sources that

---

[5]Various anthropologists have suggested that human culture has its roots in the practice of hunting (Tiger and Fox 1971, Washburn and Lancaster 1968). Claiming this view derived from a male bias within the field of anthropology, Slocum (1975) proposes that the role of Woman the Gatherer was more critical to the early development of culture than was that of Man the Hunter.

points to a strong innate propensity toward aggression on the part of human beings. Wars and expressions of cruelty have played a prominent role in nearly every known culture. Mythologies and religions throughout the world, as well as the fantasies and dreams of individuals, are replete with violent and aggressive themes. While the social environment certainly influences the form and intensity of its various expressions, there appears to be a good deal of support for the existence of an instinctual predisposition toward aggression.

From a psychoanalytic perspective, human work derives from the constructive application of the aggressive drive. As phrased by Menninger (1959), "it represents a deflection to constructive uses of energy arising originally in connection with hostile feelings and a destructive purpose" (p. 477). Through the process of sublimation these destructive impulses are neutralized by diverting them to aims that are of personal and social benefit.

There appears to be wide acceptance of the idea that aggressive strivings play a vital role in the decision to become a physician. In a discussion of his own motives for becoming a physician, Freud (1926) states, "I have no knowledge of having had any craving in my earliest childhood to help suffering humanity. My innate sadistic disposition was not a very strong one, so that I had no need to develop this one of its derivatives" (p. 253). Here Freud implies that two common unconscious motivations for becoming a physician are infantile scoptophilia, and sadism transformed into compassion.

Simmel (1926) asserts that doctoring involves a reenactment of the child's sadomasochistic misunderstanding of the primal scene. Thus, the physician unconsciously plays the role of the sadistic father sexually torturing the mother-patient, or else takes the role of the rescuer. A six-year study of the psychodynamics of a group of physicians revealed that healing was typically used as both an expression of and expiation for sadistic impulses (Zabarenko et al. 1970).

Greenson (1967) also emphasizes the contribution of pregenital sadistic drives to an interest in doctoring. He writes:

Such impulses can be detected clinically in the overt behavior of sadistic doctors who inflict unnecessary pain and mutilation, as reaction formations in indecisive, inhibited doctors, and as reparation and restitution phenomena in guilt-laden ones who are compulsive rescuers. Relatively well-neutralized aggressive drives are exemplified in the surgeon who is able to make a conflict-free decision to operate, who performs with dexterity and dispatch, and who feels neither undue triumph nor guilt afterward. [pp. 406–407]

As with physicians, an interest in becoming a psychotherapist frequently appears to be influenced in some manner by the vicissitudes of the aggressive drive. Three relevant areas—reaction formation against aggression, the expression of aggression, and masochistic tendencies—appear to coalesce in the issue of unresolved oedipal conflict, with which the discussion concludes.

REACTION FORMATION AGAINST AGGRESSION

According to Sharpe (1930), the desire to cure derives in part from the effort to defend against infantile impulses to maim, destroy, or kill. Enduring anxieties over sadistic fantasies and promptings are unconsciously transformed into compassionate concerns with healing and repairing. The psychological process by which this alteration is accomplished is the defense mechanism of reaction formation. This term refers to the development of a personality trait which is the opposite of the original, repressed trait.

Early in life, reaction formations may occur in response to the aggressive impulses generated by the many frustrations of childhood, such as weaning, toilet training, the birth of siblings, illnesses and absences of parents, rivalries, and real or fantasized deficits (Menninger 1959). The child's abiding wish to be accepted and loved, along with the need to preserve a positive image of the parents, necessitates that his anger and hatefulness be deeply repressed. It may be that such repression and reaction formations are heightened in children who are exposed to undue frustration, who are particularly sensitive, or who are born with a high degree of innate aggressiveness.

Another factor thought to influence the strength of reaction formations against aggression is that of birth order. Rosenbaum

(1963) found that the oldest child, saddled with caretaking responsibilities, often feels "unmitigated violence" (p. 515) toward younger siblings. In a study of postnatal depression, Beattie (1978) reported that firstborn females frequently experience intense anxiety that they will harm their baby. These aggressive impulses are turned inward, resulting in depression. The author links this dynamic to a history of jealousy toward a younger sibling. Seeking parental approval, "the child soon learns that she is expected to be loving towards the newcomer, and she often develops an exaggerated care for him to mask the underlying hate" (p. 247). Firstborns, it should be noted, are overrepresented among mental health professionals (Henry et al. 1973). Even when they are not the oldest, therapists tend to have played a caretaking role in relation to younger siblings (Reich 1984).

When aggressive impulses are heavily defended against, an individual's identity may center around selfless giving and self-sacrifice. Schafer (1954) maintains that the assumption of a "saintly" role is particularly seductive to those individuals with strong and pervasive reaction formations against dependent and hostile wishes. Schafer perceptively describes how, for the psychological tester as well as the psychotherapist, helping the patient can carry saintly connotations:

> Is it not so that the tester does his best to help, no matter how provocative or "ungrateful" the patient? Does not the tester give out with all he has so long as he believes it is for the patient's good? Does he not implicitly promise psychological salvation? Will he not subdue his own needs and resentments and selflessly try to understand and feel the tragedy of the patient? Is not this code like that of a saint with a sinner, a slave or a leper? It certainly is—as it is in the case of the therapist too—once we get below the level of objective, logical appreciation of reality and confront some of our magical thoughts and wishes. [p. 24]

While reaction formations against aggression appear to be a common component of the wish to heal, they can also present difficulties in regard to the treatment process. Therapists who are excessively defended against aggressive impulses may be hampered when faced with confronting patients, setting firm limits and boundaries, requiring payment, making painful interpretations, or taking decisive action. Their interventions may reflect attempts at rescue or reparation, regardless of patients' actual treatment needs. Intent on disowning any hint of hostility, such therapists will have difficulty helping their patients to face or work through negative transferences. They may be so busy attempting to provide the patient with a "new object" that they hinder any opportunity the patient may have to resolve conflicts with "old objects" or to surrender the infantile wish for an idealized parent and adequately mourn this loss. Finally, therapists who are unaware of their own aggression are likely to express such warded-off impulses in disguised and potentially harmful ways.

In certain situations, the therapist's capacity to tolerate and even to express negative feelings toward the patient may be a critical factor influencing treatment outcome. In his seminal article on countertransference, Winnicott (1949) applies the term *objective countertransference* to those feelings that are realistically induced by the patient's actual personality and behavior. He contrasts this type of reaction with the more idiosyncratic countertransference that represents the therapist's insufficiently analyzed and conflict-laden responses. Winnicott maintains that, at times, the therapist's hate for a patient can be objective and appropriate. Furthermore, he argues that modulated expressions of this hatred may promote the treatment of some highly disturbed patients, who may need to evoke the therapist's hatred before they can feel connected in a more positive way. Winnicott also suggests that such expressions may enable the therapist to endure and carry out the treatment.

Frederickson (1990) also emphasizes the importance of overcoming defenses against hateful feelings. He contends that countertransference hate can become part of an empathic position when the therapist is able to identify its object-relational sources. Frederickson presents a segment of the treatment of a 27-year-old man with a borderline disturbance, whose seething rage increasingly becomes focused upon the therapist:

> At one point he became thoroughly enraged, having concluded that since I didn't accept his screaming, I didn't accept him. In the midst

of this tirade I tried to talk. "Shut the fuck up!" he yelled, raging on. I interrupted, "You expect that you should be able to shit on people and they should like it." "Yes I do. That's it." I continued, "And you are wondering why your parents got away with it and you can't." "Yes," he said sadly. He then continued, lamenting that his mother's contempt for him would never change. The next hour he apologized for being rude. His first apology. [p. 487]

Frederickson concludes that his feelings of hatred gave him an empathic understanding of how the patient had felt with his parents. He argues that if the patient enacts the role of the abusing parent, while the therapist assumes the position of the abused child, expressions of warmth cannot be considered to be empathic. Warmth would represent an empathic failure, since the child did not feel warmth toward the parent at the time of being abused. When the therapist attempts to meet the patient's hatefulness with kindness and sympathy, the patient may come to distrust the therapist for loving him while he is acting destructively. "Feeling increasingly bad and guilty, hateful and envious, he renews his attacks. A vicious circle begins: when we hide from our hatred, the patient becomes more hateful" (p. 491).

In a ground-breaking paper, Maltsberger and Buie (1974) discuss the countertransference hatred that suicidal patients may elicit in therapists, and how difficulties managing such feelings can constitute a major obstacle in treatment. The authors distinguish between two components of countertransference hatred: feelings of malice toward the patient, and feelings of aversion. The latter often bring about impulses to abandon and thereby escape from the patient. The authors declare:

> Paradoxically, most therapists find the component of lesser danger, malice, more painful to tolerate than the component with lethal potential, the dangerous urge to abandon. In fact, there is a temptation to resort to abandonment of the patient in order not to acknowledge, bear, and place in perspective the countertransference malice. [p. 626]

Hence, tragic consequences may result from a therapist's incapacity to tolerate (rather than to fend off or act out) conscious sadistic wishes. Searles (1979) reaches the same conclusion in regard to the disguised sadism contained in an overly "dedicated" stance on the part of therapists. He states:

And the suicidal patient, who finds us so unable to be aware of the murderous feeling he fosters in us through his guilt- and anxiety-producing threats of suicide, feels increasingly constricted, perhaps indeed to the point of suicide, by the therapist who, in reaction formation against his intensifying, unconscious wishes to kill the patient, hovers increasingly "protectively" about the latter, for whom he feels an omnipotence-based physicianly concern. Hence it is, paradoxically, the very physician most anxiously concerned to *keep the patient alive* who tends most vigorously, at an unconscious level, to drive him to what has become to seem the only autonomous act left to him—namely, suicide. [p. 74]

EXPRESSIONS OF AGGRESSION

Although reaction formations against aggressive strivings are thought to be characteristic of psychotherapists, this does not mean that the underlying sadistic impulses are never expressed.

Certainly the therapeutic situation provides therapists with ample opportunities to do so. A psychoanalytic approach to treatment requires the therapist to refrain from gratifying many of the patient's yearnings, which must eventually produce a certain degree of suffering. In a discussion of the concept of the analyst's abstinence, Freud (1918) remarks that "it is expedient to deny [the patient] precisely those satisfactions which he desires most intensely and expresses most importunately" (p. 164). Moreover, in order to resolve psychic conflict fully, an optimal degree of anxiety must be sustained. Freud acknowledges the sadistic element contained in this technical requirement when he states that "cruel though it may sound, we must see to it that the patient's suffering, to a degree that is in some way or other effective, does not come to an end prematurely" (p. 163). Tarachow (1962) also emphasizes the pain and disappointment that are an inevitable result of the analytic ground rules:

We assist our patients to develop access to their real feelings, especially to the therapist, and then we refuse to treat these feelings as
real. The patient is urged to treat his love for us as real, and we snub
him for his pains. The very basis for an analysis involves *really*
disappointing the patient. In psychotherapy we do not so completely disappoint the patient. This makes the therapist's role more
bearable in psychotherapy than in analysis. [p. 381]

Many of the common clinical interventions can involve direct or
indirect expressions of aggressive and sadistic impulses. In order to
identify areas requiring treatment, therapists may point out their
patients' weaknesses, deficits, and problematic behaviors. At times
they must confront and thereby puncture patients' illusions and
expectations. Family therapy techniques often aim to subvert the
family system's equilibrium. Even silence on the part of the clinician can represent hostility, indifference, or abandonment and thus
express sadistic aims.

Interpretations are particularly likely to provide opportunities
for instinctual discharge. As Greenson (1967) notes, transmitting
insight to patients may involve libidinal or hostile impulses, depending on whether the activity of interpreting is unconsciously
felt to be helpful or hurtful. Under the guise of providing insight,
therapists can humiliate and ridicule their patients, and further
undermine their already tenuous self-esteem (Jaffe 1986). Even
when properly and therapeutically administered, interpretations
can be considered aggressive in that they rob patients of their
fantasies, defenses, and gratifications. According to Tarachow
(1962), the principal consequence of an interpretation is the loss of
an infantile object, and when correct it is followed by a mild
depression.

By rigidly adhering to the tenets of classical analytic technique,
therapists can engage in a sort of one-upmanship that may scarcely
conceal underlying hostility. Therapists frequently refrain from
answering questions, remaining silent or responding with questions
of their own. This may be experienced as frustrating and unsympa-
thetic by patients who have not been provided with a rationale for
such behavior. Some therapists do not reply to Christmas cards,

preferring to analyze the patient's motives for sending one. Others may not offer condolences to a patient who has suffered a death in the family, presumably to avoid interfering with expressions of ambivalence over the loss. While such approaches may be justifiable on theoretical grounds, the aggressive component is undeniable and is likely to result in damage to the therapeutic alliance.

Certain forms of psychotherapy display more overt expressions of aggression. Glover (1929) points to the sadistic roots of therapeutic approaches that rely on exhortation and direct or implied reproach and criticism of the patient. Treatments based on emotional catharsis, such as Primal Therapy, involve outright assaults on the patient's defenses. Somatic therapies, such as Bioenergetics and Rolfing, attempt to break through the patient's "muscular armor." Aversion Therapy, in which a maladaptive response is paired with an aversive stimulus such as electric shock or a nausea-producing drug, has been used by behavior therapists in the treatment of sexual deviations, alcoholism, and smoking (Bucher and Lovaas 1968). Other behavioral treatments, such as flooding and implosion, aim to maximize the patient's anxiety through confronting the patient with real or imagined fear-inducing situations and to hold the anxiety at this pitch until it extinguishes (Levis and Hare 1977). Finally, some of the more recent approaches to short-term psychodynamic treatment involve rather aggressive prodding and confrontation of the client.

Practitioners may also find in the role of therapist a relatively safe way of mounting an attack on authority and tradition. Bugental (1964) addresses this motive:

Study and observation confirm how the needless inhibitions of society complicate the lives of all: the taboos about sexual talk and actions; the guilt about ambivalence toward parents, spouses, and others; the shame of death wishes and other hostile impulses. With the authority of being a therapist, one can strike back at these influences. Notice how often psychotherapists, particularly in their earlier years of practice, become great users of the four-letter words (Feldman, 1955). Notice how often they are flagrant in their expressions of sexual and hostile impulses. It seems quite clear that this may be an acting-out, a counter-phobic kind of behavior which represents the celebration of the licenses of being a therapist. Thus one may pay back society, hit back at authority. It is not a matter of chance, for example, that most therapists tend to be political and social liberals. We would like to think that this is chiefly because they have had an opportunity to see the crippling effect of social ills, and this is one significant reason. On the other hand, the person who is in some revolt against what he feels is social injustice may find in the· practice of psychotherapy a relatively safe way to express his rebellion. [p. 274]

Therapists who harbor unresolved anger over noxious prohibitions and taboos in their own backgrounds may also rebel vicariously by encouraging patients to ignore societal norms and conventions (Guy 1987).

As we have seen, certain aspects of the therapeutic situation, the role of the therapist, and the techniques employed in conducting psychotherapy either require or readily lend themselves to the expression of aggressive impulses. What remains to be explored is what the *therapist* brings to this equation. Hammer (1972), for example, contends that individuals with strong sadistic trends may be attracted to working with those who are emotionally disturbed, as they are often helpless and vulnerable. Such therapists, he maintains, attempt to control and to frighten patients in order to compensate for their own interpersonal fearfulness.

Defense mechanisms are thought to provide partial or disguised expressions of the very impulse that is being defended against. Thus, Searles (1967) suggests that even the therapist's dedication to his work contains sadistic features. He asserts that the therapist "is unaware of how much he is enjoying his tormenting the patient with his dedication, of which the patient, who feels himself to be so hateful and incapable of giving anything worthwhile to anyone, feels so unworthy" (p. 76). Searles expresses suspicion at therapists' attempts to fully submerge their own self-interest in the welfare of their patients, viewing this as an unconscious defense against hatred and other "negative" emotions.

Excessive therapeutic zeal on the part of clinicians can be fueled, in part, by sadism and a need for power and control. Main (1957) applies this notion to both medical and psychological treatments:

Refusal to accept therapeutic defeat can, however, lead to therapeutic mania, to subjecting the patient to what is significantly called
"heroic surgical attack," to a frenzy of treatments each carrying
more danger for the patient than the last, often involving him in
varying degrees of unconsciousness, near-death, pain, anxiety, mutilation or poisoning. Perhaps many of the desperate treatments in
medicine can be justified by expediency, but history has an awk-
ward habit of judging some as fashions, more helpful to the *amour
propre* of the therapist than to the patient. The sufferer who frus-
trates a keen therapist by failing to improve is always in danger of
meeting primitive human behavior disguised as treatment. [p. 129]

In describing the dynamics of the sadistic therapist, Glover (1929)
reaches the same conclusion: "The patient's illness is a source of
inner irritation to the therapist and since the latter cannot escape by
flight, i.e., by refusing to have anything to do with the case, he aims
at an immediate and violent cure, viz. the cure by attack" (p. 14).

Taking a Jungian approach, Guggenbuhl-Craig (1971) suggests
that underlying sadism is typically a part of the psychoanalyst's
shadow, Jung's term for the unconscious opposite of what the
individual stresses in his consciousness. Once the patient and analyst have established a relationship, the analyst begins to have
fantasies concerning the patient. The author continues:

At this point a destructive trait very often shows itself in the analyst.
Strange, negative fantasies may crop up which persist and even give
a certain kind of satisfaction. They may revolve around a possible
suicide by the patient, or the outbreak of psychosis. They may be
destructive images of the patient's family or professional life, or his
health. Such images exert a strange fascination on the analyst. Instead of positive concern for the patient, they show an enthrallment
with his negative potentialities. This is frequently expressed, in conversations between analysts, by the obvious relish with which one
tells the other about the grave danger facing a particular patient.
[pp. 50–51]

The therapist's conscious or unconscious sadism can clearly have
an adverse impact on the patient and on the therapeutic process.
Rather than helping the patient to overcome fears and mistrust of

others, therapy is likely to reenact past traumas and to reinforce maladaptive defenses. Rather than promoting moderation of a harsh superego, the sadistic therapist is likely to intensify the patient's self-criticism and sense of guilt. Left unchecked, the therapist's sadistic impulses may lead to blatant exploitation of patients: As noted earlier in this chapter, Marmor (1976) found that a common characterological feature of therapists who seduce female clients is the presence of unconscious hostility toward women.

Aggressive and sadistic impulses can also be generated by the therapeutic interaction itself. Dealing with especially resistant, uncooperative, or self-defeating clients may leave clinicians feeling frustrated and angry. Therapists who work with addictions and other disorders of impulse control frequently feel thwarted by repeated relapses in their patients. Hostility may also accompany feelings of envy toward patients. Whitman and Bloch (1990) note that therapists may experience envy of the patient's therapy and of the nurturance being provided, of the patient's physical, emotional, financial, or occupational freedom and of the patient's youth or success.[6] As the patient grows and matures, envious feelings can intensify, and the therapist may even envy a successful termination. These various forms of envy may also contribute to what Klauber (1976) describes as "almost a tendency" (p. 288) among psychoanalysts to sabotage relationships with analysands following termination. Klauber attributes this phenomenon to the high degree of instinctual restraint demanded of the analyst.

When reflecting on past treatments, therapists may also burden themselves with guilt and self-reproach when they conclude that some ideal standard was not met. As exemplified by Bugental (1964):

---

[6]Therapist envy is such a neglected topic that it appears to warrant the distinction of being "a far dirtier little secret than sex or money" (Elliott 1974, p. 17). As with so many other issues that are shunned in the professional literature, Searles is one of the few authors to address it. He states, "But what I had not realized until the last very few years was how competitive I am with the patient in his analysand role—how much I envy him for being an analysand, and how much I assume that if I had the freedom to be in his place on the couch, I would do a vastly better job of being an analysand" (Langs and Searles 1980, p. 92).

This is a story of the therapist's guilt. If I am to be a growing, evolving person, each old patient I see again is an accusation; each patient of former years will be in some measure someone who trusted me, and whom I failed by today's standards. If I become despondent or self-punitive, I am acting out a neurotic-type guilt; but if I recognize the legitimate responsibility I had in this matter, I am revitalized in my own growth.

But there is yet one further way in which this guilt operates. When I recognize that I am continuing to try to grow, to increase my awareness, skill, and competence in effectively being in the relationship with my patients, then I must look at my patients today and know that each one is getting less than I hope I will be giving his successor 5 years hence. There is guilt in this too. [p. 276]

MASOCHISTIC TENDENCIES

A discussion of unconscious aggressive strivings on the part of the psychotherapist is not complete without a consideration of masochistic motives. According to the *Encyclopedia of Psychoanalysis*, "sadism and masochism occur in pairs of opposites in the individual, and represent the active and passive aspect of partial instinctual drives which pass through psycho-sexual developmental stages" (Eidelberg 1968, p. 386). It was Freud (1920) who identified the two as component instincts, viewing masochism as complementary to sadism. Essentially, he regarded masochism as sadism turned against the self, although Freud did not rule out the possibility of primary masochism.

Certain aspects of the therapeutic setting can encourage the therapist's masochism and lead to related countertransference difficulties. Greif (1985) points to the high degree of self-denial that is required, citing such examples as the physical inactivity, abstinence from acting out or responding to the patient in kind, the delay required to formulate interpretations, and the social isolation. Highlighting the martyrlike aspect of the therapist's need for restraint and obligation to maintain confidentiality, Kottler (1986) states, "We suffer in silence so that others may be released from pain" (p. 61). Greenson (1962) refers to the constant assault on the therapist's narcissism caused by the patient's projections and resistance to change, as well as to the depressive pull to identify with patients in the process of empathic listening. Schafer (1954) also notes that therapists can be masochistically gratified by patients' demands, abuse, and non-compliance, and may actually exacerbate such behaviors by unconsciously provoking anxiety in patients.

Upon reflection, there appears to be a masochistic element to the very desire to expose oneself to those who are ill and disturbed. In a discussion comparing aspects of shamanism with psychoanalysis, Lewin (1946) remarks, "The shaman was in danger. The whole history of primitive medicine testifies to the primitive unconscious feeling that in the presence of the sick one is in danger. Clinical psychoanalysis, studying germ phobias and morbid fears of disease, substantiates the widespread existence of this thesis in the unconscious" (p. 198). The same notion is encountered in a passage of Freud's (1901) in which he asserts that "no one who, like me, conjures up the most evil of those half-tamed demons that inhabit the human breast, and seeks to wrestle with them, can expect to come through the struggle unscathed" (p. 109).

Not only do therapists subject themselves to an unconsciously feared situation, they also risk taking on the psychological disturbances of their patients. As noted earlier, Jung (1946) warns that patients' illnesses can be transferred to their therapists by activating their own latent conflicts. Jung claims that such "psychic infections . . . are in fact the predestined concomitants of [the therapist's] work, and thus fully in accord with the instinctive disposition of his own life" (p. 177). A masochistic orientation must clearly be an important component of such an instinctual disposition.

Similarly, Schafer (1954) suggests that masochistic tendencies may attract an individual to spending large portions of the day with persons who are seriously limited in the capacity to give of themselves and to tolerate anxiety or frustration. Such an orientation may be essential, moreover, in order to make bearable the more demanding and punishing aspects of the work, such as dealing with negative transferences.

In the psychoanalytic approach to treatment, the therapist encourages the patient to reexperience and to verbalize the most potent and disturbing feelings and experiences of the patient's past, as though the therapist were cause and object of them (McLaughlin 1961). Wheelis (1959) emphasizes the stressfulness of being the object of intense transferences on such a continuous basis. He states that the analyst

> cannot expect his secretary to mollify the patient who has come to hate him, or call on God to extricate him from a transference impasse. There are only two persons in the consulting room and the analyst has been tagged. He's "it" and must handle as best he can a demand for a magical performance that continues—fearful, angry, trusting, or frantic—hour after hour, day after day. [p. 178]

As the patient's past is relived in the course of treatment, the therapist must withstand the onslaught of the patient's rage. In a sense, there must be a certain degree of masochism in the therapist to accept and endure the patient's hostility and other strong feelings without reciprocating. This temporary masochistic stance is described by Tower (1956): "There developed in me, on a transient basis, an amount of masochism sufficient to absorb the sadism which he was now unloading, and which had terrified him throughout his life" (p. 248).

While masochistic tendencies in the therapist may be useful at times in promoting the therapeutic process, when excessive they can also hinder and disrupt it. Masochistic therapists may unconsciously collude with their patients' resistances, fostering them rather than attempting to dispel them through interpretation. Racker (1953a) notes that the analyst often perceives resistance as the patient's hatred toward him: "For the analyst *believes* the patient when the latter unconsciously attributes badness to him; that is to say, he believes himself to be as bad as the patient's introjected objects which have been projected upon him and which account for the patient's main resistances" (p. 321). Thus, by accepting and identifying with the patient's projected bad objects, the therapist may unwittingly heighten resistances to the treatment process.

It is widely maintained that masochistic therapists unconsciously provoke patients into abusing them. They typically invite attack by unconsciously failing to understand the patient, causing confusion and frustration to mount, and thereby encouraging the patient to focus angry feelings on the therapist (Hammer 1972). In a 1958 paper on unconscious masochism in the analyst, Racker writes that masochism "induces the analyst to allow the patient to manage the analytic situation, and even to collaborate with his defenses, preferring, for instance, to let himself be tortured and victimized rather than frustrate the patient" (p. 561). Masochistic analysts, he asserts, tend to abuse or misapply such analytic techniques as the one recommending that the analyst be relatively passive and nondirective. Submitting to their patients, they become excessively passive and interpret too little, resulting in a reduction of therapeutic gains.

Maltsberger and Buie (1974) also describe masochistic therapists as subjecting themselves to continued expressions of material meant to devalue and degrade them. They unconsciously avoid challenging or interpreting such material because it provides punishment and thereby relieves guilt concerning their own hostilities. In brief, there is an "unconscious tendency to turn the encounter with a hostile patient into a penance" (p. 629). Such therapists allow or provoke patients to "dump" on them, justifying it as part of a necessary therapeutic abreaction. Pointing to an extreme example, the authors remark:

> Under the spell of such an illusion some therapists have even permitted patients to smear them with feces for periods of time, quite unaware that they were satisfying their own craving for degradation, and further burdening a psychotic patient by inviting him to do the degrading. [p. 631]

More commonly it is verbal degradation that therapists subject themselves to. Rationalized as an attitude of tolerance and acceptance, masochistic clinicians fail to set limits and allow or encourage patients to attack and punish them. Thoroughly antitherapeutic, this serves only to frighten patients and deepen their guilt. As Wishnie (1977) observes, a patient can never achieve self-acceptance if he is allowed to damage and destroy others.

Therapists who set no limits on patients' abuse and aggression may also view themselves as providing a *container* (Bion 1962) for their patients' pathology. As Frederickson (1990) points out, however, therapists who passively submit to such assaults are acting as *repositories*, not containers. He elaborates: "Containing does not refer merely to holding feelings inside. Containment is the process by which we label those feelings and understand their meaning within the transference. As containers we are not simply passive receptacles; we are active digesters of experience" (p. 491).

In order to guard against the associated therapeutic hazards, therapists must become aware of their own masochistic tendencies and begin to understand their sources. While the specifics will vary for each individual, it is possible to state common dynamics. Riemann (1968) for instance, suggests that analysts who are overly self-sacrificing often have depressive personalities. They may masochistically allow patients to be overdemanding due to excessive anxiety over losing them. Racker (1958) postulates that if the analyst's activity unconsciously signifies an attempt to surpass or destroy the father, oedipal guilt may manifest masochistically by subverting the work. Racker also views the analyst's masochism as deriving from an "unconscious tendency to repeat or invert a certain infantile relationship with his parents in which he sacrifices either himself or them" (p. 561). Analysts may, for example, unconsciously seek to suffer, through their patients, what they had actually or in fantasy made their parents suffer. Or, as Roth (1987) notes, therapists who were given the family role of rescuer or parentified child may develop masochistic tendencies due to excessive guilt for having assumed responsibilities beyond their capacities. These latter dynamics may be viewed as components of the need for reparation, a motive that will be examined in Chapter 6.

Left unchecked, masochistic trends can eventually lead to serious impairment in professional functioning. In a discussion of the "burnout" syndrome in psychoanalysts, Cooper (1986) states that masochistic defenses typically manifest as discouragement, boredom, and loss of interest in the treatment process. He writes:

Self-reproaches are translated into projected aggression against the analytic work. The various tensions, uncertainties, and sources of self-doubt that plague every analyst are, for these masochistically inclined individuals, an unanswerable source of inner guilt and self-recriminations, as well as an unconscious opportunity for adopting the role of victim toward their patients and their profession. . . . It is evidence of both the attraction of masochistic victimization and of the harshness of the superego of the analysts involved that they are willing to doom themselves to a relatively pleasureless professional existence, for the sake of the deflection of the inner reproach against their talent and skill. Feeling helpless against their inner conscience which charges them with not helping their patients, they say, "Don't blame me, blame psychoanalysis." The extent of the cynicism that may be part of this defense can be startling in depth. I know analysts who have refused to permit members of their own family to enter analysis because they did not regard the treatment as helpful. [p. 593]

The end result of such masochistic defenses, suggests Cooper, is chronic anger at one's patients, one's profession and colleagues, and one's self. These profoundly discouraged analysts come to approach their patients with attitudes of sarcasm, denigration, and devaluation—ironically demonstrating the common roots of masochism and sadism.

A final point is that individuals who are drawn to the role of therapist are often ill prepared for their patients' expressions of hostility. Roth (1987) elaborates on this theme:

If any one element is underestimated in approaching a career as a psychotherapist, it is the amount of hostility and rejection that will be one's lot in the pursuit of therapeutic helpfulness. A great threat to personal integrity and self-worth will come about through open rejection of one's most heartfelt efforts to be of use, the sharing of intuitions with the patient, and the provision of great patience and forbearance; the patient may still, in spite of all these, declare the therapist inadequate, short of the mark, and uncaring. The more regressed or disturbed a patient is, the more destructive the hostility will be. All but the most farsighted of therapists never consider, when choosing therapy as a career, the major share of daily experience this open hostility will consume. [p. 2]

Surveys indicate that patients' hostility and aggression are among the greatest sources of stress reported by psychotherapists

(Deutsch 1984, Farber and Heifetz 1981). Fear of evoking rage can cause even experienced clinicians to try to appease patients, and may deter them from setting firm limits and boundaries (Ackerman 1949, Gutheil 1989). At least one study has found that therapeutic progress is impeded when therapists are conflicted about accepting their clients' expressions of hostility (Bandura et al. 1960).

UNRESOLVED OEDIPAL CONFLICT

In most mammals the male is more aggressive than the female. This aggressiveness includes not only intermale aggression, but also irritable aggression and territorial aggression (Darley et al. 1981). From as early as 2 or 3 years of age, human males behave more aggressively than human females (Pederson and Bell 1970). In the nonhuman primates, gender differences are more marked than among humans. Adult male baboons are twice as big as adult females and possess large canine teeth that are absent in the female. Similar differences in size, strength, body structure, and aggressiveness are apparent in chimpanzees, gorillas, and most other monkeys and apes.

Sex-related aggression has been found to correlate with testosterone levels. In adult male animals, castration greatly reduces all forms of aggressive behavior. For centuries, farmers have used castration to turn bulls into placid steers, and a gelded horse is considerably more docile and slow to anger than a stallion. The same effect is produced by administering estrogens and progesterone to a male animal (Moyer 1971). In countries where castration is prescribed for men who are repeatedly convicted of sex crimes, both heterosexual and homosexual aggressive attacks have been reported to disappear, along with the offender's sex drive (Hawke 1950, Laschet 1973). In one study, there was a resurgence of violent behavior when castrated men were injected with testosterone (Hawke 1950).

Human behavior, of course, is heavily influenced by social and environmental as well as physiological factors. The process of socialization fosters the development of behaviors, feelings, and a sense of self that are regarded as gender-appropriate within a given

culture (Kagan 1964, Williams 1977). Kagan summarizes this differential socialization as follows:

> In sum, females are supposed to inhibit aggression and open display
> of sexual urges, to be passive with men, to be nurturant with others,
> to cultivate attractiveness, and to maintain an affective, socially
> poised and friendly posture with others. Males are urged to be
> aggressive in face of attack, independent in problem situations,
> sexually aggressive, in control of regressive urges, and suppressive of
> strong emotions, especially anxiety. [p. 143]

In her discussion of sex-role socialization, Kaplan (1979) similarly
concludes that females are expected to be emotionally open, nurturant, and affiliative, while males are encouraged to take an emotionally inhibited, self-assertive, and interpersonally distant stance.

The foregoing suggests that many features of psychotherapeutic
work are more congruent with the biologically and socially based
roles of females than of males. Indeed, numerous authors contend
that becoming a therapist requires the full development of the feminine aspects of one's personality. Burton (1972), for example, writes:

> Intuition, sensitivity, affect, feeling, artistry, color, all highly relevant
> to the work of the therapist, are better realized as feminine qualities
> and they are most certainly correlated with success and gratification
> in work as a therapist. This does not mean that masculinity has no
> place in psychotherapy, only that a primary focus on the phallus and
> its expressions leaves something to be desired. [p. 17]

Similarly, in a paper on the selection of analytic candidates, Eisendorfer (1959) insists that, for the male applicant, the most crucial
indication of aptitude to become an analyst involves the degree of
accessibility of his "latent femininity and his correlated passivity"
(p. 375). This, according to Eisendorfer, is what determines a
man's capacity to be in touch with his own unconscious and those
of others, as well as the capacity to be patient enough to allow the
client's unconscious to emerge. He states that "the aggressive masculine tendency 'to be doing' must be subordinated to this passive
capacity to listen and understand" (p. 375).

We may now pose the following question: What motivates certain men to choose a vocation that is in many ways at odds with the attributes commonly associated with their gender? In keeping with the widely held view that gender identity is consolidated during the oedipal phase of development, speculation on this question has centered around the Oedipus complex. In essence, it has been suggested that male therapists possess an unusual capacity for passivity and greater access to their latent femininity due to an atypical or incomplete resolution of the oedipal situation.

Much of what has been written on this topic focuses on psychiatrists and other physicians. In a discussion of the childhood histories of physicians, Kasper (1959) notes that sex-role confusion is typical:

> What we do find with considerable consistency is a strong bond with an encouraging, even seductive mother, and an ambivalent relationship with a father seen as aloof, distant, but masculine and strong. There are more than ordinary doubts about sexual role, and womanly aspirations to feed, care for, and make happy are frequent. We find indications of not feeling equal to other boys, not wanting to be like father, being bookish and curious about nature. Conscious fear of competition and feelings of physical inadequacy are also more common in future doctors than in other children. [p. 263]

According to psychoanalytic theory it is during the oedipal stage of development, from about 2½ to 6 years of age, that gender identity crystallizes and the degree of aggression versus passivity of the personality is largely determined. As generally formulated, the young boy's increasing awareness, during this phase, of the sexual significance of his genitals leads him to desire his mother and to envy and fear his father as a rival for mother's affection. In normal male development the resolution of the oedipal conflict brings about an identification with the father and a repudiation of feminine tendencies. A passive attitude, especially toward other males, is strongly repressed and often overcompensated against, because it is unconsciously associated with castration.

Based on their study of the psychodynamics of physicians, Zabarenko and colleagues (1970) state that many physicians exhibit a "unique partial and deferred resolution of the oedipal conflict. . . .

This oedipal unresolution leads to a career choice which sanctions and/or requires the integrated exhibition and use of maternal and paternal introjects" (p. 106). The authors assert that their findings support the hypothesis that a self-concept as one who repairs the defective and castrated serves to bind castration anxiety. Their results, they add, were in close agreement with the few cases reported in the psychoanalytic literature concerning the treatment of ill physicians (Glauber 1953, Lewin 1946, Nunberg 1938, Simmel 1926).

Based on his experience in training psychiatric residents, and his summary of twenty-five autobiographies written by male residents, Ford (1963) presents a psychodynamic formulation of ego development in children who later become psychiatrists. He postulates a series of affective crises in the young child involving seductive demandingness on the part of the mother and a great deal of phallic-aggressive hostility toward the father during the oedipal years. These constitute threats to ego integrity and result in several trends. An incomplete resolution of the oedipal conflict seriously interferes with paternal identification. Heightened libidinal and aggressive drives remain largely unbound, until tenuous control is achieved by means of a harsh and demanding superego and by the displacement of intense castration anxiety to the intellectual sphere. In a similar vein, McLaughlin (1961) views the role of healer as an enactment of a "pregenital identification with the nurturing, suffering mother and as an avoidance of the guilt and anxiety of the competitive erotic and aggressive struggle with the internalized father" (p. 121). He too states that, unconsciously, the use of the intellect is equated with forbidden libidinal and aggressive strivings. Therefore the analyst's intellectual powers must be used primarily in the service of others. McLaughlin notes that the role of physician, and especially that of the analyst, involves extreme renunciation of instinctual gratification. He interprets the Hippocratic Oath as a formalized statement of this renunciation:

> The swearer is to replace oedipal rivalry, sibling competitiveness, and paternal preeminence with a nurturing regard for father, siblings, and sons. More generally, egocentricity, exploitiveness, self-aggrandizement, sexual rapacity and seductiveness are all fore-

sworn, as well as direct expression of aggression in the service of the self. *Then and only then* may the healer hope to achieve satisfaction in life and the respect of his fellow man. [p. 108]

McLaughlin views psychoanalysis as the medical specialty that both demands the greatest renunciation of instinctual discharge and provides the most exposure to evocative circumstances. One might infer, therefore, that those physicians who become analysts are the ones who have the greatest need, for defensive purposes, to renounce the use of their aggressive capacities primarily in their own behalf.

Finally, Searles (1966) regards the decision to become a psychotherapist as a way of clinging stubbornly to oedipal aspirations. Thus, in addition to providing a defense against oedipal strivings and conflict, the role of therapist furnishes the practitioner with repeated exposure to the "forbidden" erotic aspirations that naturally develop within the therapeutic dyad. Through their work, then, therapists may be "focusing on our patients the demands which our parents failed to satiate, and the ungratifiability of which we refuse to accept" (p. 322).

To summarize, there appears to be some support for the hypothesis that in many male psychotherapists the choice of profession may be associated with an incompletely resolved oedipal complex. For these individuals, the role of therapist represents a continuing maternal identification as well as a way of dealing with unconscious anxiety and guilt regarding aggressive and libidinal impulses.

Few authors have had much to say regarding oedipal development as it may relate to women who become therapists. This is partly a function of the relative neglect of female psychology in general, but may also reflect the general lack of clarity that exists in regard to the oedipal phase in girls. As typically described, the girl's oedipal phase begins when she discovers that the mother, contrary to the infantile beliefs of both boys and girls, lacks a penis. The girl concludes that the penis has been lost or mutilated, resulting in a depreciation of the mother and of femaleness in general. This devaluation of the mother, when combined with anger at her for not giving the girl a penis (and thus, in the child's mind, leaving her "deficient"), leads to a turning away from the original object of attachment. The mother now becomes a rival for the attention and affection of the father. The wish for a penis is gradually supplanted by the wish for a baby from the father. In the normal course of development, the girl eventually relinquishes her disappointed oedipal aspirations and identifies with the ambivalently held mother. Positive feelings toward the mother typically return with the resolution of the Oedipus complex.

When resolution of the oedipal stage is incomplete, the girl continues to disparage the mother and never fully identifies with her. As depicted by Horner (1990):

> Clearly feminine, with a stance of compliance toward a loved and idealized father, oedipally fixated daughters are stuck with the de-valued image of the mother, and thus of themselves and of women in general. Consciously rejecting an identification with the devalued mother, they may identify with the idealized father, often through their intellects, while maintaining the sense of femininity that came from the primary identification with the mother of attachment and symbiosis. They may experience the triangle intrapsychically, feel-ing torn between the conflicting identifications parallelling feelings of being torn between the two other points of the interpersonal triangle. [pp. 227-228]

It may be that the practice of psychotherapy provides the oedi-pally fixated woman with a unique opportunity to reconcile her conflicting identifications. The role of therapist encompasses both an *authority* dimension (Langs 1973) and an *empathic* dimension (Little 1951). As Kaplan (1979) notes, the authority dimension re-quires such personality characteristics as independence, assertive-ness, and emotional distance—all of which are consistent with masculine patterns of sex-role socialization. The empathic dimen-sion, on the other hand, involves the nurturant and socially compe-tent traits promoted by the feminine socialization process. Thus, the role of therapist enables a woman to integrate authority and empathy, or, as Horner (1990) puts it, power and femininity.

A related oedipal dynamic involves the fear of success. Freud (1924) linked fear of success with guilt feelings arising during the oedipal phase, when the child perceives growth and development as rivalrous and fraught with danger. Competitive aims of any sort are repressed due to their close association with oedipal strivings. The young woman who remains oedipally conflicted may struggle with continuing fears of surpassing her mother. If her parents have encouraged professional aspirations, such an individual faces a dilemma. Becoming a psychotherapist may provide an answer to such a quandary, in that career aspirations are met within the context of a professional role that in many ways requires a maternal, nurturing stance.[7] Thus, for certain women as well as men, the role of psychotherapist may represent a compromise by which they attempt to reconcile the various conflicts engendered by the oedipal phase of development.

---

[7]Burnside (1986) found that female psychologists in private practice set their own fees significantly lower than those of male colleagues, regardless of level of experience or training. This may reflect a continuing fear of competition and success in female therapists.

5

MOTIVES RELATED TO NARCISSISM AND THE DEVELOPMENT OF THE SELF

In the Greek myth, the young Narcissus fell in love with his own image reflected in a pool, and, unable to possess the object of his desires, killed himself. Taking the name from this mythological figure, Freud (1914) uses the term "narcissisim" to refer to the state of self-directed libido, or, in other words, a concentration of psychological interest upon the self. While he notes that excessive narcissism provides a major predisposition toward psychopathology, Freud postulates that narcissistic operations constitute a normal stage or characteristic of early development. He also suggests that in the course of normal development the major portion of libido remains narcissistic, or self-directed, throughout life. In the contemporary psychoanalytic literature, while narcissism is still defined as self-love, it has also been widely discussed as a matter of personal esteem necessary for relations with others. This chapter deals with therapists' motivations pertaining to narcissistic needs and the development of the self, including such issues as the regulation of self-esteem, the role of the ego-ideal, the process of identification, and the need to overcome a diffuse identity formation.

When narcissism reaches pathological extremes it results in recognizable personality configurations. Nemiah (1961) describes individuals with a narcissistic character disorder as exhibiting great ambition, highly unrealistic goals, intolerance of failures and imperfections in themselves, and a nearly insatiable craving for love, attention, and admiration, upon which their self-esteem is based. Kernberg (1967) portrays patients with a narcissistic personality as displaying excessive self-absorption, grandiose fantasies, intense ambition, and overdependence on the acclaim of others. While behavior may be superficially adaptive, their pathology manifests in chronic feelings of boredom, emptiness, and uncertainty about identity; an inability to love; exploitation of others; and "a remarkable absence of interest in and empathy for others in spite of the fact that they are so very eager to obtain admiration and approval from other people" (p. 654).

Given these descriptions, one would be hard-pressed to come up with personality traits that lend themselves less to the requirements of the therapeutic role. And yet, remarkably, in the literature under review no motivation is cited more frequently or consistently than are those pertaining to narcissistic gratifications. This is not to say that therapists are generally viewed as suffering from narcissistic personality disorders. There is substantial evidence, however, that for many therapists some degree of narcissistic disturbance is present and has played a vital role in their choice of profession (Claman 1987, Finell 1985, Miller 1981, Sharaf and Levenson 1964).

USE OF THE PATIENT AS A MIRRORING OR IDEALIZED SELFOBJECT

Kohut's (1977) model of human psychological functioning is built around his concept of the *self*, an independent center of initiative and perception that accounts for an individual's sense of continuity in space and time. For Kohut, the self emerges from the infant's interaction with an empathic, responsive human milieu. Initially fragile and amorphous, the nascent self depends on others to bestow upon it a sense of cohesion and constancy. Because the infant has yet to differentiate these others from the self, Kohut refers to them as *selfobjects*. "Selfobjects are objects which we experience as part of our self; the expected control over them is, therefore, closer to the concept of control which a grown-up expects to have over his own body and mind than to the concept of the control which he expects to have over others" (Kohut and Wolf 1978, p. 414).

In order for adequate fulfillment of basic narcissistic needs to occur, the infant's early selfobjects must perform two crucial functions. The *mirroring selfobject* must provide empathic and admiring responses to the child's display of his or her evolving capabilities and confirm his sense of vigor and greatness. This affirmation is thought to be vital to the consolidation of a secure sense of self. The *idealized selfobject* provides an idealized image with which the child can merge. If the inevitable parental failures to mirror the child or to permit idealization are incremental and nontraumatic, the resulting disillusionment supplies the impetus for the child's gradual internalization of the selfobject relations. This means that the child progressively learns to carry out functions previously performed by the selfobjects. Archaic grandiosity and needs for mirroring are transformed into mature forms of self-esteem maintenance and strivings for success and mastery. Similarly, archaic idealizations are transmuted into mature ideals and attainment of self-soothing and drive-channeling capacities.

Kohut proposes that inadequate or absent mirroring or idealized selfobjects during early childhood can result in a narcissistic disorder in adulthood (Kohut and Wolf 1977). Such an individual is left with a defective sense of self and an inability to maintain self-esteem on a relatively consistent basis. Unfulfilled longings to be mirrored and to merge with idealized figures eventuate in a persistent use of others as selfobjects.

The idea that therapists may at times make use of their patients as selfobjects is not a new one. In a paper first presented in 1938, Fenichel (1980) warned that analysts might make "impersonal use of the relationship to the patient for some unconscious purpose, such as smoothing over of anxiety, satisfaction of narcissistic needs, easing of intrapsychic conflicts" (p. 27). Virtually the same notion is expressed in the language of self psychology by Eber and Kunz (1984): "An avowed wish to help may, in part, mask an excessive need for, and use of, selfobjects for maintenance of self-esteem and self-cohesion" (p. 133).

What exactly is entailed in the use of patients as selfobjects? Eber and Kunz suggest that this takes place whenever the patient is employed "as an object who confirms or enhances the analyst's sense of self-confidence and well-being" (p. 295). Put this way, it becomes clear that such a motive cannot be regarded necessarily as either pathological or inimical to the treatment process. Parents certainly derive a sense of confidence and well-being from facilitating the development of their offspring, as do teachers from their students. For therapists, as Adler (1985) points out, this need for patients to function as confirming selfobjects may be an expression of a healthy narcissistic involvement in one's work. "Relatively mature therapists and analysts," he notes, "require some validation from their patients that they are competent and effective clinicians. They receive this validation from experiences of understanding their patients and being useful to them" (p. 177).

For therapists, as well as parents and teachers, the critical factor appears to be the maturational level of their use of selfobjects. The therapist's fulfillment of average expectable narcissistic needs within the treatment setting will not necessarily hinder the therapeutic process, and may actually promote it by stimulating the therapist's interest and emotional investment in the patient. When developmental deficits in self-formation are present, however, the therapist's selfobject needs may be of such intensity that they serve to contaminate the treatment process (Eber and Kunz 1984). This can be assumed to occur when the therapist's needs consistently take precedence over those of the patient, or when they significantly interfere with the therapist's capacity to maintain a therapeutic stance (Marsh 1988).

The role of psychotherapist can place an individual in a unique position to receive admiration and idealization from others. Due to the prestige and elevated status commonly associated with the profession, clients are apt to approach the therapist with an attitude that contains some measure of reverence and awe. The power differential that is inherent in the therapeutic relationship can contribute to the therapist's sense of superiority and promote a deferential attitude on the part of the client. In addition, the therapist's use of silence and of interpretive comments may lend an air of mystery to the proceedings, further increasing the likelihood of idealization.

Shepard and Lee (1970) refer to aspects of the therapeutic situation that allow for and foster the therapist's narcissism and need to be iconized. They remark that most therapy clients are plagued with self-doubt and low self-esteem, predisposing them to take a subservient position and to elevate the therapist to a grandiose, idealized position. Dubbing this the *pedestal syndrome*, they write that the client "is the mortal in relation to the god, or the child in relation to the parent. *Feed me*, he says or feels; *take care* of me; *love me. And in return, I will worship you*" (p. 21).

This tendency toward idealization of the therapist is expected in psychoanalytic approaches to treatment, and is attributed to the patient's transference onto the therapist of feelings and attitudes originally experienced in relation to parents and other important figures. While the development of infantile transferences is a crucial part of the therapeutic process, it also constitutes a potential narcissistic snare for the psychotherapist. As described by Lampl-de Groot (1954), "The analytic situation, in which the analyst is the leader, the patient's confidant, the object of the patient's love, admiration, and infantile adoration, is a real temptation to the analyst to mobilize his own feelings of grandeur and to overrate himself" (p. 187). The author regards this overvaluation of the self as a defense against outer disappointments and inner feelings of inferiority; in other words as a compensation for narcissistic injuries. Hammer (1972) also contends that certain individuals become psychotherapists to compensate for unconscious feelings of worthlessness, usually due to not having felt loved or valued as a child. "They envision being a therapist as the optimal means of gaining love and thereby boosting their self-esteem" (p. 30). Such therapists try to enhance the positive transference by being overly supportive, reassuring, and complimentary, thereby attempting to gain their patients' affection and admiration.[1]

---

[1]The following passage from Guntrip's (1975) account of his analysis with Winnicott suggests that, at least when treating colleagues, Winnicott did not shy away from acknowledging his own narcissistic gratifications as an analyst: "You too have a good breast. You've been able to give more than take. I'm good for you but you're good for

A passage from Ellis (1978) contains the identical theme with regard to his Rational Emotive Therapy (RET):

> Some RET therapists, however, who themselves have their own dire need for love, including the love of their clients, go to unusual extremes to support and care for these clients—not merely to gain rapport and to help them accept themselves but to win the clients' strong allegiance and approval and thereby raise the therapists' "self-esteem." [p. 331]

Ellis maintains that this sort of treatment tends to be iatrogenic, and largely reflects the therapist's own personality features and disturbances. In this context, it is of interest to note that in a study entitled "Iatrogenicity in Psychoanalytic Psychotherapy," Usandivaras (1982) found three types of iatrogenic analysts, two of which pertain to narcissistic neediness. The first group depended on their patients' external accomplishments to feed their own self-esteem. The second group were thought to have narcissistic personalities, and consciously and unconsciously tried to instill in their patients their own outlooks on life. (The third group identified by Usandivaras was incapable of keeping adequate emotional distance from patients, which, in extreme cases, resulted in erotic or aggressive acting out on the part of these analysts.)

Therapists may, due to their own narcissistic needs, focus primarily or entirely on transference interpretations, viewing patients' communications only in terms of how they reflect the relationship with the therapist. This is illustrated by the response of a psychoanalytically oriented psychologist to a questionnaire exploring the influence of therapists' personalities on their choice of theoretical orientation and practice: "I like being the center of attention and find that transference phenomena that are facilitated through psychoanalytic techniques allow me to become the focus of attention" (Chwast 1978, p. 371).

A trend in modern analytic technique toward increased, or ex-

---

me. Doing your analysis is almost the most reassuring thing that happens to me. The chap before you makes me feel I'm no good at all. You don't have to be good for me. I don't need it and can cope without it, but in fact you are good for me" (p. 153).

clusive, emphasis on transference interpretations has, in fact, been noted (Valenstein 1980). Furthermore, Lampl-de Groot (1976) cautions that viewing the transference as a goal in itself rather than as a tool can tempt the analyst to overestimate the special importance he or she has for the patient. "Pleasant as this may be for the analyst, it may stimulate his hidden grandiosity and prevent the countertransference from becoming conscious. In this case it often becomes the obstacle to the course the analysis should run" (p. 293). Thus, the fostering of positive transferences or the excessive emphasis on transferential phenomena may serve to enhance the therapist's grandiosity and self-esteem rather than meet the treatment needs of the client.

Applying a Kohutian perspective to the issue of therapist–patient sex, Claman (1987) proposes that *mirror-hunger* (Kohut 1971) is a central dynamic in the psychological makeup of practitioners who repeatedly "fall in love" with clients. In such cases, the client functions as a selfobject, gratifying the therapist's longings for mirroring and admiration. Claman elaborates:

> With mirror hunger as the underlying dynamic, the therapist falls in love with his mirroring self-object, rather than with the patient as a separate and individual person. The sexual act that evolves is for the therapist a palpable manifestation of the reality of the encounter, the singularly concrete proof that the self-object is actual and not simply a fantasy or projection of his needs. According to the model proposed, sexual intimacy with patients is a paradigm of self-object countertransferential acting out. [p. 38]

It is the absence of mutuality, Claman asserts, that differentiates such a relationship from genuine romantic love. The repetitive and insistent nature of the therapist's involvement could be characterized as addictive, consistent with Kohut's description of mirror-hungry personalities who "must go on trying to find new self-objects whose attention and recognition they seek to induce" (Kohut and Wolf 1978, p. 421). Also noteworthy in this respect is Kohut's suggestion that lustful feelings and aims can serve a self-restorative function by providing eroticized replacements for an inadequate selfobject experience (Stolorow 1986).

In their depiction of the lovesick therapist, Twemlow and Gabbard (1989) address these same narcissistic elements in this subset of abusive practitioners. They add the notion that the therapist's tendency to fall in love with the patient-as-selfobject reflects an unconscious yearning to unite with split-off aspects of the self. Through sexual union, the lovesick therapist thus hopes to achieve a feeling of wholeness. Projecting his own idealized self-representation onto the patient, a tacit agreement appears to be enacted:

> I like you to the extent that you are like I want you to be, and like I want to be myself. Provided we do not let mundane external reality to intervene and spoil what we have, we can actually achieve a state of perfection as long as we maintain this special and unique relationship. What we have between us cannot be put into words, but we each know that when we are together, we experience a unique sense of wholeness. [p. 82]

Twemlow and Gabbard also note that the lovesick state involves some degree of ego boundary disturbance. In what they describe as a transient, nonpsychotic loss of reality testing, the participants regress to the comfort of a merged, boundaryless condition. This emotional fusion with the patient compromises the therapist's judgment, promoting still further the likelihood of boundary violations.

Maintaining the therapist's self-esteem and providing a sense of wholeness or oneness are just two of the many functions that may be performed by the patient-as-selfobject. The therapist may use the patient's vitality and buoyancy to invigorate a depleted, deadened self. The vivacity and emotional liveliness characteristic of patients with histrionic trends may be particularly appealing in this regard. Patients who engage in impulsive, thrill-seeking behaviors can also provide the therapist with a sense of excitement and aliveness. Perhaps depressive clients, among others, furnish a soothing, calming capacity. By employing adjunctive treatments, such as biofeedback, hypnosis, or medications, clinicians may, in part, attempt to assuage their own fears and anxieties.

The therapist can also gratify narcissistic needs vicariously. By identifying with the recipient, the clinician can vicariously enjoy the admiration and affirmation that he lavishes upon the patient, which may not be in line with the patient's actual needs. A patient requiring, for example, confrontation or interpretation may only be able to elicit "empathic mirroring" from such a therapist. Rogers's (1951) concept of *unconditional positive regard* can be similarly misapplied in order to fulfill vicariously the therapist's narcissistic needs.

Less obvious, but still of importance, are the ways in which psychotherapists can make use of their patients as *idealized selfobjects*. As indicated above, unfulfilled longings to merge with an idealized selfobject may persist into adulthood and contribute toward a narcissistic disturbance. By serving as the "screen" onto which therapists project their idealizations, patients may function as idealized selfobjects.

An example of this process is what Searles (1965) terms the *Pygmalion complex*. Here, the therapist derives gratification from seeing improvement in the patient, who is viewed as his narcissistic extension. Searles remarks that the therapist "tends to fall in love with this beautifully developing patient, just as Pygmalion fell in love with the beautiful statue of Galatea which he had sculptured" (p. 300). This dynamic is nicely illustrated by a passage from Allen Wheelis's (1987) novel, *The Doctor of Desire*, when the protagonist, a psychoanalyst, realizes that he has fallen madly in love with a female client:

> So that's the way it is, he thinks. She is no *other*, she is I. In loving her I love myself, in rescuing her I redeem a part of myself—weak, frightened, feminine—of which otherwise I must be ashamed. . . . I have found an idealized portrait of myself. . . . This is the secret of all that swooning; it is not *they* whom I have loved; they have been but the gilt frames within which I have discovered and swooned over—myself. [p. 112]

Instances in which patients have been idealized by clinicians can be found throughout the history of psychotherapy. A striking example is that of the antipsychiatry movement of the 1960s and 1970s. Authors such as Laing (1960) and Cooper (1967) seemed to exalt schizophrenia as a creative adaptation to an insane world.

Glossing over the suffering and limitations that psychosis involves, schizophrenic patients were viewed as taking a romanticized, enriching voyage into inner realms. The level of idealization focused upon the patients at Laing's Kingsley Hall is illustrated by a passage from the book *Mary Barnes: Two Accounts of a Journey Through Madness* (Barnes and Berke 1971). When his patient, in the midst of a regressive period, started painting on the wall with her feces, therapist Joe Berke praised her work: "Mary smeared shit with the skill of a Zen calligrapher . . . I marvelled at the elegance and eloquence of her imagery, while others saw only her smells" (p. 249). While the potential benefits of promoting regression in the treatment of certain patients continues to be debated, such unmitigated glorification suggests selfobject idealization on the part of the therapist.

A different sort of idealization of patients is illustrated by Langs (1976). In his descriptions of the therapeutic interaction, Langs frequently extols the exceptional sensitivity and unconscious perceptiveness of patients. He refers to an inherent unconscious capacity to be "exquisitely in touch with the nature of the therapist's interventions and his failures to intervene" (p. 99). Not only is the patient on some level aware of the therapist's difficulties in treating him, but also unwittingly offers the therapist a kind of supervision and attempts to cure the treater through the unconscious use of interpretations. Although many of Langs's points are well taken and are supported by case material, an unmistakable tone of idealization emerges in his descriptions of patients. In the process he appears to devalue the abilities of the supervisee-therapists, who often come across as inept.

THE ATTEMPT TO REALIZE AN AGGRANDIZED EGO-IDEAL

As we have seen, inadequate mirroring and idealized selfobjects in early life may account for the heightened narcissistic needs of many psychotherapists. A related approach to understanding this important issue involves what Freud (1914) termed the *ego-ideal*.

According to Freud, narcissism originates in the young child's attempts to recover an initial state of harmony with the mother.

Repeated ruptures of this earlier "primary narcissism" (p. 88) lead to the formation of an ego-ideal. This "new ideal ego . . . like the infantile ego, deems itself the possessor of all perfections" (p. 94), and thereby serves to protect the child from parental rejections and other blows to the child's sense of omnipotence. The ego-ideal, usually considered part of the superego, is based on identification with the parents and other early figures, as they actually were and as they were idealized by the child. To the extent that the actual self does not measure up to the ego-ideal, the person's self-esteem suffers (Moore and Fine 1968).

In normal development, the ego-ideal becomes an important guiding force of the personality, constituting those standards of behvior toward which the individual aspires. However, in certain distortions of the early developmental process the ego-ideal can form in such a way that it becomes unrealistic and grandiose. Nemiah (1961) postulates:

> If the parents set standards for behavior and make demands on the child beyond his capacity to comply, the child develops an exaggerated sense of inadequacy and helplessness. . . . As his superego develops, it adopts the parents' unrealistically high standards and ideals, as well as their punitive, critical attitudes, which now internalized, are turned upon the self. [p. 160]

Such an individual is a "prisoner of his aspirations, his needs, and his harsh criticism" (p. 163) and requires constant reassurance, admiration, and love to bolster his or her self-esteem.

According to Kernberg (1975), narcissistic individuals are left emotionally needy as children by cold, unempathic mothers. Feeling bad and unloved, these children project their rage onto their parents, who are then perceived as even more hurtful and depriving. Kernberg proposes that by fusing the actual self with the ideal self and the fantasized image of a loving mother, the narcissistic individual achieves an inflated self-image that functions to deny the need for anyone else. And by projecting unacceptable parts of the self onto others, who are then devalued, narcissism perpetuates a "vicious circle of self-admiration, depreciation of others, and the elimination of all actual dependency" (p. 235).

An individual's ego-ideal comes to play an important part in the choice of profession. As Milrod (1982) states, "The struggle to achieve realistic likeness to the wished-for self-image fires ambition and motivates work" (p. 107). Those with narcissistically inflated ego-ideals are likely to be drawn to vocations that hold the promise of fulfilling their unrealistically high expectations and ambitions. The profession of psychotherapist, allowing as it does for fantasies of omnipotence, grandiosity, and perfection, appears to fit the bill nicely.

Some support for such a scenario can be drawn from a study by Ford (1963), who had psychiatric residents write autobiographies and keep journals throughout their training. Ford reports that most of the residents were aware of a striving for self-realization that was "quite unremitting, as though under pressure from a strict superego. They seemed to need to become something worthwhile, and this worthwhileness increasingly assumed the form of psychologic medicine" (p. 473). Developmentally, many of the residents had suffered strong anxieties as children resulting from rebuffs and separations from their mothers. The lost intimacy was later sought by identifying with a series of idealized figures. Ultimately, the journals indicate, it was psychiatry that provided the residents with an ideal, omnipotent model that did not let them down. Further support for this notion comes from a 1972 study by Perlman, which found that the practice of psychotherapy by trainees resulted in increased congruence between therapists' self-concepts and their ego-ideals. Thus, it appears that by becoming psychotherapists certain individuals may be attempting to realize, or live up to, an aggrandized self-image that took shape in early childhood.

Narcissistic overaspiration and self-overestimation appear to be nearly universal among beginning therapists (Sharaf and Levinson 1964). To what, specifically, do they aspire? Maltsberger and Buie (1974) contend that the three most common narcissistic snares are the aspirations to heal all, know all, and love all—all doomed to failure and leading therapists to resort to magical and destructive responses. They state that, of all the helping professionals, psychotherapists are the most inclined to these aspirations because it is their own person that constitutes the therapeutic tool. "The psychiatrist is therefore prone to confuse the limitation of his professional capacity to heal with his sense of personal worth" (p. 627). In his depiction of the *grandiose professional self*, Brightman (1984–1985) discusses this same triad of narcissistic aspirations: omniscience, omnipotence, and benevolence.

Omniscience

Omniscience, including the power to divine the future, has long been associated with the healing arts. Indeed, it appears that such an association has at times been actively cultivated. Guggenbuhl-Craig (1971) cites the eleventh-century physician, Archimatheus of Salerno, as providing the following advice to aspiring practitioners: "To the patient promise a cure, and to the members of his family give warning of grave illness. If the patient fails to recover, it will be said that you foresaw his death; if he is cured, your renown will grow" (p. 22).

In a discussion of the various roles involved in psychological testing, Schafer (1954) refers to the *oracular* aspect. The tester, and, one might add, the therapist, "'sees into' hidden meanings, predicts turns of events, implicitly or explicitly advises" (p. 23). Schafer contends that certain individuals may enter the field of clinical psychology in search of just such an oracular role. He states:

> Testing—or therapy—may be to him a royal road to omniscience—short, broad, smooth and well marked. One sees this conception in blatant form in many young graduate students of clinical psychology for whom there is no response they cannot interpret, no contradiction they cannot resolve, no obscurity they cannot penetrate, no integration they cannot achieve. . . . But in all of us, even if well repressed or well controlled, there is this longing for omniscience, for oracular powers. [p. 23]

It could be that the mental health sciences as a whole attract students who are unconsciously seeking to fulfill strong wishes for omniscience. The initial fantasy may be that, by studying human behavior and psychological functioning, one will eventually attain a perfect understanding of oneself and others. Confronted with the actual limitations of current knowledge, such individuals may eschew research and take refuge in the role of psychotherapist, which can at least preserve the illusion of omniscience. Marmor (1953) describes how the reactions of patients and the public in general can foster the therapist's fantasy of knowing all:

> The psychotherapist has become the shaman of our society, the all-seeing father with the Cyclopean eye. He is endowed with God-like perceptiveness. "I'd better be careful or you'll read my thoughts," is a constantly encountered reaction. The assumption that the psychotherapist merely by a glance can understand any variety of dream, behavior problem, or emotional disturbance is one that is often shared by patients and public alike. [p. 371]

Thanks to the power of transference, patients can usually be counted on to view the therapist as possessing the same sort of omniscience attributed by young children to their parents. Through the use of professional jargon, the practitioner can further enhance such attitudes. Other ways of promoting a sense of omniscience in the clinical setting, as noted by Guggenbuhl-Craig (1971), may be more subtle and covert:

> When the patient tells him of his troubles, the analyst lets it be seen that he already understands everything. Through the use of certain gestures, such as sage nodding of the head and of pregnant remarks interjected among the patient's statements, the analyst creates an impression that, while he may not be prepared to communicate all his knowledge and profound thoughts, he has already plumbed the depths of his patient's soul. [p. 39]

Salzman (1968) describes the attempt to achieve omniscience through an emphasis on intellectuality as a central aspect of the obsessional defensive style. The key dynamic appears to be a striving for control over oneself and one's environment in order to overcome intolerable feelings of helplessness.

> The obsessional can be comfortable only when he feels he knows everything or is in the process of trying to know everything. He is

convinced not only that this is absolutely necessary but also that often it is possible, even in the face of his intellectual grasp of the impossibility of achieving the goal. He demands of himself that he be capable of anticipating his own reactions and the emotional responses of others by rational and logical means. He requires that he be able to control the uncontrollable. [p. 17]

Those individuals whose childhood experiences resulted in the development of an unrealistically inflated ego-ideal may therefore strive for omniscience as an obsessional defense against feelings of being out of control or helpless. The role of psychotherapist may enable such people to gain a sense that—at least through the eyes of their patients—they are fully in control and "in the know."

It is of interest that such strivings for omniscience may extend to the therapist's family as well. According to Maeder (1989), many children of therapists report having shared in the parent's narcissistic gratification of being privy to secret knowledge. He writes:

By living within the privileged domain and being included on the parents' side in discussions of what "we" know and what other people do not, there is an unspoken assumption, if the child chooses to adopt it, that he is somehow entitled, by some sort of birthright, to a position above everyone else. This feeling of belonging to the priest class is sometimes explicit and is quite often detected as an underlying current. The psychotherapist's family is special. [p. 192]

Although some clients may feel reassured by a therapist's omniscient stance, the drawbacks are apparent. Such clinicians are unlikely to tolerate the anxiety and uncertainty inherent in authentic therapeutic inquiry, instead taking refuge in preconceived and dogmatic explanations. While this approach may provide clients with intellectual insight (accurate or otherwise), it cannot provide the kind of vital and transforming self-knowledge that emerges from the give-and-take of joint exploration. In addition, clients will have more difficulty relinquishing their idealizations of the seemingly all-knowing therapist, further hindering the therapeutic process and a successful termination.

Omnipotence

In their study of the psychodynamics of physicianhood, Zabarenko and colleagues (1970) conclude that feelings of omnipotence and omniscience, derived from residual infantile megalomania, often fuel the desire to practice medicine. The authors report that, for the doctors in their sample, the attempt to heal had become the vehicle through which they expressed the unconscious fantasy of magical omnipotence in adult life. They note that many of the physicians appeared to use their patients' positive transferences to enhance these derivatives of their own narcissistic wishes.

Gill and Brenman (1959) discuss the unconscious motivations of the hypnotist, based on the supervision and analyses of hypnotists, as well as on written statements by experienced practitioners of hypnotism. The authors report strong confirmation of Pardell's (1950) hypothesis that the hypnotist has an unconscious wish to be an omnipotent parent-figure who allows the client to satisfy regressive longings. Gill and Brenman contend that the same dynamic functions in many psychotherapists. They quote one psychiatrist-informant who emphasizes the hypnotist's infantile wish for magical omnipotence, adding, "But we must not forget that such motives undoubtedly play an important role in the initial decision to become a physician at all, and certainly in the specialty choice of psychiatry. The only trouble is that with the use of hypnosis this all becomes so naked" (p. 450).

Marks (1978) maintains that in rejecting the technique of hypnosis, Freud was setting aside his own narcissistic satisfactions derived from dominating the patient and effecting prompt removal of symptoms. This point is questionable, however, in view of reports that Freud was not an especially gifted hypnotist (Jones 1957). Moreover, there is little to indicate that the role of psychoanalyst provides less narcissistic gratification than does the role of hypnotist. A study of first-year analytic candidates, in fact, revealed an initial conception of the psychoanalyst as a largely idealized and omnipotent figure (Keller and Schneider 1976). Burton (1975) also refers to a persistent feeling on the part of all psychotherapists that "something terribly important is involved in the psychotherapeutic process, and that no one else—certainly not the clergy, the artist, or the philosopher—can provide it. The psycho-therapist thus feels he is the chosen one" (p. 121). This grandiose feeling of importance may develop (or, assuming all infants make some use of this defense, fail to be attenuated) in early childhood, as exemplified by Natterson's (1991) personal account: "As a child, one of my delusions was a sense of messianic importance that I was necessary for the entire universe, and at the same time another laughable conviction that nothing but me really existed in the universe" (p. 7).

Hammer (1972) posits that certain individuals are drawn to the career due to a "savior complex" (p. 27), in which unconscious strivings for omnipotence compensate for intense feelings of fearfulness and vulnerability. Such therapists present themselves to patients as being always correct. They maintain an ideal of being able to heal anyone who comes for help, and when unsuccessful are likely to blame the failure on the patient. Hammer summarizes: "These therapists envision therapy relationships as providing them with an opportunity, via the patient's adoration, reverence and growth, to substantiate the illusion of their own personal worth and omnipotence" (p. 27).

In his 1913 article "The God Complex," Jones suggests that an unconscious identification with God and resulting unconscious feelings of superiority might be one of the factors contributing to a strong interest in psychology and psychiatry. He states that this God complex is characterized by fantasies of omnipotence and "a colossal narcissism" (p. 247). Jones notes that this superiority complex generally manifests not in the form of conceit or vanity, but, through reaction formation, as excessive modesty, self-effacement, aloofness, and the tendency to cloak oneself in mystery—all fully compatible with the role of the analyst.[2]

Mullan and Sangiuliano (1964) describe the endeavor to change another human being as "omnipotent in its formulation and omniscient in its design" (p. 91). Indeed, there is a certain amount of

---

[2]Given Jones's description, it may be that the need to identify with God, at least in males, derives from the inability to resolve the oedipal complex and thereby identify with father.

audacity in the presumption that in a relatively short span of time one can alter patterns of behavior and thought that have been an integral part of the personality since the patient's early years. Add to this the fact that the therapist is in a position to attribute all positive changes to the treatment, disregarding all other influences in the patient's external life, and it becomes clear how gratifying the role can be to an individual's need for omnipotence and grandiosity.

Ultimately, therapists may view their work as enabling them to evade death and to achieve some measure of immortality. Kottler (1986), for instance, addresses the motive of "leaving spoors":

> I suspect that deep within my own heart is the desperate need to influence others. I am afraid of dying, and worse, of being forgotten. I feel as though I am in the process of immortalizing myself with every disciple who goes out in the world with a part of me inside them. It is as if I can cheat the terror of death if only I can keep a part of me alive. [p. 53]

In an informal survey of older psychoanalytic colleagues concerning the preparations they had made for their practice in the event of their death, Fieldsteel (1985) found that denial was the most frequent strategy in dealing with the issue. Similarly, a study of patients whose analysts had died during their treatment revealed that the subject of the analyst's mortality was rarely broached, even when a terminal illness had been diagnosed (Van Raalte 1984).

The attempt to vanquish death can also be seen in therapists who try to cure patients who are dying of terminal illnesses. McWilliams (1987) provides a case in point:

> Grandiosity takes many forms in psychoanalysis. One analyst in my community virtually exhausted himself a few years ago under the pressure of a belief that since there is evidence of emotional contributants to cancer, he should be able to cure a patient with terminal leukemia. He entered a crazy race with time, reaching for any interpretation that might make a difference to his dying patient, regarding all remissions of the cancer as evidence of interpretive skill and all deteriorations as evidence of his own failure to hear the unconscious correctly. The patient naturally died, and the analyst

went into a depression, vacillating between feeling responsible for
the death and trying to tell himself that without the analytic work,
the patient would have died even sooner. [p. 99]

A similar dynamic may be at work when clinicians treat patients
suffering from severe mental illness. As Burton (1970) remarks:
"The psychotherapy of schizophrenia is a Lazarus-like affair in
which the patient is analogously returned to life. The microgenesis
of those who have briefly died and been resuscitated is not unlike
the catatonic schizophrenic who again accepts human existence"
(p. 199). Thus, by bringing about a psychic rebirth in his patient,
the therapist may achieve a sense of power over life and death and
temporarily assuage his own existential dread.

Benevolence

Hammer (1972) discusses differences between individuals who
approach psychotherapy as a science and those who view it as an
art. He states that the student who needs to identify with the role of
an absolute scientist is "usually one who needs to see himself as
being powerful, masterful, intellectual, self-controlled and masculine, rejecting all traits of weakness, passivity, and emotionality"
(p. 35). Such an individual, according to this author, uses the discipline of science as a means of exerting control and domination in
order to deny an underlying conviction of weakness and vulnerability.

Hammer compares this position to that of the student who
strongly identifies with the role of an absolute artist. The latter

tends to try to gain a feeling of personal superiority by trying to
confirm an image of himself as someone who is tender, gentle,
affectionate, emotional, sensitive, intimate, noncombative, esthetic,
altruistic and nonmaterialistic. He identifies with all of these feelings
as a value but does not really experience them or live them as a
reality. [p. 36]

Thus, the scientist-type attempts to achieve a sense of security
through a powerful and omnipotent self-image, while the artist-

type attempts to achieve it through another form of godliness—selfless, loving attributes. This formulation helps to clarify how the same narcissistic needs can manifest in antithetical personality styles via divergent ego-ideals. So different on the surface, the two styles share a common foundation: a grandiose self-image that compensates for and protects against narcissistic injury.

For many therapists, an attitude of benevolence constitutes an important feature of their ego-ideal. The term refers to the desire to do good to others and is synonymous with kindness, compassion, and charitableness. Because it tends to be so ego-syntonic for therapists, and is apparently so congruous with a wish to help, the defensive aspects of the striving for benevolence may not be immediately apparent. Left unanalyzed, however, it can contribute to a significant "blind spot," limiting the therapist's capacity to conduct psychotherapy effectively.

This striving for an idealized, all-good image again recalls the myth of Narcissus. As Miller (1981) writes, "His reflection deceives him as well, since it shows only his perfect, wonderful side and not his other parts. His back view, for instance, and his shadow remain hidden from him; they do not belong to and are cut off from his beloved reflection" (p. 49). It is Narcissus's denial of the totality of his self, his insistence on being nothing but the beautiful youth, that "leads to a giving up of himself, to death or, in Ovid's version, to being changed into a flower" (p. 49).

As previously indicated, narcissistic needs center around the preservation of self-esteem. Hammer (1972) posits that those who have a compulsive need to nurture and give to others may use an ego-ideal of *unselfish giver* as a means of raising chronically low self-esteem. The therapist's gain, however, may be at the expense of the client. In assuming a virtuous and selfless stance, the therapist assures that all of the "evil" in the office is situated in the client. Templer (1971) notes how this sort of disparity emerges from the therapist's attempt to remain tolerant of the client at all times. "Such tolerance," he writes "may further imply that the tolerant person is superior to the person being accepted, and is displaying great magnanimity in his unconditional positive regard for an inferior" (p. 235). By showering the client with love and kindness, the therapist fails to elicit the client's retentive and negativistic attitudes, thus precluding any opportunity to understand or to modify them (Strupp 1959).

Epstein (1983) refers to the perfectionistic ideals contained in the role of psychoanalyst. He contends that analysts commonly exhibit a need to suppress patients' destructive tendencies, noting that hostile feelings often do not enter into the transference neurosis. Epstein asserts that the major reason for this is that patients' hate and destructiveness evoke similar feelings in the analyst, and that for most analysts such feelings are abhorrent because they contradict their own narcissistically invested self-idealizations. These are described as follows:

> For one thing, historically, analysts have shared a self idealization which includes such values as a high degree of rationality, objectivity, and highly developed capacity for controlling impulses and detaching themselves from personal feelings and needs, in the service of the analytic task. In other words, such a self idealization requires them to be, vis-a-vis their immature and emotionally disturbed patients, something like a paragon of mature functioning. [p. 219]

Epstein goes on to comment that the patient, typically burdened with feelings of being a bad, hateful, and inferior person, will naturally experience an intensification of such feelings when faced with the sharp contrast of the all-good therapist. This results in attempts on the part of the patient to reverse this imbalance by dissociating and disowning hated aspects of the self and projecting them onto the therapist. Epstein concludes that the therapeutic process can be seriously hindered if the therapist suppresses or deflects the patient's hatred in order to preserve his or her own self-idealizations.

Searles (1966) also warns against the dangers of trying to maintain a self-image of an unambivalently loving person. He states that this leads to a constriction of the therapist's responsiveness, in that the therapist is essentially relating to warded-off aspects of his or her own self rather than engaging in a genuine relationship with the patient. Any attempt to accept the patient wholeheartedly, Searles insists, is an unrealizable and omnipotent goal: "We could unambiv-

alently love and approve of and accept our patient only if he were
somehow able to personify our own ego-ideal—and in that impossible eventuality, we would of course feel murderously envious of
him, anyway" (p. 323).

The pursuit of benevolence appears to involve a religious or
spiritual dimension. Kohut (1971) contends that a "deep feeling of
inner saintliness" (p. 222) may play a role in therapeutic successes
with very disturbed patients. Such fervor, on the part of a charis-
matic therapist or treatment team, can provide the necessary lever-
age to reach those who are highly regressed. Kohut continues:

> Not only the messianic or saintly personality of the therapist, however,
> but also his life history seems to play an active role in the therapeutic
> successes, and a myth of having—like Christ—risen from death in an
> ascendancy of self-generated, life-giving love appears at times to form
> a particular part of the effective charisma. [p. 223]

In his novel *The Doctor of Desire* (1987), Wheelis also draws a
parallel between the psychotherapist and Jesus Christ:

> Does not something like this happen in analysis? The analyst makes
> it possible for the patient to recover and express the previously split-
> off anger; and though himself the innocent object of that anger
> (innocent? who is innocent?) he remains attached, thereby enabling
> the patient to integrate that anger with the rest of his emotional life
> and so become whole?
>
> Such a view of therapy echoes the Christian scheme of salvation.
> Christ offered himself as a sacrifice to man's demonic rage. "Father,
> forgive them; for they know not what they do." His unconditional
> love redeems those who believe, they recover their true selves, are
> born again. [p. 165]

This spiritual dimension also plays a role in the narcissistic aspiration of the perfected self.

The Perfected Self

Since the therapist's instrument is his or her own person, the clinician who expects to fulfill some ideal standard of practice must

have access to a perfected self. Omniscience, omnipotence, and benevolence are, in this sense, three common components of a broader aspiration—the attainment of perfection. There are indications that, for many therapists, such an ambition predates their choice of profession. Professional training may thus hold the promise of a kind of spiritual transformation. In an account of his psychoanalytic training, Farber (1966) recalls an orientation meeting in which he and his fellow neophytes were given a "sermon" by one of the institute's training analysts. Farber writes that, between himself and this senior analyst, ". . . there seemed to be an impossible gulf—not only of esoteric skills and knowledge but, more important of a quality of being that I assumed was the most important reward of this long period of training I was yet to undergo" (p. 209). Twenty years later, he was still painfully aware that this gulf remained untraversed: "When pressed I find it hard to designate my insufficient person as that of a psychoanalyst. . . . my experience cannot be too different, say, from that of the proselytes of the Catharist heresy in the Twelfth century, who were divided into the Pure and the Impure" (pp. 209–210).

One of the central ways in which therapists attempt to achieve this fantasied purity is through personal therapy or analysis. The trainee may adopt the conviction that, by undergoing a "complete" analysis, all flaws and imperfections will eventually be eliminated from his or her character. Roth (1987) refers to this myth of the perfectly analyzed therapist as "a childish idealization rekindled out of disappointment, a sense of inferiority, and a need for restitutive, narcissistic perfection" (p. 9).

Whether or not the trainee ever attains this grandiose goal of being "fully analyzed," the role of therapist continues to hold the promise of inducing a sense of perfection. The idealized image of the psychotherapist is that of a paragon of health and maturity. Sublimating or transcending the base instincts, the therapist maintains a focus on the needs of the client, yet never acts to manipulate or exploit them. Fully self-contained and self-sufficient, yet exquisitely attuned to others, this prototypical superperson somehow manages to balance and resolve all of the conflicts and contradictions of human existence that plague lesser mortals. The therapist sustains, all the while, a demeanor of perfect calm and composure, drawing upon the underlying emotional currents, yet refraining from any unwarranted expression of affect.

Despite Freud's insistence that psychopathology be viewed as a continuum, theorists and clinicians alike often speak or write about patients as if they were a separate breed. Finell (1985) comments that analysts frequently strive to maintain the *analyst-ideal-self*, which is regarded as "structured, conflict-based, and essentially oedipal *except* in so far as preoedipal issues are activated by patient pathology" (p. 439). Whereas patients, she notes, are said to suffer from pathological narcissism and grandiosity, the analyst's own narcissism is referred to as mere "residues" provoked by that of the patient. Yet another way in which the idea of the perfected self is reflected in the literature is the near absence of references to the fact that therapists grow older over the course of their professional lives (Hinze 1987).

Therapists' own fantasies of perfection are, of course, mirrored and fed by the idealizations of patients and the public at large:

> Therapists are considered to have wonderful marriages, impeccable children, total balance in their emotional lives, outstanding work relationships, astounding intellectual achievements, scintillating social activities, fascinating friends, boundless energy (why else would patients not apologize for calling in the wee hours of the morning?), and, of course, an unlimited capacity to give. [Whitman and Block 1990, p. 481]

To the extent that they are viewed as narcissistic extensions, family members may also be expected to live up to the therapist's perfectionistic ideals. Condit (1987), who interviewed psychoanalysts regarding the parenting of their own children, suggests that projection of a highly critical superego frequently results in extreme concern with how others view their offspring:

> Several described in vivid terms how excruciating it was for them when their children were misbehaving in front of other people. They all felt that they were being watched and secretly criticized for their inability to control their children. They imagined a rather gleeful response on the part of the onlooker, who sees that "shrinks" have the same problems that everyone has. [p. 73]

The author speculates that analysts "harbor secret fantasies [of producing] the perfectly psychologically healthy child" (p. 73).

Returning to the clinical setting, it is apparent that the therapist's pursuit of perfection can have deleterious effects on the treatment process.[3] Therapists who practice in an overly stilted, studied manner and attempt to deliver the "perfect interpretation" or to avoid "errors" at all costs, may demand that their patients meet a similarly unrealistic set of standards and may prolong treatment unnecessarily. Therapists who need to maintain a grandiose professional self will attribute to the client all of the difficulties encountered in the therapeutic process, will never admit to blunders or empathic failures, and will be seriously hindered in their capacity to explore honestly transference and countertransference issues. Treatment failures may be ascribed to "unsuitable" clients, as the therapist's case load eventually comes to consist entirely of clients who adequately accept and gratify the therapist's self-idealizations.

PARENTAL NARCISSISTIC DISTURBANCE

In her book *The Drama of the Gifted Child*, Miller (1981) conducts an extensive examination of narcissism as it relates to the field of psychotherapy. She suggests that, for most psychoanalysts, a narcissistic disturbance forms the basis for both their interest and aptitude in clinical work. This derives, Miller maintains, from their having been raised by parents who were themselves narcissistically deprived. These parents looked to the child to gratify their continued longing for what they themselves lacked as children: the presence of someone who was fully aware of them, who admired them and otherwise confirmed their sense of self and of worth.

---

[3]The clinical *utility* of blunders and imperfections on the part of the analyst was emphasized by Ferenczi in his clinical diary in 1932: "One could almost say that the more weaknesses an analyst has, which lead to greater or lesser mistakes and errors but which are then uncovered and treated in the course of mutual analysis, the more likely the analysis is to rest on profound and realistic foundations" (1988, p. 15). Also pertinent in this regard is Levenson's (1983) statement: "Clever analysts have always known that their function is paradoxical. It is the goal of the therapist to fail the patient's expectations, not to meet them" (p. 121).

Due to the infant's total dependency, the child of such parents quickly learned as a survival tactic to apply all of his or her resources toward the implicit demand of maintaining the parent's narcissistic equilibrium.

We cathect an object narcissistically when we egocentrically experience it as part of ourselves, rather than as the center of its own activity and autonomy (Kohut 1971). Miller elaborates on some of the characteristics of narcissistically cathected children. While their intellectual capacities are left to develop undisturbed, their emotional lives remain quite narrow. Miller describes grandiosity and depression as two aspects of the counterfeit or *false self* (Winnicott 1965). Although appearing outwardly as opposites, both can be viewed as defensive reactions to the deep pain over the loss of the self, over not having been loved for what one truly was. Miller elaborates: "Both are indications of an inner prison, because the grandiose and the depressive individuals are compelled to fulfill the introjected mother's expectations: Whereas the grandiose person is her successful child, the depressive sees himself as a failure" (p. 45). In reality, the two generally coexist, as the person alternates between these two extremes.

Based upon numerous analyses of analytic candidates, which she either conducted or supervised, Miller formulated the following generalizations:

> There was a mother [or primary caretaker] who at the core was emotionally insecure and who depended for her narcissistic equilibrium on the child behaving, or acting, in a particular way. This mother was able to hide her insecurity from the child and from everyone else behind a hard, authoritarian, and even totalitarian facade.

> This child had an amazing ability to perceive and respond intuitively, that is, unconsciously, to this need of the mother, or of both parents, for him to take on the role that had unconsciously been assigned to him.

> This role secured "love" for the child—that is, his parents' narcissistic cathexis. He could sense that he was needed and this, he felt, guaranteed him a measure of existential security. [p. 8]

This unconscious perceptiveness and intuition grows as the child takes on the role of confidant and comforter of the mother, and possibly assumes responsibility for siblings. Miller contends that this acute sensitivity to the needs of others eventually leads to a natural aptitude for and interest in practicing psychoanalysis. She goes so far as to question whether anyone lacking this sort of developmental history could muster the interest needed to spend day after day attempting to discern what is taking place in the unconscious of others.

Groddeck, an early contemporary of Freud's, described his conception of the therapist in a way that, in a somewhat exaggerated fashion, illustrates Miller's point. Groddeck (1928) notes that the word "therapy" originally meant service, rather than treatment. Consistent with this, he views the proper role of the therapist as that of "servant" to the patient-"master." He writes:

> A person who serves knows that he has to do what his master says; he knows that he is in service with his whole being and not just with his knowledge or with his skill, that he is obliged to guess at the wishes and needs of his master, that he has to adapt himself in everything, in his deepest nature to his master's nature. [p. 212]

This exquisite sensitivity to the emotional vicissitudes of others is an indispensable quality of the psychotherapist. As Azorin (1957) remarks, "This constant attempt to interrelate our reactions and even our associations with what is going on in the patient and what is coming at us from the patient, is an essential step in the process of helping another human being toward his self-realization" (p. 38). Miller's findings suggest that there may be specific parent–child dynamics, involving narcissistic deprivation, which contribute to the development of this degree of empathy and emotional responsiveness. Thus, the professional role of therapist may be viewed as an attempt to overcome the narcissistic damage caused by having been inappropriately "used" by the parent as a supporting self-object at a point in development when the roles should be just the reverse (Brightman 1984–1985).

MATERNAL IDENTIFICATION

The concept of identification has been defined by Moore and Fine (1968) as follows:

> An automatic, unconscious mental process whereby an individual becomes like another person in one or several aspects. It is a natural accompaniment of maturation and mental development and aids in the learning process (including the learning of speech and language), as well as in the acquisition of interests, ideals, mannerisms, etc. . . . By means of identification with a needed person an individual can often provide for himself the satisfaction of the needs desired from that person. Separation from a loved person becomes more tolerable as a result of identification with him. [p. 50]

As discussed in Chapter 4, many male psychotherapists report childhoods reflecting an incompletely resolved oedipal conflict in which a paternal identification was not fully achieved. Some degree of maternal identification enabled these individuals, as children, to ward off threatening libidinal and aggressive strivings. Another consequence of such maternal identification, it appears, is to enhance the individual's capacity for such traditionally feminine attributes as nurturance, emotional sensitivity, and empathy. Greenson (1967) notes that empathy, required by the psychoanalyst, develops from the nonverbal and intonational aspects of the earliest mother–child relationship, and therefore has a "feminine cast" (p. 383).

A number of sources confirm the presence of strong maternal identifications in those who become healers (Greenson 1967, McLaughlin 1961, Menninger 1959). In a discussion of the unconscious factors contributing to the choice of a medical career, Menninger (1959) cites an identification with the mother's nurturing and healing qualities, as well as the wish to please the mother, who may or may not have married a physician. (Although, if the father is a physician, there must clearly also be some degree of *paternal* identification.) Similarly, Greenson (1967) notes that the role of doctor may involve an identification with the nursing mother, alleviating pain by suckling the child. He also remarks that "the ideal analyst is a motherly father figure or fatherly mother, the duality existing in regard to functions and not as a sexual characteristic" (p. 106). McLaughlin (1961) concurs, stating that an important part of the psychodynamics of a healer is the "need to conceal his sexual and aggressive thrusts behind a healing, succoring way of life" (p. 114), via an identification with the nurturing mother.

Various empirical studies provide additional evidence (Donnay-Richelle 1971, Donnay-Richelle et al. 1972, Eagle and Marcos 1980, Ford 1963, Racusin et al. 1981). In a review of the literature on personality factors correlated with the choice of psychiatry as specialty, Eagle and Marcos (1980) state that psychiatric residents tend to identify more with their mothers than fathers, and to score higher than other medical students on measures of nurturance and intimacy. Ford (1963) reports that the fathers of male psychiatric residents "usually were revealed as passive, noninteracting men contributing little psychologic strength to the family and certainly not to the son" (p. 474). These fathers were described as either highly passive or as overcompensating through defensive bullying; none provided a strong masculine model. Ford concludes that the "earliest known factors initiating movement toward a career in psychiatry are primitive identifications and objects from preoedipal and oedipal years. Of these, involvement with mother and the mothering functions seems most common" (p. 482).

Similarly, Racusin and colleagues (1981) conducted in-depth interviews with seven male and seven female clinical psychologists, nearly all of whom reported having felt closest to their mother. The authors hypothesize that, as children, the psychologists had allied with their mothers against basically nonnurturant fathers, thereby identifying with the role of the underdog.

Donnay-Richelle (1971) presents the results of psychological testing on approximately fifty psychiatry residents. One of the characteristics found to differentiate the residents who were rated the most competent on various measures was a strong maternal identification. In a related study (Donnay-Richelle et al. 1972) this investigator compared psychiatry residents and clinical psychology students. Interpretation of projective tests revealed that both groups of males exhibited anxiety regarding masculinity, as well as emotional conflict centering around the mother figure.

Thus it appears that, as children, therapists tend to have identified more closely with their mothers than with their fathers. While many authors apparently assume that such maternal identifications result in an enhanced capacity for empathy, the reverse could also be the case. Roth (1987), in fact, suggests that an inborn talent for nurturance and empathy, largely the mother's domain, may *lead to* strong female identifications. Either way, it is clear that male or female clinicians who are uncomfortable with their maternal identifications will have difficulties in providing their patients with a supportive and caring therapeutic environment.

The literature does not appear to address the issue of maternal identifications in female therapists, presumably because such identifications are considered to be the norm in women. As discussed in the previous chapter, the role of psychotherapist may provide oedipally fixated women with an opportunity to reconcile and integrate their conflicting identifications. This is a neglected topic that clearly warrants greater attention, and may help solve the chicken-and-egg puzzle contained in the question of the origins of empathy.

IDENTITY DIFFUSION

In order to empathize adequately with clients, psychotherapists must be able to project themselves into the selves of others through a process of partial identification. As Weigert (1954) remarks:

> The analysts's empathy puts him into the patient's shoes, enables him to read between the lines, to take his clues not only from the patient's verbal communications, but also from the intonation of his voice, changes in breathing, his facial expression, gestures, automatic movements that are taken in on the preconscious level. [p. 243]

According to Weigert, this capacity for empathy requires an ability to expand one's ego-boundaries.

In full accordance, Greenson (1962) states that the individual's aptitude for empathizing depends on one's ability to give up one's identity temporarily and partially. "People with a rather narrow sense of identity, rigid and fixed, are unwilling or unable to empathize. The analysts's self-image has to be flexible and loose" (p. 16).

There are a few indications in the literature that, for many healers and psychotherapists, the self developed in such a way that the individual's identity remained rather unconsolidated, allowing for this chameleonlike flexibility. For instance, in their study of the psychodynamics of the initial phase of psychoanalytic training, Keller and colleagues (1976) report that candidates manifested clear evidence of "a general uncertainty about their identity" (p. 36), later referring to this as "identity diffusion" (p. 37). In another study, regarding the psychodynamics of physicianhood, Zabarenko and colleagues (1970) found that their sample of doctors had, as children, attained a partial oedipal resolution that was sufficient to sustain developmental progress, but "considerable portions of ego-identity remained diffuse until the choice of medicine as profession" (p. 106). The authors note that these doctors appeared to have preserved both maternal and paternal introjects. Rather than having been synthesized, they seemed to manifest alternately, in a shift between maternal and paternal roles. Similarly, several of the psychiatry residents who were studied in depth by Ford (1963) indicated that "it was as though intense and conflicting identifications within them were battling for dominance and control of their life energy and role" (p. 476).

Schafer (1954) also contends that clinical psychology is particularly attractive to individuals with a chronically diffuse self-concept. He further describes these prospective psychologists as

> persons who are unsure what sort of individual they want to be, what kinds of relationships to cultivate, which of their impulses and feelings to accept and express and how to express those they can accept, which of their assets to develop and which traditions and values to adhere to. [p. 26]

In short, the attraction to the work of the psychotherapist may stem, in part, from an uncertain sense of identity and the search for personal identity solutions. Via the role of therapist, individuals with a diffuse self-concept can, in a sense, be "all things to all people." Coming into contact with a wide range of personalities, they may vary how they relate to others according to the needs of the situation. Depending upon the type or the phase of treatment, the clinician may function as teacher, healer, advisor, confidant, psychic masseur, devil's advocate, audience, or teddy bear. Through the vehicle of the transference, the therapist may assume the role of a parent or child, man or woman, sage or fool, ally or enemy, and, according to Searles (1965), even an inanimate object. As if this were not enough to satisfy even the most chameleonlike of individuals, therapists may, through empathic listening, lose themselves altogether—if only temporarily—in their clients.

6

MOTIVES INVOLVING OBJECT RELATIONS

In addition to viewing the therapist's motivations in terms of instinctual aims and in terms of the development of the self, we can also examine them from the vantage point of the individual's relationships to others. Freudenberger and Robbins (1979) remark that the psychoanalytic profession "tends to attract individuals who suffer from more serious and specific psychological problems related to emotional relatedness" (p. 277). In this chapter some of these problems shall be explored. Because the instincts are gratified, and the self develops, within an interpersonal context, there is a good deal of overlap among these three perspectives. The focus here, however, will be more exclusively on the interactional realm.

According to Brenner (1974), the term *object* is used "to designate persons or things of the external environment which are psychologically significant to one's psychic life, whether such 'things' be animate or lifeless" (p. 98). The term *object relations*, therefore, refers to the individual's attitudes and behaviors toward such objects. The concept derives from psychoanalytic instinct-theory; the object of an instinct, usually another person, is the agent through which the instinctual aim is achieved. The mother is generally regarded as the infant's first object, and psychoanalytic theories postulate that interpersonal relations originate in the infant's dependence on her.

DEPENDENCY

Due to the human infant's protracted period of nearly total helplessness, our first relationships are characterized by dependency. The infant is virtually immobile; all needs must be met by the parents or other caretaking figures. Although maturation and development generally bring an increasing degree of autonomy, issues related to dependency often continue to play an important role in the psychological functioning of the adult.

What sorts of dependency needs do therapists tend to have, and how do such needs relate to their choice of profession? In their study of the family backgrounds of clinical psychologists, Racusin and colleagues (1981) cite a key factor involving deprivation of parental nurturance. Such a history, they note, could be expected to result in prolonged dependency needs, as well as defenses erected against becoming aware of their painful reality.

Traumatic events, such as personal illness, parental death, and parental separation or divorce, have been found to be common in the early histories of clinicians (Hafner and Fakouri 1984b, Henry 1966). Burton (1972) summarizes the childhood backgrounds of twelve noted psychotherapists who contributed autobiographies to his volume. He points out that early and sustained physical illness was nearly universal among the sample. This usually involved lengthy periods of inactivity and dependency. Burton writes:

> Beds, white sheets, nurses, doctors, medication, the attention of helpful people, all help slant the ego toward the melioration process. This strange milieu then becomes the one of comfort, and if one cannot become a perpetual patient, one can at least become the doctor. [p. 312]

Strean, an analyst who has treated both therapists and their children, is quoted by Maeder (1989) as stating that "a person who becomes a therapist, I think, is very hungry to be parented himself or herself" (p. 205). How, then, might therapists attempt to meet their own dependency needs within the clinical setting? Therapists may rely on their clients in ways that are similar to the reliance of children upon their parents. They can, for example, look to their patients to furnish them with a holding environment that sustains them (Buie 1982–1983). Clinicians with dependent orientations may obtain receptive gratifications through their professional roles due to the one-sidedness of the communication, and due to the esteem and appreciation expressed by patients. In this sense, such therapists "feed" on their patients, satisfying dependent and narcissistic cravings (Schafer 1954).

Clients are more likely, of course, to assume the role of child than that of parent, potentially resulting in further frustration and intensification of practitioners' dependency needs. Ironically, this may be the case even when the client is the therapist's *actual parent*, as is seen in a rather curious account by Kramer (1987), in which he describes the analyses he conducted with his own mother and father:

> I have a great ambivalence about treating my parents. Some patients are interesting; these are not. They induce in me feelings that remind me of the neglect and deprivation I experienced with them as a child. They are self-absorbed, fixated at the oral stage. Their sessions often seem interminable. They rarely make contact with me and I would find that difficult work even if they were not my parents. At the present time, my mother maintains a strong resistance to transference. [p. 213]

Two critical factors appear to prevent the therapist–patient dyad from consisting of a colossal mismatch. The first is that many therapists are heavily defended against dependency needs by means of denial and reaction formations. Thus, they tend to be largely unaware of their own dependent longings, and may even exhibit a counterdependent defensive stance. Such trends can be inferred, for instance, from an autobiographical account by Ellis (1972), who declares: "I do not believe that the events of my early childhood greatly influenced my becoming a psychotherapist, nor oriented me to becoming the kind of individual and the type of therapist that I now am" (p. 103). Ellis proceeds to relate a background "replete with poor circumstances" (p. 104) and characterized by parental neglect. His father was largely absent and left for good when Ellis was 12. His mother was self-centered, self-aggrandizing, and manipulative. He nearly died of tonsillitis, and was in and out of the hospital for a number of years because of complications. Ellis's background, in fact, reveals many of the circumstances that are typical of those who develop an interest in psychotherapy. It is likely that he developed profound dependency needs that may have played a role in his development of a short-term therapy approach. This approach shifts the focus away from emotions and the therapeutic relationship and otherwise minimizes dependency ties between therapist and client.

Defensive distancing from dependency needs may also be professionally and institutionally reinforced. In an article entitled "Giving up Martyrdom," Ephross (1983) addresses what he considers a lack of self-esteem within the social work profession, reflected in an inadequate concern with work conditions and other needs of practitioners. He writes:

> Unique to social work may be a pattern of expecting staff to treat clients in a way quite different from the way they are treated themselves. To illustrate the dichotomy: perhaps somewhere there exists a stern and punitive memorandum to social work staff that *orders* them to be warm, accepting, and outgoing to consumers of the organization's services. [p. 31]

The second factor that helps to prevent a mismatch is that therapists may vicariously gratify their dependent longings by playing a caretaking role vis-à-vis their patients (the term "caretaker" is, itself, quite ambiguous—just who is receiving the care?). Marmor (1976), for instance, states that strong dependency needs on the part of therapists may lead them to respond as a loving, affectionate parent to the patient's inner, emotionally deprived, child.[1] Marmor declares

---

[1]Therapists have, at times, been very explicit in their assumption of a parental role in relation to patients. Schwing (1954), for example, makes the following recommendation for treating schizophrenic individuals: "The way to accomplish a positive transference

that this is what led Ferenczi to experiment with hugging and kissing female patients, and impels other therapists to rationalize further physical intimacies. Similarly, Menninger (1957b) notes that psychiatrists deal with lonely, eccentric, and unloved people, and suggests that this interest is likely to involve a projection of their own repressed sense of loneliness, unlovableness, and rejection. In this regard, writes Menninger, psychiatrists are constantly healing themselves in their attempts to cure others.

In one of the few descriptions in the literature focusing on female professionals, Norwood (1985) refers to the same dynamic:

> Women from dysfunctional homes (and especially, I have observed, from alcoholic homes) are overrepresented in the helping professions, working as nurses, counselors, therapists, and social workers. We are drawn to those who are needy, compassionately identifying with their pain and seeking to reduce it in order to ameliorate our own. [p. 17]

Thus, through unconscious identification with the cared-for patient—who may also serve to contain the therapist's own projected neediness—clinicians may indirectly satisfy their warded-off dependency needs. The same goal may be reached by becoming indispensable to an organization, clinic, or university department. In general, the underlying wish appears to be to provide what one failed to receive from one's parents, or one's therapist. As noted by Whitman and Bloch (1990), "Therapists can sometimes hear themselves making certain interpretations, and timing them in certain ways, that arouse the profound wish that their own therapist had responded similarly and had been equally understanding, helpful, and empathic" (p. 481).

No matter how strong the therapist's wish to play the role of "good parent," the futility of this endeavor must eventually become apparent to both participants. Perhaps this helps to explain

---

relationship is, as we have noted, a very simple one. We must give to the patient that motherliness which he lacked as a child and which the patient, without knowing it, has searched for all of his life. . . . *All of my patients have grown up*, in the deepest sense of the word, motherless" (p. 51).

why many therapists are reported to hide their pregnancy from patients for as long as possible (Imber 1990). Certainly the wish to maintain anonymity comes into play. But the therapist's pregnancy does not merely reveal that she has a personal life; it abruptly exposes the illusory nature of the therapist-as-parent metaphor. When the *real* infant arrives, there is little question as to who will receive the mothering and who will have to wait, or receive a referral elsewhere.

The motivating wish to outdo the patient's or one's own parents may also contribute to the "parent-bashing" attitudes that are so frequently seen in clinical theory and practice. In a discussion of such biases among family therapists, Wylie (1989) notes how often mothers are blamed for the pathology of their children, or of the entire family system. He writes:

> Traditionally, mothers have been excellent candidates for therapy, dutifully or desperately presenting themselves before a therapist in order to be "cured" or at least taught how not to botch up the job so badly. And training "good mothers" has been a kind of crusade for family therapists from the beginning, a task the field's originators often approached with the zeal of missionaries converting the heathen. [p. 45]

As with their patients, clinicians' conflicts regarding dependency needs appear to arise in early childhood. Psychotherapists are significantly more likely than average to be the oldest sibling; firstborns constituted 57 percent of a random sample of over 4,000 mental health professionals (Henry et al. 1973). Reich (1984) states that even when they are not the oldest, therapists tend to have taken on that role with respect to younger siblings. Most learned to take on responsibility very early; to sacrifice, to protect and nurture, to be cautious and careful, and strive to be the ideal child. Such behavior, Reich maintains, represents an identification with the parenting role. This role results from, and further contributes to, their own deficits in regard to nurturance. Highly sensitized to the needs of others, they never learn to meet their own.

This scenario may be especially common among social workers, the great majority of whom are women. In a survey of over 1,500 social workers, Lackie (1984) found that more than two-thirds appear to have been assigned and to have played roles that promoted seeming self-sufficiency: the parentified child, the overresponsible member, the mediator or go-between, the burden-bearer. A recent study of social work students (Marsh 1988) also found that for half of the sample, "a developmental model entailing precocious caretaking responsibilities within the family, and sacrifices of the self, appear to offer some explanation for their choice of career" (p. 98). The way in which this caretaking role can take on central significance in the person's self-image and self-esteem is nicely illustrated in the following excerpt from an interview with a social work student:

> This young woman stated with pride that she was the only member in her family who had influence over her father's alcohol consumption. She served as her mother's confidante, and was called at college by siblings when a family problem arose. On weekends she was drawn home by what she believed to be her role as helper to the family. When asked who was there to be helpful to her, a momentary sadness descended over her, and it seemed that she had touched the loneliness within herself. She quickly rebounded, stating that her affinity for helping others was rewarded by a very special sense of acceptance and approval from others, which meant more to her than anything else (Blumenstein 1986, p. 241).

The results of the study by Henry and colleagues, referred to above, also indicate that more than half of all mental health professionals marry individuals who were raised in unhappy family environments. Respondents frequently implied that this was an expression of their own need to nurture and treat, making remarks such as, "I guess I married my first 'patient,'" and "My first marriage was a rescue mission, I married a 'patient'" (p. 145). Children of therapists, on the other hand, are frequently described as feeling somewhat neglected by the therapist-parent, who may be emotionally depleted after a long day in the consulting room. When asked what he wished to be when he grew up, the son of a psychiatrist is reported to have replied: "I want to be a patient" (Cray and Cray 1977).

Numerous authors address the potential therapeutic hazards of an excessive need for caretaking on the part of the therapist. Weinberg (1984), for instance, warns that the therapist who is overly eager to help the patient and relieve distress can easily become overprotective and hinder the patient's development, just like the parent who cannot let her children make their own mistakes and learn from the consequences. Weinberg sees this as the reason why many therapists fall into the trap of giving advice to patients, a practice that may gratify the therapist's need to be "giving," but ultimately fosters dependency and deprives the patient of the chance to mature. A proclivity to "give too much" may also lead the therapist to be too quick to offer extra sessions, to prolong sessions, to prescribe medications, or to do all of the interpretive work for the patient.

Wolstein (1959) also refers to analysts who are overly nurturing and protective, wanting to feel needed and to play the role of the "good" parent they believe the patient never had. Impelled by strong maternal feelings, these analysts require continued dependency and infantilization from patients. Thus, seemingly nurturant motives can paradoxically interfere with clients' growth and separation. Money-Kyrle (1959) cautions, as well, that analysts playing the part of the good parent may try to offer patients love instead of effective interpretations. Additionally, they may foster a split in their patients' minds between the analyst as good parent versus the real parents as the bad ones. This can hinder patients from becoming aware of their guilt toward their parents and from working through their ambivalence, the conflict between feelings of hatred and love.

A caretaking orientation may also bias clinicians in their choice of therapeutic modalities. Blumenstein (1986) proposes that many therapists underutilize family therapy, despite avowed support for the treatment model, because of developmental experiences as a parentified child. He explains:

> Use of the family treatment modality is ego dystonic to the therapist who brings to the treatment relationship an internalized frame of reference based on his/her own parentification. His/her function is to guide treatment, not to be the therapeutic tool. He/she fosters communication between family members, rather than communicate

for them as the central source of knowledge and caretaking. This framework divests the worker from inclinations to engage individual family members in isolation from the rest of the group and to be the most prominently recognized caretaker in the treatment relationship. These deprivations create frustrations and tensions within the therapist, often leading to reducing the family to subsystems or individuals as a way of dealing with the discomfort. [p. 243]

The same argument can be made in relation to group therapy, another modality that may be underutilized.

In dissecting clinicians' motivations, it is possible to overlook such basic human components as compassion and generosity of spirit. Holt and Luborsky (1958b) express concern over this issue, suggesting that, in an attempt to screen out overzealous candidates, admissions committees have underemphasized the importance of a "more truly loving kindness" (p. 336). As these authors point out, it is crucial to distinguish between genuine helpfulness and "pseudo-kindliness" based on guilt or on reaction formations against hostility and dependency.

SEPARATION

Another essential component of object relations that appears to play a role in the wish to practice psychotherapy is the struggle for separation and autonomy. Mahler (Mahler et al. 1975) provides a widely accepted developmental model that helps to clarify the concept of separation. Mahler postulates that infants go through a symbiotic phase (approximately 2–10 months) in which they are merged psychologically with the mother and view her as an extension of themselves. During the separation-individuation phase (lasting until 2–3 years) there is a gradual differentiation as the child begins to establish a separate identity. This culminates in the achievement of libidinal object constancy, in which the child is able to maintain internalized images of others.

Even under ideal conditions, the process of separation and individuation is an ongoing one, which continues into adult life. As Fine (1983) puts it:

This separation-individuation process provides a paradigm for all
later development. Individuation proceeds to a point where there is
a period of self-consolidation involving attachment to some other
person. From there it then goes on again to separation from the
person (or internalized image) and eventual individuation. Thus the
attainment of a sense of the self is never a single process attained
overnight. [p. 114]

An important aspect of the therapeutic gains made by individuals
in psychotherapy can be conceptualized in terms of increased capacity for separation and individuation. What has not been as widely
recognized is that the therapeutic relationship also provides *therapists* with opportunities to develop further along these lines. For each
of the participants, the treatment setting appears to provide unique
opportunities to experience both symbiosis and differentiation.

As in most developmental models, Mahler's developmental
stages are viewed as building one upon the other. Unless the young
child has an adequate chance to merge symbiotically with the
mothering figure, later attempts at differentiation will be impeded.
The therapeutic relationship can furnish the practitioner with repeated occasions in which to achieve what Racker (1968) describes
as a "psychological symbiosis" (p. 143) with clients. This sense of
closeness and connectedness may serve to allay the therapist's own
separation anxiety. Buie (1982–1983) proposes that this is a central
motivation for becoming a psychotherapist:

> Specifically, the therapist hopes, consciously or unconsciously, to be
> relieved of his sense of aloneness; prior to his own therapy or
> analysis he is unable, however, to conceive of the possibility of
> achieving for himself a comfortable sense of security as an autono-
> mous human being. Instead he implicitly hopes that in meeting his
> patient's needs his own need for the kind of sustaining togetherness
> that mitigates depressive aloneness will be fulfilled. Even when his
> own treatment is successfully completed, he continues to yearn for
> comforting closeness with his patients, but his yearning is less a need
> and more simply a wish. [p. 227]

Every analysis involves, to some degree, a regression on the part
of the patient to a symbioticlike transference relationship, which

may be gratifying to the analyst and difficult to relinquish (Marks 1978). Some degree of regression must clearly also take place on the part of the analyst. In a discussion of the role of regression in the empathic process, Jaffe (1986) states that it is through a transient identification that the analyst experiences a temporary oneness with the patient, followed by a sense of separateness. More precisely: "The analyst thinks *with* the patient (oneness) and then *about* the patient (separateness)" (p. 229). For both the patient and analyst the analytic situation recapitulates the early mother–child dyad, as the "interplay is between merging pressures and those of redifferentiating, separating, individuating" (p. 231).

Greenson (1962) contends that the urge to understand a patient originates in the desire to get inside another human being. He views this propensity as deriving initially from the infant's longing for symbiotic fusion with the mother. Analysts' empathy enables them to reestablish contact with a lost love object, the patient they have yet to understand. "It may be in part an attempt at restitution for the loss of contact. This seems to be borne out by my experience that the best empathizers seem to be those analysts who have a tendency to depressions" (1967, p. 383).

If the clinical setting offered only opportunities for merging, it might help to soothe away anxieties but would do little to promote growth. In actuality, when the therapeutic process is on track, it allows for movement toward greater separation and differentiation. As Searles (1965) writes in regard to his treatment of schizophrenics, both therapist and patient may benefit from this aspect of the therapy relationship:

> The therapist finds himself involved so deeply in the same conflict concerning individuation in the treatment relationship, that the individuation which eventually results can truly be called a mutual one. . . . These are aspects of what I have described in earlier papers as the phase of therapeutic symbiosis. The mutual individuation which follows, again by dint of many ambivalent weaning struggles by both patient and therapist, leaves each deeply changed. The patient will never again, presumably, be so vulnerable to psychosis. But neither will the therapist ever again need to repress so fully his own more primitive processes which include the kind of nonintegra-

tion and nondifferentiation of experience that have comprised the defenses of the formerly psychotic patient. [pp. 25–26]

This dynamic is in no way limited, however, to work with highly disturbed patients. The same theme appears, for example, in Ruderman's (1986) account of a therapist who, in helping her patient resolve gender-identity conflicts encountered several issues involving her own difficulties separating from her mother:

> Every move I made in the service of individuation was like a cardinal sin. And so this female patient reminded me of myself, and of the girl I would wish to be . . . I helped her to realize herself as my mother could never comfortably help me. . . . In helping her [the patient] to individuate from a controlling, martyring, self-sacrificing mother, I identified with her to an extent, I'm quite sure, and I maybe further freed myself in the process of freeing her. [p. 113]

Stone (1961) remarks that a state of "intimate separation" (p. 86) is implicit in the psychoanalytic situation. He suggests that certain features of the setting and the relationship closely parallel the phase of separation-individuation:

> As an alternative to Spitz's proposal (1956) that the analytic setting tends to reproduce many aspects of the earliest (i.e., objectless) phase of mother–child relations, I would suggest that, except in certain aspects of the physical arrangements, the psychoanalytic setting in its general and primary transference impact tend to reproduce from the outset, the repetitive phases of the state of relative *separation* from early objects, and most crucially, via the phenomenon of extreme exaggeration, that period of life where all the modalities of bodily intimacy and direct dependence on the mother are being relinquished or attenuated, *pari passu* with the rapid development of the great vehicle of communication by speech. [p. 86]

The process of separation-individuation appears to be somewhat different for girls than for boys. Chodorow (1978) notes that the father, as currently culturally defined, does not tend to experience himself as being merged with the infant, nor does the infant feel as totally dependent on the father as on the mother. Rather, the father represents separation and otherness to the growing child. Whereas little boys typically shift their attachment from mother to father, girls never really give up their earlier preoedipal tie to their mothers. According to Chodorow, this continuing attachment keeps girls from experiencing themselves as fully separate and differentiated; instead, their sense of self is one of self in relation to other.

These gender differences may affect how male and female therapists deal with separation issues. In terms of transference and countertransference, female therapists are more likely to be in touch with and to elicit preoedipal feelings. Moreover, by virtue of their gender role, they may feel drawn toward symbiotic closeness with clients, and find it more difficult to deal with separateness and boundaries (Schachtel 1986).[2] Thus, the therapeutic situation may be especially useful to female therapists in developing a more differentiated sense of self, as is seen in the following passage:

> I personally like the kind of deep, but limited intimacy that thera-
> peutic relationships have. As a woman who in her past easily found
> herself merging or wanting to merge with others once I became
> emotionally involved, I need to learn about boundaries and detach-
> ment. Being a psychotherapist has helped me work with the contra-
> diction of longing for closeness but needing separation too. I find it a
> valuable model for other kinds of relationships (Chaplin 1989,
> p. 182).

An important indication that many psychotherapists have had significant problems in achieving separation and autonomy comes from the large-scale study of Henry and colleagues (1973). Late adolescence is a critical juncture in the individuation process, when the individual commonly achieves increased independence from parental figures. These investigators had psychotherapists describe how their parents reacted to their attempts during adolescence to move toward independence, referred to by many respondents as

---

[2]This notion appears to be contradicted, however, by the incidence of sexual boundary violations, which are far greater among male than female therapists.

their "break from home" (p. 181). Of over 4,000 mental health professionals surveyed, 63 percent portrayed their mothers as having fought or disapproved of it, and 45 percent portrayed their fathers similarly. The authors note that the significant discrepancy between these two figures is consistent with the therapists' descriptions of their mothers as possessive, dominating, and demanding. Similarly, for the 60 percent who reported strained relationships during their transition to adulthood, the mother was cited twice as frequently as the antagonist. Overall, the results indicate that many psychotherapists had intense struggles for independence from their families during adolescence and early adulthood. Once again, however, the absence of comparable data on other groups of professionals brings into question to what degree, if any, this is outside the norm.

It was noted earlier in this chapter that many psychotherapists, as children, took on parental roles in their families. Searles (1979) refers to the intense emotional distress that results when such parentified individuals attempt to leave home and establish a separate identity, thereby "abandoning" family members. The explanation for this, according to Searles, is that "the young person's individuation needs have come into unbearable conflict, that is, with his therapeutic strivings toward family members" (p. 437).

Another way of understanding therapists' difficulties with separation and autonomy involves Bowen's (1976) concept of triangulation. According to Bowen, there are three ways in which psychological dysfunction is commonly expressed in nuclear families: marital conflict, dysfunction in a spouse, and projection onto one or more of the children. Typically, one child is "chosen" as the recipient of the major portion of parental projections. This child is the one who is most emotionally attached to the parents, and is the one who, due to this projection process, emerges with the lowest level of differentiation of self.

Bowen adds that the triangulated child is also the one who becomes the most emotionally reactive, who grows up with the greatest fusion of emotional and intellectual functioning, who is most sensitized to disturbances in the family system, and is the most vulnerable to developing mental, physical, or social problems. Given this description, it also appears likely that the triangulated child, the one who receives the bulk of the parental projections, is the one most likely to become a psychotherapist. Moreover, such individuals can be expected to possess a greater-than-average level of conflict regarding issues of separation and individuation.

Returning to the clinical setting, if therapists do indeed tend to have difficulties with separation, this would become most evident during the termination phase of treatment. In fact, numerous authors have commented on the noticeable dearth of literature and lack of study concerning all aspects of the termination phase of psychotherapy (Hiatt 1965, Kauff 1977, Levinson 1977, Weddington and Cavenar 1979). Particularly ignored are the emotional reactions of therapists to terminating clients. As Klauber (1983) notes: "And practically no word ever appears in the literature about how the analyst manages to form relationship after relationship of the most intimate kind with patient after patient, of the mourning which he must feel for each one of them, and of how he discharges it" (p. 46). The very word, termination, appears antiseptically free of all affective connotations.

Martin and Schurtman (1985) hypothesize that this important area has been largely avoided because it is especially conflictual and therefore elicits much anxiety in therapists. They maintain that termination anxiety in therapists may involve separation anxieties stemming from their own personal histories; particularly, a flawed or incomplete separation from mother. Related to this are guilt feelings in the therapist deriving from a sense of abandoning the client. These feelings may be dynamically linked to early guilt over childhood attempts at separating from the mother.

These authors suggest that many therapists, in response to intense separation anxieties evoked during termination, deviate unnecessarily in a countertransference-based effort to allay their fears. Langs also notes that many analysts tend to introduce modifications of the treatment during the termination phase—such as sitting the patient up, or developing a social relationship—as a way of softening the trauma of separation (Langs and Searles 1980). Excessive separation anxiety on the part of clinicians may also lead them to avoid termination by blocking their clients' moves toward autonomy and unduly prolonging treatment. McWilliams (1987) concludes, "Thus, like a mother who keeps reminding her children how unprepared they are for life without her, the analyst unwittingly contaminates the separation process with even more guilt and ambivalence than separation ordinarily contains" (p. 95).

It could be that therapists' difficulties with termination are especially marked in the treatment of adolescent clients. A recent empirical study found no support for the widely held view that adolescents show a pronounced tendency to drop out prematurely from individual psychotherapy (Suzuki 1989). The author contends that the adolescent client's decision to end treatment is more likely to be made unilaterally, and thus labelled premature, due to a reenactment within the therapeutic relationship of the adolescent's attempts to separate from his parents.

For some psychotherapists, the decision to enter the field may be directly related to their difficulties in fully terminating with, and thus separating from, their own therapists. Glover (1929) declares as well-known the observation that, at a particular stage in analytic treatment, many patients express the desire to become analysts themselves. Glover characterizes this attitude as essentially defensive, involving an identification with the analyst to avoid submitting to the analysis.

Could those who go on to become analysts and psychotherapists be carrying this defensive process one step further? This rather frightening notion has, in fact, been entertained. Milner (1950) suggests that analysts bypassed their own termination by identifying with their analysts' profession and acting out the identification. The New York analyst with the alias of Aaron Green (Malcolm 1981) clearly concurs:

> If the full experience of termination is a kind of existential rite of passage . . . then analysts never grow up and never have to die. The people who instruct others on serious and final things themselves remain Peter Pans, indefinitely staving off adulthood and extinction in the Never-Never-Land of analytic practice and institutional politics. [p. 155]

Finally, and further intensifying the cause for concern, it has also been advanced that psychoanalysts as a whole have yet to separate from, relinquish, and otherwise come to terms with the death of the founder of their movement (Klauber 1983, Wallerstein 1983). Wallerstein writes that "Sigmund Freud remains our lost object, our unreachable genius, whose passing we have perhaps never properly mourned, at least not in the emotional fullness that leads to intellective accommodation" (p. 271). This reluctance to separate from Freud has resulted in rigid adherence to his ideas and in a continuing dependency that has been "infantilizing and stultifying" (p. 271).

POWER AND CONTROL

Boswell (1791) quotes Samuel Johnson as declaring that "no two men can be half an hour together but one shall acquire an evident superiority over the other." It would surely be naive to suppose that the therapist's office is the one place where power struggles do not enter into human interactions. The lust for power and control can, indeed, play a central role in an individual's wish to practice psychotherapy.

In his influential volume, *Listening with the Third Ear*, Reik (1948) suggests that even the wish to understand another individual derives from this power motive. He traces the roots of the desire to comprehend to the primitive urge to devour and incorporate, noting that the infant's only means of possessing an object is to consume it. Reik points to the remnants of this origin in the tendency of children to open their mouths when surprised, as well as in such verbal expressions as "thirst for knowledge" and "lapping up a story." Reik goes on to suggest that the psychological comprehension of another person involves a sublimated form of this wish for incorporation, representing, in a sense, "psychological cannibalism" (p. 232). He elaborates:

> The other person is taken into your ego and becomes, for the time being, a part of your ego. Thus in the process of psychological comprehension man's craving for power is satisfied, not only in its most refined and sublimated form, but unconsciously in its crudest. [p. 232]

The role of psychotherapist clearly permits various expressions of the need for power. Because of the inequality inherent in the relationship, the therapist is in a position to dominate and control the patient. As Schafer (1954) points out, the fact that the patient comes to the therapist for assistance assures this inequality from the start. The nature of the professional relationship contains the implicit assumption that, of the two people in the office, the therapist is the one who is strong, healthy, and in command of the situation. Langs notes that his idea, that patients may unconsciously attempt to cure their treaters, has met with considerable resistance: "The notion that there is only one person with curative powers, abilities or interests, and that he is the analyst, is fiercely maintained—in large part because of strong countertransference-based needs" (Langs and Searles 1980, p. 164). Even the common use of the possessive pronoun in such phrases as "my patient," or "I have a patient who . . . ," reveals this wish for control (Shepard and Lee 1970).

In his discussion of power in psychotherapy, Guggenbuhl-Craig (1971) draws parallels between the Inquisition and modern-day social work:

> Now it naturally cannot be maintained that today's social welfare endeavors are directly descended from the medieval Inquisition; there is no torture, no burning in social work. But there are certain obvious parallels. An attempt is made to combat unhealthy family situations, to correct unsatisfactory social structures, to adjust the maladjusted—in brief, we try to enforce that which we consider "right" for people. And we often do this even when our help is rejected by those concerned. In our own way we frequently force a certain view of life upon others whether they agree to it or not. We do not choose to acknowledge a right to sickness, unhealthy family relations, social degeneracy and eccentricity. [p. 7]

Partly because the therapeutic relationship has been founded on the medical model, the psychotherapy patient is generally afforded a low status. As Guggenbuhl-Craig comments, a polarity is established, "with the regressed, childish, fearful patient at one end and, at the other, the superior, proud physician, aloof though perhaps still somewhat coolly courteous" (p. 84). Particularly when hospitalized, patients are likely to feel powerless and bereft of dignity. Only since the patients' rights movement, beginning in the 1970s, have such basic issues as the right to refuse treatment been addressed.

The power motive can be inferred from some of the metaphors found in Freud's writings. This is most clearly seen in his use of the surgeon analogy, but may also come into play when he discusses the analyst-as-sculptor, with the patient providing the "raw material" (Freud 1905b). Freud claimed that "compared with other psychotherapeutic procedures, psycho-analysis is far and away the most powerful," while observing cautiously that "psycho-analysis really is a form of therapy, just as other methods are. It has its triumphs, its defeats, its difficulties, its limitations, and its indications. . . . The proportion of recoveries which have been effected give us ground neither for boasting nor for feeling ashamed" (1933, p. 112).

Other reflections in the literature of the power motive range from the exalted to the depraved. Eissler (1952) describes the Swiss analyst, Schwing, who was a pioneer in the treatment of the severely disturbed, in the following terms: "Like a medieval saint, she released the schizophrenics from their strait-jackets, and patients who had just been howling immediately quieted down when she turned to them" (p. 165). Also in reference to the treatment of schizophrenics, Burton (1970) writes:

> The deep encounter with the schizophrenic patient is of great and sublime magnitude and it is a position of personal privilege. It is as though the healer were permitted to be present at the birth of creation and participated in it. It is feeling magnified to the 10th power, and it is the best proof that one is himself alive and living. [p. 196]

The debased aspect of the power motive involves wishes to humiliate, degrade, and violate the helpless patient. In his novel, *The Doctor of Desire*, Wheelis (1987) has the analyst-protagonist describe such urges:

Violation is part of my desire, the dark underside. Might be better not to know. But I do know. The garden must be secret, guarded, mysterious. Access must be hidden or difficult or denied. I seek to enter where, though I be desired, I'm not altogether welcome. Resistance must be overcome. Some advantage, not entirely fair or honorable, must be taken. [pp. 158-159]

Even more extreme, and far less poetically described, is an account of an analyst who ordered his client to "duck-walk across the room, unzip his pants with her teeth, and then perform oral sex on him" (Walker and Young 1986, p. 4).

Hammer (1972) maintains that many students are drawn to the field out of a need for power: "They essentially become manipulators of their patients and are incapable of really caring about them or seeing any beauty in them" (p. 24). The situation, he notes, is further complicated by the fact that these individuals may also find it difficult to accept supervision or to submit to their own personal therapy. Empirical findings to substantiate such claims are hard to come by, but two reports are worth noting. In one study comparing the unconscious motivations of psychiatric residents and clinical psychology students, projective testing revealed that the wish to have power and to dominate others was frequently present in both groups (Donnay-Richelle et al. 1972). Another study of three medical schools found that *High Machs*—manipulative, exploitive individuals—were overrepresented among students specializing in psychiatry, when compared to various other medical specialties (Christie and Geis 1970).

What sorts of needs might therapists be attempting to satisfy in their wish to command power over their patients? It may reflect a need to alter the behavior of a recalcitrant self or that of a past figure (Edelwich 1980). Omnipotent fantasies of producing magical transformations may also be involved. Hammer (1972) contends that therapists with a strong need to dominate were, as children, excessively dominated and controlled by their parents. By dominating and controlling their patients, they compensate for underlying feelings of powerlessness and vulnerability and defend against an inability to trust and to relate deeply to others. Such therapists strive to be in the superior position in relation to clients and equate the inferior role with humiliation and, unconsciously, with castration:

> They are trying to undo all of the humiliation they felt toward themselves for submitting and permitting their parents to dominate them, and for this reason they harbor a secret revulsion toward all their patients for putting themselves in the inferior position of having to ask for help. [p. 22]

Early relationships with siblings may also contribute to the development of these needs. Based on extensive interviews and data from questionnaires, Henry and colleagues (1973) state that therapists view themselves as having occupied the superior sibling position twice as frequently as an inferior one and three times as frequently as an egalitarian one. The authors point to the similarities between the role of therapist and that of dominant sibling, described by respondents as including "such nurturant behaviors as protecting and defending, giving support and encouragement, and attempting to 'straighten him out,' as well as manipulation" (p. 187).

Henry and colleagues also refer to a significant difference on this issue between psychoanalysis and the other three professions studied: psychiatry, psychology, and social work. While 82 percent of the analysts who discussed it identified themselves as having been in the dominant role, only 50 percent of the other three professions did so. The authors view this as consistent with the dominant position of psychoanalysts—both in terms of their prestigious position within the mental health field, and in terms of the greater inequality in relation to patients fostered by the psychoanalytic approach. Psychoanalysts, they contend, are used to occupying a position of dominance, having played such a role within the family context.

Whatever its source, the power motive can clearly distort the treatment process, or contribute to an impasse in which therapist and patient wind up in a mutual standoff. As this case example from Brightman (1984–1985) illustrates, therapists' attempts to gain control over their patients' behavior impede empathic understanding:

A female trainee was working with an adolescent girl with anorexia nervosa. The patient defined her therapy goals as eating normally and gaining weight, which the trainee readily accepted as her own aspirations for the treatment. The patient's weight quickly became the scale by which the trainee evaluated her own professional power and knowledge. The trainee felt "good" (proud, loving) about herself and the patient when the weight went up, and "bad" (ashamed, angry) when it fell. She became increasingly committed to controlling the patient's weight in order to preserve her own professional self-esteem, thereby recreating the struggles that the patient had with her mother around having anything (a feeling, thought, or body) of her own. What was strikingly absent from the trainee's representation of the patient in supervision was any mention of the patient's *own* experience or understanding of her illness. It was only when the trainee could, with supervisory support, tolerate her own feelings of utter confusion, anger, and helplessness (initially unacceptable to her grandiose professional self) about the patient's symptoms that she could "give up" her attempts to control them, and see for the first time the complementary sentiments the patient had about her illness, her self, and her life in general. The patient's perception that the therapist could "let go" of her eating and weight, and "hold" her truest feelings, allowed a stronger treatment alliance to develop between the two. [pp. 313–314]

Resistant patients and therapy failures can inflict significant blows to the therapist's sense of omnipotence. Guilt, self-recriminations, and depression may follow, unless—as Searles (1979) advises—the therapist comes to understand that both participants are involved in a process that in some manner transcends their individual wills:

The more experienced and confident the therapist becomes in this work, the more deeply does he realize that this process is far too powerful for either the patient or himself to be able to at all easily deflect it, consciously and willfully and singlehandedly, away from the confluent channel which it is tending—with irresistible power, if we can give ourselves up to the current—to form itself. When the therapist sees this, he realizes how illusory has been his subjective omnipotence, but also how groundless has been his subjective guilt. [p. 559]

THE WISH TO DRIVE
THE OTHER PERSON CRAZY

In a controversial and thought-provoking article published in 1959, Searles explores the unconscious attempt to drive another person crazy as an element in the etiology and treatment of schizophrenia. He describes a mutual struggle of this sort, between parent and child, as a key dynamic in the child's eventual descent into psychosis. A similar struggle between therapist and patient is viewed as a necessary and inevitable part of the curative process.

Searles describes a variety of motives for wishing to drive someone crazy, and suggests that the range of underlying motives is as broad for therapists as it is for patients. Such strivings on the part of the therapist may be determined primarily by the patient's transference or by the therapist's countertransference. That is, they may involve a complementary reaction to the patient's drive-and-be-driven type of relatedness, or may derive from a character trait of the therapist's. Searles contends that such an unconscious tendency varies in strength from therapist to therapist, but is probably never entirely absent. With characteristic candor, he reveals that he discovered this trait in himself, late in his own analysis.

Why would therapists unconsciously wish to drive their patients crazy? Some of the general motives elucidated by Searles could clearly apply to the specific case of the therapist. One of these is the desire to externalize, and thereby dispose of, the threatening craziness in oneself. Langs (1980) addresses this motive as well, describing how the therapist may misuse the therapeutic situation to re-create his or her own pathogenic past in the interaction with the patient. These tendencies, Langs observes, are "in part related to unresolved motives to make the patient sick or sicker, and to interfere with his growth and the resolution of his symptoms" (p. 382).

Another related motive, clearly applicable to the therapeutic situation, involves a conscious or unconscious desire to aid another person in attaining better integration and a healthier closeness. Searles explains:

Here, that is, the conscious or unconscious effort is to activate dissociated or repressed elements in the other's personality, not with

the goal of his ego's becoming overwhelmed by their accession into
awareness, but rather with the goal of his ego's integrating them.
[p. 11]

This rather paradoxical-sounding impulse appears consistent with
the seemingly contradictory notion, implied in psychoanalytic
treatment, that the therapist must first weaken the patient's defenses, and increase intrapsychic conflict and resulting anxiety, in
order to bring about a fuller integration and balance.

A third motive, emphasized by Searles as the most powerful of
all of these, is "the attainment, perpetuation, or recapture of the
gratifications inherent in the symbiotic mode of relatedness"
(p. 11). This manifests in therapists as an unconscious effort to
drive patients crazy, or to perpetuate their craziness, in order to
obtain the gratifications offered by the "crazy" symbiotic mode of
relatedness. These include both feelings of infantile satisfaction as
well as omnipotent-mother fantasies. Searles suggests that such
gratifications on the part of both patients and therapists are often
responsible for therapeutic impasses.

Finally, Searles states that for a large number of therapists and
analysts, and especially for those with obsessive-compulsive tendencies in which reaction formations are prominent, the unconscious desire to drive the other person crazy is especially strong and
constitutes an important determinant of vocational choice. Here,
Searles merely expands on the frequently encountered notion that
the desire to heal often derives from reaction formations against
unconscious sadistic wishes:

> That is, just as we would not be surprised to find that a surgeon
> brings forth, in the course of his psychoanalysis, powerful and here-
> tofore deeply repressed wishes to physically dismember other per-
> sons, so we should be ready to discern the presence in not a few of us
> who have chosen the profession of treating psychiatric illness, of
> similarly powerful, long-repressed desires to dismember the person-
> ality-structure of other persons. [p. 15]

Searles maintains that such impulses may be revealed in the tendency to make premature interpretations, or in the use of any

therapeutic technique that fosters further disintegration in the patient.

In *On Being a Therapist*, Kottler (1986) makes the following remark: "It would almost seem that even with the hardships of being a therapist, we have a great thing going. If only we did not encounter those clients who push us to the brink of our own madness" (p. 65). This notion is reminiscent of a comment by Woody Allen, along the lines of his having worked enthusiastically for the Gay Rights Movement until discovering to his dismay that it was thoroughly infiltrated by homosexuals. Could it be that therapists on occasion induce craziness in patients in order to keep from going crazy themselves?

INTIMACY

The psychotherapy setting provides opportunities for a level of human contact and closeness that is rarely achievable in ordinary social situations. It stands to reason, therefore, that the profession would attract individuals who have strong needs for, and conflicts over, intimacy.

Menninger (1957b) remarks that medical students who choose to specialize in psychiatry react to feelings of loneliness and rejection in such a way that they become more concerned with human relationships than do their peers. Hammer (1972) also contends that some students are drawn to the profession due to loneliness and a need for people. He describes them as having had isolated childhoods, often as only children, resulting in an intense hunger for companionship. "They envision a career as a therapist as providing them with a constant source of interpersonal relationships to relieve their panic of being lonely and isolated" (p. 28). Having scheduled appointments brings the assurance of predictable client company (Pollak 1976).

Empirical validation is, once again, in short supply. Roe and Siegleman (1964) report on two studies comparing the early experiences of social workers versus engineers. The results indicated that both the male and, to a lesser extent, the female social workers experienced greater stress and less affection from their parents than did the engineers. The parents of the former group also exhibited a higher frequency of personality disorders and other psychological problems. The authors conclude that the choice of social work as occupation may be, in part, an attempt to achieve more satisfying personal relations. The results were viewed as consistent with the hypothesis that "some unsatisfying early experiences may lead, not to giving up the quest for such satisfaction, but to a further search for sources of such satisfaction" (p. 66).

The results of the study by Henry and colleagues (1973), in which over 4,000 mental health professionals were interviewed or responded to questionnaires, provide some support for the hypothesis that therapists tend to have difficulties with personal relationships, and therefore attempt to achieve intimacy in the controlled setting of the consulting room. Of the respondents who mentioned the social timeliness of when they began dating, 92 percent of the psychoanalysts and 90 percent of the psychiatrists considered themselves to have been late. The authors note that the responses to questions concerning relationships with spouses and children were relatively sparse and restricted compared to other areas of inquiry. Changes in the style of delivery of interviewees were also noticed:

> The typical affective posture of the psychotherapist when speaking of his spouse or children was one of cool placidity, in striking contrast to the involved excitement that distinguished discussion both of the family relationships of childhood and of the current patient–therapist relationships. [p. 143]

It appears that, for many therapists, the intensity and intimacy of their professional encounters with clients are balanced by relatively subdued interpersonal interactions in private life. Henry and colleagues conclude that "typically, the relationship between husband and wife, while generally satisfying, lacks emotional intensity. . . . For most, the emotional interaction with spouse, while positive, is temperate" (p. 158). Some of the respondents accounted for this by suggesting that the intimacy achieved in therapeutic interactions compensates for the lack of, or inability for, intimacy in their personal life.

Burton (1972) describes a meeting he attended of the Division of Psychotherapy of the American Psychological Association, in which there was a workshop for therapists' wives. Discussion revealed that marital problems were frequent and that the wives often felt lonely, as well as jealous of their husbands' patients. Similarly, Carey (1977) reports that children of psychiatrists tend to feel that the parent is distant, and both children and spouses complain that they receive less attention than do patients.

Despite the intense emotional involvement that often characterizes the therapeutic relationship, the intimacy that is achieved must remain asymmetrical. This is a pivotal aspect of the clinical situation, on which the entire therapeutic enterprise rests. In the words of Tarachow (1962):

> The therapeutic task for the therapist is his struggle with his need for objects and with the self-imposed therapeutic barrier. The problem of spontaneous and unplanned acts of the analyst arise from this consideration. The temptation to breach the barrier will assail the therapist at all times. If the patient pleads for help he wants to extend himself; if the patient is hostile he wants to fight; if the patient is unhappy he wants to console him; if the patient is in need he wants to give. The therapist's task is to restrain himself from regarding these phenomena as real and thus destroying the transference "as if" potential. This restraint separates him from the patient as object and imposes upon him the task of tolerating loneliness. [p. 381]

Greben (1975) warns that if the therapist does not have adequately close personal relationships, this can prolong treatment and interfere with the patient's attempts to separate. Moreover, he contends that when the need for intimacy is a major underlying motive, the vocational choice of psychotherapist may prove disappointing and self-defeating. The profession itself can impose a great deal of isolation, and if the practitioner adheres to a rigid technique, it will severely limit the intimacy that can be achieved with patients. This dilemma is seen in Wheelis's (1959) artful description of the longing that may stir within the analyst when enticed by the patient's transferential love:

Lean hands within him reach out hungrily. He longs to touch, to feel, to warm himself by this bright fire, so close, so near to hand, so unutterably far away. One slight movement and he could touch her hair. But he has so designed his life that it is as though there were a continent between them. [p. 184]

In an excellent overview of the impact of therapists' work on their personal lives, Guy (1987) lists the many ways in which the practice of psychotherapy can increase one's sense of isolation and estrangement. Certain factors contribute to an experience of *physical isolation*: being confined to an office, isolation from colleagues and the external world, isolation from family and friends (difficult to reach by phone), environmental deprivation, physical inactivity, and isolation imposed by confidentiality. Other aspects of the work may contribute to *psychic isolation*: maintaining a focus on clients, withholding personal information, setting aside personal concerns, need for emotional control, one-way intimacy, maintaining interpretive stance with little room for spontaneity, clients' idealization and devaluation, strains of terminations, professional competition, and public perceptions and stereotypes.

Guy also describes how such factors as emotional depletion, excessive psychological-mindedness, loss of identity, grandiosity, secrecy, and emotional preoccupation can have deleterious effects on the therapist's relationships with friends and family members. Ultimately, the clinician's capacity for intimacy may wane:

The blend of the personal and professional life of the therapist results in a blurring of the boundaries, causing one existence to flow into the other. Over time there often appears to be less and less distinction between roles and persona, with the therapist becoming increasingly "clinical" and less real. Life is lived vicariously, and the therapist becomes an observer rather than a participant in the events and experiences of everyday living. [p. 194]

While the wish for intimacy appears to be an important motivation for engaging in psychotherapeutic work, the fear of intimacy may play an equally significant role. In discussing the proper attitude of the analyst, Freud (1912) explains his rationale for using the analogy of the surgeon, who subordinates all personal feelings in order to concentrate fully on the technical operation:

> The justification for requiring this emotional coldness in the analyst is that it creates the most advantageous conditions for both parties: for the doctor a desirable protection for his own emotional life and for the patient the largest amount of help that we can give him today. [p. 115]

Thus, the professional role of the psychotherapist is designed to provide distance as well as closeness.

In Malcolm's *Psychoanalysis: The Impossible Profession* (1981), the analyst called Aaron Green describes his need for emotional distance, viewing it as deriving from excessive self-absorption and an inability to immerse himself in another person. He declares:

> I was attracted to psychoanalytic work precisely because of the distance it would create between me and the people I treated. It's a situation of very comfortable abstinence. A situation of *not* taking responsibility for the other person's behavior, but only for one's own. Psychoanalysts talk quite frankly about the defensive comfort of analytic silence, passivity, and neutrality. It fits in with certain profound motives. [p. 110]

Wheelis (1959) provides a succinct account of how the role of analyst offers an exquisite defense against intimacy:

> An analyst is not to become involved with his patients; very well, he will remain uninvolved. He will require his patients to lie down; he will sit, unseen, behind the couch. He will direct his patients to talk continuously; he will speak infrequently, and not on demand, but only at his own discretion. The conditions optimal for psychoanalysis appear to fit the conditions optimal for personal security with a rare precision. A more fortunate concordance could hardly be imagined. [p. 181]

Greenson (1967) asks what might impel an individual to want to take on the role of blank-screen anonymity and emotional restraint of the analyst. He concludes that although it might stem from relatively healthy traits, such as modesty and a sense of privacy, it can also derive from more pathological ones, such as excessive shyness, isolation, and tendencies toward generalized emotional withdrawal and lack of involvement. He states:

> My experience with candidates suffering from such problems indicates that they are persons who are struggling against great hostility, rage, and anxiety. They need to remain remote in order not to explode with anger or panic. These people are not suitable for psychoanalytic work, yet they sought it out because superficially it seemed to offer them a haven from the fearful direct contact with people. [p. 400]

Riemann (1968) addresses the need for distance in analysts with schizoid traits. He remarks that they tend to be overly intellectual, remain uninvolved emotionally, and unconsciously discourage positive transferences. They do not assume enough of a partnership with patients, who may feel like objects of scientific investigation. A rigid rule prohibiting therapist self-disclosure, which may be of use with certain patients, also suggests excessive self-protection and discomfort with intimacy. Finally, Lindner (1978) speculates that psychiatrists with schizoid tendencies may prefer dispensing medications to engaging in intensive psychotherapies requiring more personal involvement.

For the majority of psychotherapists it appears that there exists some combination of the wish for and fear of intimacy, and that their professional work provides a balance between the two. A study by Gill and Brenman (1959), for example, indicates that an important determinant of a career in psychiatry, which is particularly apparent in the hypnotic relationship, is "the paradoxical need for simultaneous intimacy and distance" (p. 452). The professional rules of psychotherapeutic practice provide a context in which the need to engage in a close, and even "merging," relationship can be kept within safe bounds. One analyst in their sample comments on

> the curious situation where I sit behind my analysand who is supine and thus symbolically "helpless," who has to tell me his most inti-

mate thoughts and feelings and to whom, *in this controlled and circumscribed situation, I react with intimate feelings and comment*—and to whom a few seconds later I behave in a somewhat cool and professional manner as he leaves my office. [p. 452]

Hammer (1972), likewise, maintains that many who enter the profession crave intimacy, yet require distance because they fear getting hurt or becoming engulfed and overwhelmed. "Because their own identity or sense of self is not clearly established they unconsciously fear that intimacy will produce a state of fusion which will result in the loss of their individuality" (p. 26). Thus, intimacy becomes bearable only within the controlled setting of the therapeutic relationship, in which they expect to be protected from overinvolvement or loss of self.

The asymmetrical nature of the therapeutic relationship further reduces, for the therapist, the risks associated with intimacy. Only the patient is expected to be revealing. As Henry and colleagues (1973) note, "The psychotherapist is not only free to determine what he will reveal and conceal about himself, but also to choose how to react to what the patient is saying, if indeed he decides to respond at all" (p. 218). Only the therapist, moreover, is supposed to interpret the patient's remarks and to assign meaning to them. As the authors conclude:

In sum, the therapeutic relationship is a highly circumscribed, personal relationship conducted in accordance with ground rules laid down by the therapist. These rules result in a relationship in which the therapist comes to know all about the patient as a person while the patient never comes to know the therapist as anything but a therapist. Thus, from the therapist's standpoint, the therapeutic transaction provides intimacy and close personal familiarity without, at the same time, involving the risks entailed in revealing one's inner thoughts and feelings to another. [p. 219]

Hence, in their professional role, psychotherapists appear to have the perfect *compromise formation* for dealing with their conflicts over intimacy. Just as a patient's neurotic symptom allows for partial satisfaction of both the threatening impulse and the defense against it, the work of the psychotherapist enables both the wish for, and the fear of, intimacy to coexist.

RESCUE FANTASIES AND
THE NEED FOR REPARATION

A rescue fantasy refers to the wish to be rescued or to rescue someone else. As noted by Eidelberg (1968), "It seems to represent an immediate elimination of the infantile helplessness or the magic ability to save others from such predicaments" (p. 376). In this sense, it is closely related to other interpersonal issues discussed above, such as dependency, separation, and power.

In a discussion of therapists' rescue fantasies, Grey (1988) recounts the following tale:

> There is a story about a man who reluctantly made love to his dying wife, to fulfill her last request. He was astonished to see her revive in his arms. She even rose from their bed and whirled joyously around the room. When the recovered woman looked again at her husband, it was her turn to be amazed. "Why are you crying?" she asked. "Oh," he moaned, "had I only known, I might have saved mother." [p. 484]

Numerous authors have suggested that, at bottom, the practice of psychotherapy derives from a wish to "save mother."

Perhaps the earliest reference to such a theory comes from Jones (1913), who suggests that an unconscious identification with God, and the resulting unconscious feelings of superiority, may be a contributing factor to a strong interest in psychology and psychiatry. Jones contends that a particularly common form of God-complex is what he calls the "Christ type" (p. 264), which involves the following unconscious themes: a revolution against the father, rescue fantasies directed toward the mother, and masochism. Essentially this is an oedipal situation, in which the hero-son is a suffering savior, who, through great self-sacrifice, desires to save an individual or all of humankind.

The recent literature on therapists' motivations also indicates that underlying rescue fantasies are an important and relatively common dynamic. For instance, Kaslow and Friedman (1984), reporting on their interviews with fourteen clinical psychology graduate students, state that "a number of trainees referred to the unexpected unearthing of their own rescue fantasies" (p. 42). Gutheil (1989) views rescue fantasies as nearly universal among trainees, and suggests that they are especially likely to emerge when treating patients with borderline personality disorder. Greif (1985) also asserts that a frequently observed motive to become a psychotherapist involves "a deep and abiding wish not only to cure oneself but also to heal the suffering of one's parents" (p. 491). Noting that this wish to cure the parents is typically manifested in a highly sublimated form, he states that it is associated with a profound sense of the interdependence and mutuality between people—a perspective that serves the psychotherapist well.

The family dynamics of many therapists appear to have been conducive to the formation of rescue fantasies. As Rollo May stated in an interview:

> Psychotherapists generally come from families where there's been quite a lot of trouble. And they become psychotherapists later on because they had to be psychotherapists for their families. They picked up the idea, perhaps unconsciously, that "I can make my mother happy by doing such and such" or "This is how I can quiet my brother." [Cunningham 1985, p. 15]

Based on his compilation of therapists' autobiographies, as well as the previous literature on the lives of therapists, Burton (1972) states that the majority of them were given the responsibility, as children, for the happiness of their families. Their early role was to resolve conflict and bring peace to the family which, without such ministrations, was believed to be likely to fall apart. Burton conceives of the following scenario as typical:

> A child is in some way selected to provide happiness for all, and to him is given the role of healer. Obviously a grown-up is better prepared to handle such a mandate than a child, so the child, in the

face of the impossibility of the task, carries it over to adulthood. The demand becomes a latency and is repressed but remains as a draft on the currency of the personality. How else do we explain the total acceptance of unbridled venom from some clients, the terrible vicissitudes of doing psychotherapy with chronic regressed schizophrenics, the endless complaints and victimization of the neurotic, the narcissism and infantility of the character disorders? On the face of it, no therapist would rationally submit to psychotherapy for any of the rewards now extant. [p. 10]

The urge to rescue should not be assumed to be purely altruistic, or simply the result of pressures exerted by the family system. As cited earlier, Kramer (1987) embarked on the unorthodox (and ethically questionable) experiment of conducting analyses with his own parents. Here we seem to have the professional rescue fantasy par excellence, stripped of all pretense or camouflage. Using the telephone, Kramer held individual sessions with each parent, for which he charged no fee. Although painfully laborious to him at times, these sessions were apparently successful in improving family relationships by increasing both psychological separation and emotional closeness. The author found that he stopped blaming his parents for his own difficulties and stopped seeking revenge for the deprivation, excessive demands, and interference with his autonomy that he had experienced from them. In reflecting upon his motives, Kramer concludes: "My unconscious agenda was simply to experience less pain in my relationship with them. . . . I suspect that I might have wanted to be their analyst so that I could finally help them to be good parents to me" (p. 213). Thus, an important aspect of rescuing seems to be an underlying wish to obtain better parenting for oneself by restoring the parent's equilibrium.

Perhaps the most detailed description of the origin of therapists' rescue fantasies is provided by Olinick (1980). He contends that many psychiatrists and psychoanalysts are powerfully motivated by "the genetic effect of a rescue fantasy having to do with a depressive mother, the latter having induced such rescue fantasy in her receptive child" (p. 12). The fantasy is elicited by a mother who is not only prone to depression, but is also characterized by oral dependency, strong narcissistic needs, and feelings of deprivation. Olinick indicates that there is often an effort on the part of the mother to provoke guilt and thereby force the child to come to her rescue. He writes:

> The child will be pressed into becoming the idealized mothering one and into additionally becoming one day the rescuing champion of the distressed woman or man, for the sexualizing and gendering of the rescue motif may cut across and interpenetrate male-female lines. [p. 160]

In a related passage, Olinick suggests that what differentiates psychoanalysts from those in the other helping professions is the extent to which they are "willing and expectant of regressive immersion in the service of the other, as distinguished from service without such regression" (p. 46). Just as the mother must regress in order to immerse herself in the needs of her infant, the analyst must be able to engage in a controlled and reversible regression in order to empathize properly with the regressed patient. An important motivation for the analyst to enter into this regressive relationship, according to Olinick, is the presence of an early unconscious rescue fantasy involving a depressed mother. The analyst's work may in this way substitute for internalized conflict involving the wish to save the mother. The resulting motivation is ongoing, notes Olinick, in that this wish can never be satisfied:

> To be sure, no amount of rescuing or healing, however successful, is going to satisfy a therapeutic ambition and master a conflict whose wellsprings are in a child's rescue fantasy. It is the internalized conflict and the introjected object that must of course be mastered. [p. 47]

Closely related to the concept of the rescue fantasy is that of reparation. While the former more often refers to external objects (i.e., actual persons), the latter typically applies to internalized object-representations. To examine the concept of reparation, it is first necessary to discuss some of the developmental theories of Melanie Klein.

According to Segal (1981), Klein divides the oral phase into two stages, termed the *paranoid-schizoid* and the *depressive* positions.

The depressive position commences when infants begin to recognize their mothers as whole objects, rather than as collections of parts, such as breasts that feed them, hands that hold them, and eyes that frighten or cheer them. A corresponding and complementary integration takes place in their perception of the self, allowing for the capacity for ambivalence, that is, that it is the same self who both loves and hates the mother. As explained by Segal, this shift in object relations brings about a change in the nature of the infant's anxieties: "While he was previously afraid that he would be destroyed by his persecutors, now he dreads that his own aggression will destroy his ambivalently loved object. His anxiety has changed from a paranoid to a depressed one" (p. 13).

The major defensive mechanisms operating during Klein's depressive position are ambivalence, gratitude, and reparation. Kernberg (1980) defines reparation as "an effort to reduce the guilt over having attacked the good object by trying to repair the damage, express love and gratitude to the object, and preserve it internally and externally" (p. 30). The mother's absence is now interpreted by the infant as a death. The infant omnipotently concludes that his aggression has destroyed the mother, leaving the infant overcome with feelings of loss and of guilt. Reparation represents the expression of the infant's wish to restore and regain the lost or injured object.

A profession that involves healing the sick appears to be typical of those individuals with strong reparative needs. As Menninger (1959) notes, the rescuing, restoring, and attempting to make whole, characteristic of physician and therapist alike, can thus represent a symbolic attempt at restitution or atonement. Seen from this perspective, the desire to heal constitutes a "way of undoing injuries which, as a child, [the therapist] inflicted in fantasy upon individuals now represented by his patients" (p. 485). Similarly, Money-Kyrle (1959) states that when the reparative motive is present, the patient represents the damaged objects of the therapist's own unconscious fantasy. Due to the repetitive and timeless nature of the unconscious, these internal objects continue to be endangered by aggression, and therefore in need of care and reparation. Put most succinctly, Racker (1968) concludes: "What motive (in terms of the unconscious) would the analyst have for wanting to cure if it were not he who made the patient ill? In this way the patient is already, simply by being a patient, the creditor, the accuser, the 'superego' of the analyst; and the analyst his debtor" (p. 146).[3]

Searles (1966) also concurs with such a formulation. In a discussion of feelings of guilt in the psychoanalyst, he questions whether the initial desire to enter the profession might amount to a guilt-based choice. Searles comments: "Thus, it may not be so much that our doing analysis tends to promote guilt in us, but rather that we originally entered this profession in an unconscious effort to assuage our guilt and that the practice of analysis fails to relieve our underlying guilt" (p. 319). Searles concludes that this unconscious guilt may derive from having failed to cure one's parents.

Winnicott (1986), as well, views the constructive activity of healing as largely fueled by the dynamic of unconscious guilt and the need for reparation. Although similar to the concept, discussed in Chapter 4, of healing as a reaction formation against sadistic impulses, in Winnicott's view the therapist's work can serve to promote integration and wholeness, and is not merely a defensive maneuver. He states:

> If you like, you can look at the way a person mends and you can cleverly say: "Aha, that means unconscious destruction!" But the world is not helped on much if you do this. Alternatively, you may see in someone's mending that he or she is building up a self-strength which makes possible a toleration of the destructiveness that belongs to that person's nature. [p. 88]

---

[3]A good example of strong reparative needs deriving from fantasized damage to others is provided by Natterson (1991), a psychoanalyst: "But I persist in my belief that I was born, therefore I was responsible for my parents' marital unhappiness and their economic burdens. I was the youngest, so I must have been parasitic and debilitating to others. My childish irritability engendered ambient unpleasantness in the family. My sexuality was dirty and sinful, sullying the noble values of the family and the neighborhood. If on the street a little friend was hurt during our play, it was surely my fault. Conversely, no one but I was responsible for my own injuries and close calls. In childish sex play, I was corrupt, the other was a despoiled innocent. And so it emerged through the epochs of my life. I have always played the role of fugitive cum victim, being pursued by the posse of guilt" (p. 9).

Winnicott proceeds to suggest that the individual who is prevented from accomplishing reparation through constructive work can no longer take full responsibility for his or her destructive impulses, and the result is either depression or projection of destructiveness onto others. Put more bluntly, by treating and helping others, therapists fend off their own potential depression or paranoia.

A number of authors have warned about the inherent dangers in the therapist's unconscious need for reparation. Greenson (1962), for instance, states that clinicians with an unconscious desire for restitution and reparation can become compulsive rescuers and behave masochistically with patients. Little (1981) points to the unconscious unwillingness of such therapists to allow their patients to get better and leave. She states:

> A patient who has been in analysis for some considerable time has usually become his analyst's love object. He is the person to whom the analyst wishes to make reparation, and the reparative impulses, even when conscious, may through a partial repression come under the sway of the repetition compulsion: it becomes necessary to make that same patient well over and over again, which in effect means making him ill over and over again in order to have him to make well. [p. 38]

The reparative motive may be particularly problematic when therapists are faced with treatment failures or impasses. Racker (1968) comments on how the patient's masochism, a frequent component of the negative therapeutic reaction, can elicit early paranoid and depressive anxieties and guilt feelings in the therapist. Faced with the aggression that the patient is implicitly directing at him, the therapist "finds himself in his unconscious confronted anew with his early crimes" (p. 145). The resulting anxieties can increase the intensity of the negative countertransference (i.e., anger with the patient), further contributing to the impasse.

It is likely that patients understand on some level that their staying stuck or regressing can generate reactions in the therapist, such as anxiety, fear, depression, guilt, anger, frustration, and despair. While the motivating wish may be hostile and retaliatory, it can also reflect an attempt to assist the therapist by eliciting (and thereby communicating) the difficult feelings with which the patient is struggling. The therapeutic alliance may be undermined when therapists ignore or misinterpret such communications and instead blame their patients and try to force them to improve.

A major hazard of therapeutic motivations involving both rescue fantasies and reparative needs is that therapists become too heavily and too personally invested in the progress of their patients. Beginning with Freud (1926), the literature is replete with warnings regarding the dangers of excessive therapeutic zeal. Ironically, the very motive that draws so many individuals to the profession can apparently become a major obstacle to its effective practice.

Therapeutic overzealousness can be described as "the *wish* to make the patient get well by whatever means" (Gitelson 1973, p. 250). Psychoanalysts in particular tend to regard any strong wishes to "cure" or "rescue" the patient as counterproductive. As Schafer (1983) puts it:

> Analysts do not view their role as one of offering remedies, cures, complete mental health, philosophies of life, rescue, emergency-room intervention, emotional Band-Aids, or self-sacrificing or self-aggrandizing heroics. It is more than likely that each of these alternatives to a primarily interpretive approach manifests countertransference. [p. 11].

Similarly, Sachs (1947) indicates that therapeutic zeal in an analyst is likely to be frustrated as well as antitherapeutic. "To those who are impatient for quick therapeutic effects, psychoanalytic technique will soon become a burden because it is neither apt to gratify their ambition nor to assuage their compassion" (p. 163).

Adler (1972) notes that therapists may become overzealous in response to patients' regressive demands for an omnipotent parent. Rather than recognizing and interpreting such expectations as an important part of the transference, therapists may react with a rescuing, smothering approach that is both gratifying and frightening to their patients. Adler elaborates:

> For many patients this provides temporary relief. But, ultimately, this therapist-response provokes increasing regression in the patient, who perceives that the therapist sees him as the helpless child who

has to be held and saved from disaster. Inevitably, demands increase, the patient regresses more, and often ultimately rejects and devalues in his increasing fury. The therapist who began as the rescuer ends up feeling as helpless and furious as the patient. The capacity of the therapist to anticipate this transference–countertransference situation is crucial. [p. 323]

Holt and Luborsky (1958b) emphasize that the desire to help the patient ought to be present in highly sublimated form, so that the analyst will be able to postpone interventions until the appropriate time and not be compelled to rescue immediately. Unsublimated, it tends to cause the analyst to act out and to obtain direct gratifications from the relationship with the patient. Additionally, as Hammer (1972) notes, therapists who constantly attempt to rescue patients during difficult times actually prevent them from assuming responsibility and unwittingly foster dependency. Although these therapists may consciously be quite devoted to helping their patients grow, "they guarantee that just the reverse occurs through compulsive ministrations of 'help'" (p. 30). In sum, therapists cannot conduct psychotherapy properly when they have the same sleepless nights over their patients that parents may experience in regard to their children (Cooper 1986).

It is of interest that *supervisory zeal* may also be problematic. Excessive fervor on the part of supervisors can blind them to the actual needs of their trainees. In a recent paper, Teitlebaum (1990) suggests that supervisors' zeal and need to view themselves as competent can interfere with the supervisory process. He writes:

If the therapist's initial priority is to feel safe and develop a sense of trust, while the supervisor's priority is to supervise (i. e., focus on psychodynamics, theory, technique, etc.), it is much like an analyst expecting to do analysis before establishing a working alliance with the patient. In their zeal to impart their knowledge in a limited number of sessions to their supervisees, supervisors frequently bypass the important step of establishing a positive supervisory alliance; a stalemate may follow. [p. 245]

This concludes the review of the common unconscious motivations involving object relations. There is clearly a wide variety of interpersonal dynamics that may predispose an individual to be attracted to the practice of psychotherapy. Moreover, due to the nature of the therapeutic interaction, therapists' own conflicts regarding their object relationships are likely to emerge in their work. Once again, this provides both the potential for greater sensitivity and insight, and, when the conflicts remain unconscious, for significant impediments to successful practice.

This also concludes the entire overview of the unconscious motivations for practicing psychotherapy. The following chapter provides profiles of the unconscious motives of nine psychotherapists, as derived from interview material.

7

THERAPIST PROFILES

The preceding chapters surveyed a wide range of motivations for becoming a psychotherapist. For heuristic purposes, each motive was singled out and discussed as an isolated entity. While this constitutes a necessary first step, it fails to take into account both the unity and the complexity of human psychological functioning. It still remains to understand how a variety of unconscious motives, of varying intensities and depths, coalesce and interact within the totality of a personality. It is likely that many of the dynamics discussed play a greater or lesser role in nearly every person who enters the field. Nevertheless, each individual therapist can be expected to present a unique constellation of underlying needs and wishes. To illustrate this point, nine psychotherapists will now be profiled, based upon in-depth interviews conducted for this purpose.

SUBJECTS

Fourteen subjects volunteered to participate in the study, and nine of these were selected for this volume. Three of the subjects were doctoral candidates in clinical psychology, and the other six were professional practitioners. One male and two female students are profiled, ranging in age from 25 to 39 (mean = 30). Each of them had from three to four years of experience practicing psychotherapy. Of the six professional psychotherapists presented, two are female and four are male. They include three psychologists, two psychiatrists, and one social worker. Their mean age was 50, and mean years of experience was 18. All six describe themselves as psychoanalytically-oriented clinicians. For all subjects, certain identifying characteristics were altered in order to assure confidentiality.

All nine subjects had undergone their own psychotherapeutic treatment, and five of them had been in analysis. Some of the insights that they provide regarding their own motivations, it should be noted, were made consciously accessible only through years of self-exploration.

MATERIALS

A semistructured interview format was employed. Subjects were asked a series of forty-eight questions (see Appendix I), dealing with six broad areas: vocational choice, experience as a therapist, experience as a psychotherapy patient, family background, personal development, and current personal life. The subjects were also allowed and encouraged to speak freely about any topic that emerged during the course of the interview. Thus, the standardized questions were used as springboards and were often anticipated by the interviewees.

One of the interview questions was designed as a projective measure. It reads: "What would you guess might be the most common unconscious motivation of your average colleague?" It was assumed that, by temporarily shifting the focus away from the subject, he or she would be more likely to address motives that might otherwise be difficult to acknowledge.

PROCEDURE

Subjects were recruited by posting a notice requesting volunteers interested in participating in a confidential interview regarding the motives for becoming a psychotherapist. Participants were informed that the interview data would be used as part of a dissertation on this topic, and informed consent was obtained in writing. Handwritten notes or audio recordings were taken during the interviews; the transcripts are largely verbatim, aside from the changes made to protect confidentiality.

Interviews were conducted by the author and lasted approximately two hours. They were held in a variety of settings, including clinic office, conference room, subject's home, and interviewer's home. Each of the subjects granted permission to include the material in the thesis, and have now graciously allowed their profiles to be presented here, thereby adding to the profession's understanding of these important issues.

RESULTS

Therapist 1: Ms. Ryan

Ms. Ryan is a licensed social worker who has had three years of post-masters analytic training and is currently in private practice. Ms. Ryan's interest in her field was initially stimulated by a neighbor "of the age that a mother to me would be," who was a social worker. She suggests that she was also influenced by working for her father, who employed individuals from a wide variety of ethnic and socioeconomic backgrounds. "He would even go to skid row to take bums off the street and give them jobs. . . . Some of the black men who worked for him were second fathers to me." It is of interest that for many years Ms. Ryan's family took in unwed mothers; this also may have contributed to her interest in entering social work, which earned her "big points" with her father. She majored in sociology, later switching to English literature when her college eliminated the tiny sociology department. Her first job was as a caseworker for the Catholic Home Bureau. "I would go to the court the day that children were taken away from their parents and placed in foster care. I would pick them up and drive them to the foster home, and then I was responsible for visiting those children and providing the link between them and their parents."

Ms. Ryan notes that as she became more involved in her own therapy and self-exploration, her professional focus shifted from that of casework with clients who were poor and highly disturbed to psychotherapy with clients more like herself. Ms. Ryan found the practice of psychotherapy highly rewarding and felt quite natural at it from the start. "It was just such a fit!" In retrospect, she views her attraction to the role of therapist as having involved "a search to heal my own problems." She mentions that a friend once joked that doing therapy all day is "like a day-hospital for the therapist."

Ms. Ryan also considered becoming an English professor and enjoys teaching. When asked what alternative occupations she might find rewarding, she replied that she would like to be an actress, a singer, or a dancer.

Psychological Disturbances

Ms. Ryan first sought therapeutic help at the age of 28, "because I was depressed after the birth of my second child." She elaborates, "I was evaluated, put on a mild medication and placed in a therapy group. The group treatment, however, never came anywhere near the deep issues that were going on for me." After reluctantly making a second move for the sake of her husband's career, Ms. Ryan experienced another depressive episode and entered individual therapy. She later entered an eight-year psychoanalysis.

Family members— "I think my mother was full of loss and self-absorbed. I think she was a disturbed and sad woman, who never knew who she was. . . . My mother dominated the family, on an emotional level, by her problems." Father is described as having "shut down his emotional life, and legislated the emotional lives of his children."

Motives Related to Instincts

Voyeurism— Ms. Ryan describes her father as having been stimulating, at times, in inappropriate ways. "There are stories of him getting home at midnight, when I'd be asleep, and then waking me up to play. Giving me dolls, and stuffed animals in the middle of the night! Which set a precedent for having affairs—intense libidinal attractions for unavailable men." It may have also contributed to her attraction toward the role of therapist, another situation in which libidinal wishes are stirred up but cannot be gratified in any direct manner.

Ms. Ryan's first exposure to therapeutic treatment was when she entered group therapy, an experience she compares to watching a soap opera. "I was utterly fascinated," she recalls. "I was this controlled, Catholic girl who sat there shaking and in shock as I listened to these women talk about things in their lives. For example, there was a woman in the group who used to try to kill herself every once in a while, and before she did she'd put her vibrator in the trash so no one would find it. I'd just sit there on the edge of my seat, thinking 'Oh my God, this is the real world? People are like this?'" She also recalls another group member, who was having an affair with her individual therapist. "It was seeing the interior lives of women that was so interesting."

Part of Ms. Ryan's attraction to the role of psychotherapist involved an identification with priests hearing confession. "I thought that might be a very interesting part of the work, a sort of private, secret, sacred chamber of therapist and patient that really wasn't so different from sharing your secrets with a priest."

Exhibitionism— Ms. Ryan's earliest memory is of "pushing a kitchen chair to the back door one summer, when I was probably about 3, unlatching the top latch, taking off all of my clothes, and running down the street—with Martha [the babysitter] chasing after me screaming, 'Stop that little girl!' . . . The feeling about it was exuberant and mischievous."

Ms. Ryan feels that her exhibitionistic tendencies have "gone underground," although teaching and creative writing provide outlets for their expression. She declares, "I think that I have *lots* of actress in me that's frustrated at this point . . . by always being cast in the script of the patient, and not being able to express or emote much." To some degree, she feels this is less the case with group therapy and her work with adolescents, which she greatly enjoys.

Reaction formation against aggression— When asked how her family had dealt with emotions, Ms. Ryan replies that they were legislated. "We could not express anger—it was a mortal sin. We couldn't even acknowledge that we were angry." Father would occasionally "blow up, but we were not allowed to be angry."

Ms. Ryan's first depressive episode followed the birth of her daughter. At the time, she attributed the depression to difficulties coping with her son's feelings of jealousy and hurt. As a first child herself, Ms. Ryan strongly identified with her son's pain and felt guilty for inflicting it upon him. She could not deal with this sense of having harmed him, or with his own expressions of anger and aggression.

During her analysis, Ms. Ryan discovered another precipitant that had been largely unconscious at the time. "The birth of my daughter opened up a trauma in my early history, when I was 11 and my parents adopted a baby sister. And I was told that I could not touch her, play with her, have anything to do with her . . . because I might hurt her. My mother had projected all that onto me. . . . She became the 'good mother' and I became the 'bad mother,' the destructive mother that might hurt her child. So having a girl child was absolutely terrifying, and my internal reaction was to keep a distance from her to protect her."

Expression of aggression— In exploring the unconscious gratifications that she may have derived from taking children out of their homes, Ms. Ryan states, "I don't know whether it may have had to do with getting myself out of my own family, or with getting rid of my sister, who had come on the scene to ruin my life with my mother. There seems to have been some primitive satisfaction in taking kids away from bad parents." Ms. Ryan notes that, as time went on, this experience taught her that it was traumatic for a child to be wrenched from his parents, and she made every effort to aid the parents and enable the child to remain at home.

Masochistic tendencies— Regarding her second individual therapist, Ms. Ryan states, "She hated me, basically, and I converted that into always trying to figure out what she was doing. And knowing I was masochistic, my mental frame on it was, 'She's trying to contain the masochism *here*, by being sadistic to me, so that I don't have to get hurt other places.'" She recalls, "When I would cry in her office, she would sometimes pick up the phone, call her husband, and say, 'I forgot to tell you that your three o'clock patient was changed to four o'clock.' Or I would cry, and she would take hard candy and throw it across the room at me and exclaim, 'Ach! I can't stand to listen to you when your throat gets all clogged up like that!'" Fairly early in the treatment, Ms. Ryan brought her husband to a therapy session in order to work on their marital difficulties. "Dr. A. saw him once and said, 'I can't see the two of you again because always, you know,'—in this wonderful accent—'one likes one partner in the marriage better than the other, and he reminds me of my favorite brother.' You would think that I would have run for the door immediately, but of course I didn't. Because it replicated my relationship with my mother so perfectly." In fact, she remained with this therapist for some six years, leaving only when strongly urged to by another analyst. "I said, 'Well, I have to terminate from her. That could take *months*.' He just laughed and said, 'Go back to her and say goodbye. You don't have to take care of her anymore.'"

When asked what she finds most difficult about her work, she replies, "Being used as an instrument who is smashed against the wall, thrown out the window, kicked, reviled . . . [laughs] . . . made to feel enormously sad. Just the enormous range of emotions I get subjected to on a daily basis in my body, mind, soul, and the cumulative effect over the years of being a container for all that intense emotion."

Ms. Ryan refers to a particular client who elicited her deepest masochistic tendencies. "Most therapists would have either let that person go in order to preserve themselves—or they might have died in the attempt, it was so extreme." She states, "I can't think of a more masochistic profession. To deny one's own needs, to contain the other person's. *Especially* when, most likely, one's been used

like that one's whole life in some way, or you wouldn't be doing it
in the first place." She adds: "Sometimes I hope that at least this
work may help *contain* my masochism, so I don't have to do it as
much somewhere else."

Unresolved oedipal conflict— There was a closeness between
Ms. Ryan and her father that, at times, seems to have extended
beyond the usual boundaries of a father–daughter relationship.
"I was the listener for my father's dreams. My father has a very
rich dream-life and told me his dreams every morning when I
was growing up. He would dismiss them, though, as 'Isn't that
silly?'"

During adolescence, when earlier oedipal dynamics frequently
resurface, Ms. Ryan fought bitterly with her mother. "She was
very jealous of my relationship with my father, and I would get
sent to my room a lot from the dinner table. . . . There's a recurring image I've had, which is at the dinner table during high
school. My father was at the head of the table, with my mother
and I facing each other on either side and my father and I talking
about books. He would quiz me. I fed him everything I learned—
he hadn't gone to college but was very bright. My mother was an
intelligent woman who had graduated from college Phi Beta
Kappa, and then never read a book after that. So my father and I
would share all I was learning, and my mother would get increasingly jealous. She would provoke some kind of confrontation with
me. There'd be an outburst, and I'd be sent to my room. I'd refuse
to leave, and then my father would chase me to my room." When
Ms. Ryan later fell in love with a boyfriend, her father's disap-
proval of the young man kept her from marrying him. "My father
was, I think, probably quite jealous of him. What was stated was
that he wasn't of our class—he was working-class. But I think that
my father sensed that he was a very powerful influence to com-
pete with."

"I have hypothesized since my analysis that I might not be able
to have a man in my life until my father dies, because the two men
I'm most attached to are my father and my son. I still need to
mourn the loss of my son and my father, so that I can free up my
life for a man of my own."

Motives Related to Development of the Self

Narcissistic needs— Because her mother was so narcissistically self-absorbed and unempathic, Ms. Ryan never experienced her as fully attentive or admiring. "I was the one who mirrored my mother, attuned myself to *her* needs." She grew up feeling that she orbited around other people, rather than developing a firm sense of self. "I was not allowed to be competent at home. I could not caretake my siblings, as I've mentioned. I was never taught any skills. So I really felt, growing up, that I had no function."

Only the babysitter, Martha, seems to have consistently met her early narcissistic needs, allowing her to feel special. "I became her favorite child of all time." Ms. Ryan also appeared to be highly invested in being among the most interesting of the therapists to be profiled and, perhaps, the "favorite." (And, indeed, she is profiled first.)

Ms. Ryan entered training to be a therapist in the midst of an unsatisfying marriage, in an apparent attempt to offset the narcissistic injuries it had entailed. "Because the marriage made me feel very bad about myself. There was absolutely no way I could heal my husband. At that point, of course, I didn't know that."

Aggrandized ego-ideal— Ms. Ryan appears to have grown up with somewhat of a split between her inner and outer selves. "As an adolescent I had a false, goody-goody self, but I did not lose sight of what I really felt. I was the Prefect of the Sodality at the Catholic school. There were these little groups that would meet, and you had these cards that showed how many masses, how many communions, how many rosaries you'd done. I was the leader, and all the while I was lying about how many rosaries I'd done, and was going out on weekends drinking and partying."

For her first few sessions as a patient in group therapy, Ms. Ryan mistakenly believed that a fellow patient was one of the group leaders. She describes this woman as having been "quite beautiful, and extremely articulate about psychology and herself. . . . There was something very fresh about her, and very well put-together, but not tense looking . . . sort of glowing." She describes her second individual therapist as "a petite woman, whom I think I saw as being about six feet tall." Ms. Ryan also notes that she developed a "God transference" to her analyst. All of this suggests that her decision to become a therapist may have been influenced by an aggrandized ideal to which she aspired. Indeed, when asked to expound on her "priest identification," she explained, "Within the Catholic Church, to become a priest is the highest achievement. Priests are the most grand, powerful, important figures. They get to wear beautiful vestments, smell of incense, and hear confessions, conduct masses, and offer communion."

Parental narcissism— Ms. Ryan grew up experiencing herself as a narcissistic extension of her parents, and had difficulty distinguishing their wants and needs from those of her own. This is apparent in her current view of what precipitated her depressive episodes. "I had not married the man I loved, because my parents disapproved of him. So I married my college boyfriend, and had depressions after each child was born because I felt trapped in the marriage since divorce was forbidden in the Catholic Church." She describes herself as having been "a container for my father's hopes for himself, put on me."

Maternal identification— Ms. Ryan describes herself as having been closer to her father, and, prior to her analysis, viewed her personality as more similar to his than to her mother's. "I was so afraid to identify with my mother that I tried to identify instead with my father and with men." Given her early sense of maternal abandonment, as well as a highly conflicted oedipal stage, it is not surprising that Ms. Ryan's identification with her mother was not particularly strong. Perhaps her sense of being a frustrated actress is related to this dynamic, in that her mother is described as highly dramatic and, in fact, worked as an actress at one point in her husband's television show. Through her work as a therapist, Ms. Ryan has been able to identify with her "good mother," Martha, a "caretaker *who got paid*, and was a strong model for me." She also notes that one of the outcomes of her analysis was an identification with her mother.

Diffuse sense of identity— Ms. Ryan felt that her mother could never perceive her as she really was. "Sometimes I was the mother who abandoned her by dying on her. Sometimes I was her wicked stepmother, who had been mean to her. She *never* knew who I was." Ms. Ryan grew up feeling that she had no function within the family, but realizes now, in retrospect, that she served *psychological* functions (e.g., as a container for her mother's negative projections, her father's dreams, etc.). Thus, her personal and professional identities seem to have coalesced around this sense of providing psychological aid. As a therapist, she believes that an important function she provides is to be a container for the feelings and projections that her clients cannot acknowledge or contain.

Motives Involving Object Relations

Conflicts concerning dependency— As a child, Ms. Ryan describes herself as having been "lost and lonely at home." She states that her major unconscious motivation for entering social work "was probably trying to heal the very needy, deprived part of myself, that I projected onto poor blacks, or children." It was, she adds, also an attempt to heal the "child–parent problem that existed in my family."

Ms. Ryan's descriptions of her mother suggest that she never had her own dependency needs adequately met. For example, "She longed for her mother all of her life, and saw my father as a mother."

Ms. Ryan clearly feels that her mother was unable to meet her needs as a child. "I think that my early childhood, as I have a sense of it, was very much based on missing my mother because she wasn't there. Waiting for her, missing her, and yet—when she was there—she was extremely intrusive, quite demanding of me meeting *her* needs, misinterpreted me, and projected onto me." She views her mother as having been, in some sense, relieved to see her children leave the home, because she then had her husband all to herself. "In my estimate, she is someone who shouldn't have had children."

Ms. Ryan's father appears to have been somewhat more responsive to her needs. "I was his firstborn. I think he loved and adored me. Baby pictures show him being very maternal, in some ways." Yet, she says, he worked long hours and was not very available to her. Ms. Ryan also notes that he has "an enormous need to depend on women, and needed my mother to take care of," suggesting that her father tends to defend against dependency needs via reaction formations.

Ultimately, Martha was the only one on whom Ms. Ryan could depend. "Martha was an extremely empathic, earthy woman who had been put out of her house when she was 13 years old, and was the caretaker of babies and children all her life. . . . To give you an example of her empathy, it was during World War II . . . and just before she'd go home sometimes I would do things like throw her makeup down the toilet, or throw her stockings—which during the war you could barely even get—down the incinerator, and she would say 'Oh! . . . Sally doesn't want me to go home!' She would always seem to get it right."

"My whole life was a search to have my mother. I went to her college, and I brought home the guy I eventually married . . . for my mother. Her father had been a doctor, and he was going to be a doctor. And it was like, 'Now will you love me?'"

Ms. Ryan notes that, before her analysis, she had a group therapy experience that was "really quite abysmal," a brief individual treatment that was "very bad," and a longer individual psychotherapy that was also injurious. Thus, Ms. Ryan's attraction to the practice of psychotherapy may have entailed, in part, a wish to give to others what she felt *her* therapists (as well as her parents) had been unable to provide. She states, "At any one time, I feel that I have a number of patients whom I love. Being able to love patients certainly meets my need . . . to have more 'children,' more people to love." The two instances in which she has fallen deeply in love with male clients were at times of serious losses in her personal life: during a separation from her husband, and as her children were leaving home.

While in treatment with a female therapist, Ms. Ryan repeatedly had dreams of bringing her food, cooking for her, and feeding her, suggesting strong reaction formations against dependency needs. Ms. Ryan hopes to return to her interest in creative writing, "but I keep allowing my needs to be preempted by those of others."

Conflicts concerning separation— Ms. Ryan's description of her early relationship with her mother is characterized by excessive enmeshment as well as abandonment, a combination that often leads to later problems with separation and individuation. "I was my parents' first child, and my mother allegedly never left me for eighteen months, and talked to me constantly while she carried me around, and then—this is *my* story, not hers—left me altogether, by going to work with my father full-time, six days a week." Ms. Ryan believes that her mother may have joined her father at work because she could not bear to be away from him. Various family stories provide further indications of her mother's difficulties with separation. "My mother describes me as having been too slow for her, and she'd carry me up the steps instead of letting me walk up alone. She also describes taking me to kindergarten, and I was the only kid who didn't cry. At that point I was hiding a lot of feelings. But *she* felt very rejected. She tells how—on one of her many, many trips away from me that occurred without notice—coming home and I didn't recognize her. And she thought '*See*, she didn't miss me.'" Ms. Ryan notes that her mother had been literally abandoned as a child. Her father left her when she was 3, and her mother died when she was 7, possibly by suicide.

As an adolescent and young adult, Ms. Ryan's difficulties in separating psychologically from her family were compounded by her father's possessive, domineering manner. She states that her father disapproved of and punished her moves toward independence.

Ms. Ryan's struggles with separation issues have at times entered into her clinical work. She notes that as a caseworker she found it difficult to separate children from their parents in order to place them in foster care. Later, as a social-work student, she worked for Child Protective Services. "My entire orientation was to keep the child in the home with the parents. I would literally put my job on the line about taking kids out of homes." Ms. Ryan formed a particularly strong bond with a young woman who had abandoned her child on a doorstep. "I just decided to put as much into her as I possibly could," and she continues to stay in touch some twenty years later.

Ms. Ryan worked with street people at a free clinic that offered clients only a limited number of visits. "I found myself either unable to let go of them, or constantly referring them on for more therapy. . . . I didn't want to refer them on. I wanted to be the one who did it."

The interview material contained a number of additional indications of the strength of Ms. Ryan's need to avoid separations. Martha died about 3 years ago, at the age of 96, and Ms. Ryan keeps Martha's ashes in her bedroom. She explains, "I was the only person left in her life. She asked me to cremate her and to scatter her ashes over Lake Michigan, but I felt badly about letting her go." In discussing the termination of her analysis, she states, "It was kind of like, 'I thought people were supposed to *want* to go' . . . [laughs] . . . and I really didn't, but it was *time* to go."

Need for power and control— Ms. Ryan describes her father as "*very* dominant . . . sometimes one could call him a benevolent tyrant." He insisted that things be done his way. "My father outlawed music from our house, in order to avoid his own sadness. He called music 'mood-altering.'" Having attempted to emancipate herself from her father with great difficulty, she now declares, "I will never be controlled by a man again."

One of the things Ms. Ryan likes about private practice is the absence of any boss. She states that she does like to be in a position of control. As a therapist, however, she feels that she is very aware of her power and its impact on clients, so she does not abuse it. She jokes, "It *is* nice, though, to be able to say 'it's time to go.'"

Intimacy— Ms. Ryan states that she became a therapist because what she found most rewarding as a social worker was forming "a much more intensive relationship with somebody. . . . What's *so* interesting is meeting such a variety of people whom you might not otherwise meet, and engaging in such a deep, really profound relationship."

Ms. Ryan describes her ex-husband as having been highly narcissistic, with little capacity for intimacy—much like her mother. The treatment setting seems to have provided a means of attaining the intimacy that was often lacking in her personal life.

Rescue fantasies and reparation— Ms. Ryan's life story and her fantasy life are replete with themes of rescue and salvation. When her mother left her at 18 months to go to work, "she turned me over to the care of a woman named Martha, who saved my life, I think." Describing her father, she states, "He was my hero, my savior, to rescue me from my mother."

Ms. Ryan's mother seemed to tantalize her with bits and pieces of her own traumatic history, leaving Ms. Ryan mystified and intent on putting together the puzzle. "My mother filled me with all sorts of stories about her horrific childhood. But she would just go to the point of giving you some clear picture or rationale, and then become quite hysterical and get mad at you—as if you'd asked—and keep hidden what actually happened." Aside from her emotional difficulties, her mother was also sickly. "My mother was chronically asthmatic. Sometimes we'd have to ship her home on airplanes from vacations."

Ms. Ryan was usually rebuffed when she tried to reach out to help or to give to her mother. "She was the kind of person who would return every gift you gave her. . . . My mother really rejected my love for her and my attempts to comfort her. She would always misread it." Such experiences instilled a deep sense of guilt in Ms. Ryan, who felt that her inability to console her mother was somehow her own fault. "I used to joke that there was this enormous neon 'G' flashing on my chest! . . . I think that there is a deep, unremitting, and always-will-be sense that I could never do enough. So I'm extraordinarily generous and have no idea where my limits are. I think that comes out of guilt."

Depressed following the birth of her daughter, Ms. Ryan had recurring dreams in which her beloved boyfriend from high school would come and save her from her unhappy marriage.

From the beginning of her career, Ms. Ryan was intent on rescuing those who were needy or endangered. She states that while working for Child Protective Services, "I prioritized my clients, and figured out who might really be saved." She stayed on with this job even after graduating.

Ms. Ryan went into training as a therapist in the midst of an unsatisfying marriage. "There was absolutely no way that I could heal my husband." Instead, her efforts at healing and rescuing were focused upon psychotherapy clients. She states, "The patient who sunk me into my most regressed, masochistic state," was one with whom she "all-too consciously" attempted to save her mother.

Ms. Ryan's favorite clients are "kids between, say, 18 and 25, because I think I keep trying to go back in time and save myself at that point. I invest *a lot* in people that age—I can really remember what it felt like. It's like going back and saving people before they make major mistakes." She also enjoys working with clients with borderline personality disorder, who presumably resemble her mother in some ways. One could state, as well, that the analyst whom Ms. Ryan consulted regarding her second therapist rescued *her*, in a sense, from a destructive treatment and took her into analysis.

Ms. Ryan struggled throughout her life with a deep sense of destructiveness, apparently an internalization of her mother's enormous aggression, which had been alternately expressed and projected. Through the practice of psychotherapy, Ms. Ryan has attempted to make reparation for her sense of damaging others. "In some sense I absolutely *had* to dispel the notion that I was such a potentially destructive mother, and I think that this is probably an important factor in my wanting to become a therapist." It is also of interest that she has felt it important that her children grow up to be creative individuals (which is indeed the case). Once again, this may serve to refute her inner sense of noxiousness. Finally, Ms. Ryan views her father as having harbored a strong need for reparation, which she may have internalized. "There was a whole history, for many generations, on his side of the family of men harming women in some way, and abandoning them with children. He was, I think, the one in his family to keep trying to do reparation for that. And that was the adoption of a child, and the taking-in of unwed mothers." At times Ms. Ryan has experienced the wish to adopt a client.

During the interview, Ms. Ryan touched on an intriguing point that will be discussed further in the next chapter. She comments that her analysis "partially took away" her need to practice psychotherapy. "It's not that I hoped my profession would be taken away, but it really did feel like it took the *need* away in such a deep sense, so that at the end I really didn't quite know what to do. I stayed doing this because I liked doing it, and didn't want to completely re-gear, although that's probably why I went to creative writing school." She concludes, "I practice now because I'm good at this work, because I find it intellectually and emotionally intriguing, and because developing and honing clinical skills can be a creative process. And sometimes it's deeply satisfying to be a part of a client's growth and development."

Therapist 2: Dr. Jacobs

Dr. Jacobs is a psychiatrist and psychoanalyst who currently practices psychopharmacology, psychotherapy, and analysis in a variety of settings. He first became interested in the field of psychology during college, and considered becoming a clinical psychologist. During the middle of a course in abnormal psychology, the instructor—a well-known psychologist whom Dr. Jacobs admired—became ill, and a local psychiatrist replaced him. This new teacher was a dynamic individual who made the field of psychiatry sound very interesting. Dr. Jacobs, who had played with the idea of going to medical school, decided to become a psychiatrist. The area of psychiatry that interested him the most was the practice of psychotherapy. Although Dr. Jacobs notes that he was intent on "understanding what made people act the way they did," he remained at that time relatively unaware of other underlying motives. "As I think back, I'm struck by how *little* I understood or even thought about what my motivations were. It just sort of happened. As much as I was interested in understanding people, it doesn't seem like I was terribly introspective concerning my own decision as to what I was going to do with my life. It was just there, and I sort of jumped into it without a lot of thought."

Dr. Jacobs notes an interest in the field of business, in terms of financial gain, and he could picture himself running a corporation. He used to wonder whether he might be able to go back and get an MBA degree. "I still have fantasies of doing that, and becoming the director of some corporation that runs hospitals, or psychiatric hospitals. On the whole, however, I'm not aware of any other job on earth that I'd rather be doing."

Psychological Disturbances

Dr. Jacobs first went into therapy shortly after he began his psychiatry residency. He notes that he entered treatment more for personal reasons than for training purposes. The presenting symptom was that of anxiety. He entered twice-per-week psychotherapy with an analyst, and switched over to analysis about a year later. This analysis, which lasted nearly three years, led to an interest in obtaining analytic training for himself. This meant changing analysts, however, since the person he had been working with was not a training analyst. At that time, Dr. Jacobs was still experiencing some difficulties with anxiety and mild depression involving "questions about where my life was heading, as well as things stirred up from the previous treatment, especially about my parents."

Family members— "I think my father would qualify for some sort of narcissistic diagnosis. My mother, although she's never talked openly about it, probably has some sort of anxiety disorder and is kind of counterphobic. If something is going to cause her to have an anxiety attack, she'll just go out and *do it more*. Gritting her teeth and having an anxiety attack, but never admitting to anyone that she's uncomfortable." Dr. Jacobs adds, "Within the extended family there are plenty of loony people. I'm sure that had something to do with my going into psychiatry, too.'

Motives Related to Instincts

Indirect sexual gratification— In discussing the feelings that can be generated in the clinical setting, Dr. Jacobs states, "I've certainly had patients that, at one point or another in the therapy, I felt like, 'I wish that I had met this person under different circumstances, because I'd like to be their friend . . . or to have an affair with this woman.' Indeed, there have been one or two incidents in which some of the sexualized feelings have been very intense, and it's like, 'Am I going to lose control and act out in some way?' And I always found that, just by sitting with it over a period of time, by a few months later I was wondering to myself, 'How could I have ever thought that about this person? I don't even think that she's *attractive* now, and I thought that she was the most beautiful woman on earth,' and there were clearly some other things going on."

Dr. Jacobs also comments on the voyeuristic aspects of doing psychotherapy. "Wanting to know what other people really think about. It's a little like reading the letters in *Penthouse*, to hear about a person's fantasy life in some stimulating kind of way. And not just sexual things, but other kinds of daydreams as well. Sort of, 'What really goes on in there?'" Asked whether he has any discomfort with these voyeuristic aspects, Dr. Jacobs responds, "Only in the sense that sometimes it can get me off the track of listening to other things, too. Like I'd rather have the person talking about *that* than about something else that might indeed be more important for them at the moment. Or that patients might learn they could avoid painful affect by switching to talking about their sexual fantasies, because they might pick up that I'm interested or stimulated."

Expression of aggression— Dr. Jacobs saw his mother as the aggressive one, the one who always won the arguments, while his father was at bottom "a big softy." His mother "could pull the trigger on someone who was standing in her way, and never blink an eye. You'd better not cross *her!*" When crossed, "she became enraged, or wrote them off. There was no such thing as forgiveness." He and his mother "would get into terrible fights, screaming and yelling and swearing. She would sometimes explode at me, and she threw things at me a couple of times. Things would get very intense."

Dr. Jacobs is clearly comfortable with his own aggression, and notes that he admires people who get what they want without undue regard for others. He also expresses some disdain for those clinicians who are burdened by guilt feelings and have difficulty being assertive. These traits seem to be common among therapists, and when asked whether he thought that his sense of being relatively guilt-free influenced his desire to engage in therapy, Dr. Jacobs replies, "That's part of why I'm working on a medically oriented hospital unit, and not sitting at home seeing a whole lot of analytic patients."

Masochistic tendencies— In terms of his clinical work, Dr. Jacobs suggests that masochistic tendencies may account for his "taking on impossible situations that I'm not going to get much out of, and that drag on for years and years." At times patients withhold payment and he continues to see them, "because I feel that I should, as if it's some sort of charity."

Unresolved oedipal conflict— There are numerous indications that as a child Dr. Jacobs had an atypical oedipal situation in which he and his mother remained allied against his father. "My mother was the powerful one, and to some extent I sided with her in belittling my father as a rather ineffective and powerless person."

There was little affection between his parents, and Dr. Jacobs always had the sense that his mother did not value his father in many ways. Even within the work sphere, where he focused most of his time and energy, father came to be perceived as somewhat weak and passive. When mother returned briefly to work outside the home, as the family story goes, "she walked in the door of a large corporation, and when they offered her a job as a secretary she said, 'you've got to be kidding,' and within a month or two was again the office manager and overseeing two or three hundred other secretarial workers." On the other hand, "although my father succeeded, he was fairly passive and probably didn't do nearly as well as he might have because he didn't look after himself. A lot of people got very rich on what he was doing—but he didn't—because they would always say, 'Well, you do this and we'll give you some stock someday,' or something, and never got anything in writing and it never happened."

When asked about his own relationship with his father, Dr. Jacobs replies, "I didn't have much of a relationship with my father. I didn't admire him much, other than around this specific talent that he had. I think that I wanted to see myself as the man of the house, and I *got to do that*, once he started traveling. Then it became my mother and I as this couple, and he got excluded. And he got excluded in our verbalizations about him, too. My mother would say, 'Well *you* can do that much better than your father can.' Probably not true. Or certainly not true, *most* of the time, because there I was this 10- or 11-year-old kid. But I certainly liked to hear it and wanted to believe it, as if Mom and I could do fine without him." Thus, it appears that he had become an *oedipal victor* who had effectively vanquished his father. Only after meeting up with his first analyst was Dr. Jacobs able to fully identify with a father figure.

Motives Related to Development of the Self

Narcissistic needs— Dr. Jacobs states that the most common unconscious motivation of his average colleague is, "The sense of being admired by someone for helping them out. Wanting to be idealized by the patient, because you've made them feel better and because of the transference issues of being the good parent."

In the eyes of his mother, Dr. Jacobs was "ultimately perfect. I could do no wrong—I could do anything I wanted to do. And it just always seemed that everything revolved around me. And my father would complain about that some, too. What was served for dinner always depended on *my* preferences. The story I heard growing up was that as soon as my mother found out that she was pregnant, the world came to a halt. She had to be calm, and she had to be waited on, and she had to do nice things because that would somehow result in having a nice kid."

Looking back on his unconscious motivations for entering the field, Dr. Jacobs focuses on the importance of fulfilling a strong need to feel exceptional. "As an only child, there was very much of an emphasis on being special. And that somehow medicine was very much seen as *the* profession that the Jewish, only child would go into—the most valued by my parents. Within their circle of friends, all of the males were professionals of one sort or another, but it seemed that the doctors were the most respected and prestigious." Although he felt distant from his father in many ways, Dr. Jacobs's earliest memories center around "wanting to do something for Daddy." For instance, "His being outside, painting the house, and my wanting to paint with him. Or washing the car. He would see that I had done a good job, or done something *for* him in some way."

Dr. Jacobs views himself as sharing some of his father's narcissistic tendencies in terms of "focusing on things *looking* a certain way or *being* a certain way, or that only the best is acceptable." While he wished for siblings at times, "it was sort of nice having everything to myself."

Dr. Jacobs notes that, in looking back, he is glad that he did not become a neurologist or internist, the other specialties in which he had shown an interest. "In reality their practices seem pretty boring. I mean, most internists are not doing these fascinating things of figuring out some esoteric case, like a case reported in the *New England Journal of Medicine*, but are rather treating peoples' colds and whatever, which doesn't sound very interesting at all."

Aggrandized ego-ideal— Even within the extended family,

Dr. Jacobs played the role of "the special kid." As the youngest of the grandchildren, he was the favorite of his paternal grandfather, the patriarch, and the only one with whom he would play. "I was supposed to achieve a lot, to do a lot, to make everyone happy with my accomplishments."

On an unconscious level, the idea of becoming an analyst "tapped into a fantasy of almost being a detective of some sort." As a child he had enjoyed the *Tom Swift* books. "The idea that someone could, by sitting around and thinking about things, help other people out and thereby gain some fame and notoriety for . . . saving mankind, almost. The Sherlock Holmes sort of image of being able to sit there in a chair and think about things and solve the problem."

This Sherlock Holmes fantasy entails grandiose aims (e.g., saving mankind) as well as a wish for omniscience. Dr. Jacobs had been interested in physics and chemistry, "but this seemed even more complicated in some ways than trying to solve an equation or figure out how to make something new. I'm still not aware of anything more complex than trying to understand the mind and brain on all the different levels *at once*, and trying to catch some concept of development and family background and current issues and dynamics and ego psychology and biochemistry." Feeling somewhat confined by the practice of psychoanalysis, Dr. Jacobs has branched out into inpatient work with people who also have medical illnesses and neurological deficits. "I find myself going back to relearn all of that, so that I can try to understand *everything*." He finds it frustrating that "sometimes the puzzles are unsolvable. Or that you can solve the puzzle, know what the issues are, and no matter how you present them to the person it doesn't make them change *anyway*."

Dr. Jacobs's strong identification with his first analyst played a major role in his decision to enter analytic training. His idealization of this man can be viewed as a projection of Dr. Jacobs's own ego-ideal. "His office was in his house, so I'd seen his house and glimpses of his family, and I saw them as this sort of perfect little family. That everybody must be so happy all of the time, and love one another so much. That he must have such a nice life." This attitude toward the analyst parallels early images of the family doctor, whom his mother seemed to idealize. "He was also a friend of the family, so I did know his wife and children, and they always seemed like such a nice, happy family."

Parental narcissism— Dr. Jacobs views his father's financial success as undermined at times by his narcissism. "He was more interested in the corporation giving him this unlimited expense account—so that when he traveled around Europe he could do it in this grand style—rather than thinking about the future. Those stock options would have been better than a $50,000-per-year American Express bill." There was a standing joke within the family that "when we were getting ready to go out it would be my *father* that we'd be waiting for because he'd take longer to get dressed, since he was so focused on how he looked, and that everything be just so."

Dr. Jacobs also sees narcissistic trends in his mother, in terms of her emphasis on appearances, and her determination to do what she wanted regardless of what anybody else felt or wanted.

Maternal identification— He describes himself as having been "closer to my mother all along," and shares more qualities and interests with her than with his father. "I think I'm more like my mother. I'm driven, the way she is, and always wanted to *do* things, to achieve. And somewhat cold and calculating."

Dr. Jacobs describes his first analyst, with whom he came to identify, as having been "very warm and kind of maternal, and very different from my image of men prior to that. I'd had a father whom I never doubted loved me or wanted me, but certainly was not able to express emotion very much and was fairly distant in many ways. He went to work and came home and sat around and watched television and went to bed, and didn't get too involved in things."

Dr. Jacobs's history of anxiety attacks also seems to parallel a difficulty that he believes his mother has concealed.

Motives Involving Object Relations

Conflicts concerning dependency— Dr. Jacobs's mother, with whom he identified, was very active and involved in cultural interests, yet also quite dependent. "I don't think she saw herself as someone who could go out and make it . . . going to college and getting her own degree, and so on . . . It's like she had to go out and find someone to marry who was going to make it big."

Given that Dr. Jacobs's mother tended to be overbearing and intrusive, and his father quite distant, it is unlikely that his dependency needs were adequately met. The extent of Dr. Jacobs's alienation from his father can be seen in this remark: "My father died last year. Even that, on the outside, I had little reaction to. I feel sad sometimes, but sad more about what I never had than really missing him."

One gets the impression that, while growing up, Dr. Jacobs was not given much of a chance to be a child. "My parents would have a lot of parties and things, and I'd be the only child there. I'd sort of become the host, running around to everybody, serving the drinks."

It appears likely that Dr. Jacobs coped with unmet dependency needs via reaction formation, that is, by turning the tables and caring for the needs of others. One of the central satisfactions he derives from clinical work is, in fact, the gratification of feeling needed.

Conflicts concerning separation— Dr. Jacobs notes that as a child "I didn't much like being alone, and would spend a lot of time with my mother. The image I remember is often of just the two of us being alone in the house. Even if I had to study, I would take my books and study at the kitchen table while my mother was doing the dishes, rather than wanting to be alone in my room." He continued to have somewhat of an aversion to being alone as an adolescent. "I was very much into girls, and had very intense, one-at-a-time relationships with girlfriends, and very short periods of time between relationships. I always had to find another one pretty quickly."

When Dr. Jacobs was about 10 years old, his father switched careers. "He went from a regular job where he'd get home at six o'clock every evening and work Monday through Friday, to a career where he worked late and traveled a lot, and would be away for five or six days at a time."

In regard to his mother, Dr. Jacobs states, "I saw her as somewhat smothering, so in adolescence got into a terrible battle with her around wanting to separate and be independent. I felt that she was trying to hold me close to home, and didn't want to let go, and didn't want me to grow up or to move away. She got terribly upset when I was applying to colleges if any of the ones I applied to was more than fifty miles away from home. She had an awful time with the idea that her only child was trying to leave the nest, which led me to go off to college—sixty miles from home, but with the compromise that it was far enough away that I would at least get to *live* there—and be fairly radical. In minor sorts of ways—like growing long hair, wearing the same pair of jeans for a year, and joining some slightly left-wing movements—but in ways that drove my parents crazy."

Dr. Jacobs suffered from anxiety attacks that started soon after leaving home to begin his residency. "I had gotten married and moved away from home . . . a couple hundred miles away from where I'd grown up, and started having some anxiety attacks. That may be too strong a word, but some waves of . . . heart racing and feeling like I wanted to get out of the place I was in, so I guess you could call them little anxiety attacks. I felt they were sometimes interfering with my doing things." Although he had lived away from home while he attended medical school, that had not triggered any problems with anxiety. "I think it was a matter of the permanency of finishing school, getting married, moving away, and really being on my own. Somehow that separation was much more potent than just going off to school."

Dr. Jacobs's difficulty separating from his first analyst seems to have interfered to some degree with his subsequent relationship to the training analyst. He reports feelings of dissatisfaction at the completion of his training analysis. "I at first felt somewhat disappointed, kind of angry, and still felt misunderstood in some ways, and it really took about two years after termination before whatever had been stirred up had been worked through. . . . Looking back, I think I almost did some splitting; I was sort of angry that the institute was making me terminate with this first person, and I think I went into the first session with the new analyst starting off on the wrong foot, sort of saying, 'I wish I was still seeing Dr. P.' Because I had felt very warm support from that person, and had gotten quite attached." In retrospect, Dr. Jacobs views the entire experience—

including the transfer—as having been very helpful. "It got me to look at this tendency I have of idealizing and belittling, and was sort of a replay of my own situation with my parents."

In relation to terminating with clients he says, "I find it difficult. One of my problems as a therapist or analyst is the trouble letting go. . . . I've made some of my biggest mistakes in the termination phase, saying things that I probably shouldn't have said. Things that were motivated by my own wish to avoid thinking about never seeing this person again—this person to whom I've become attached in some way. . . . The fantasy that—not that I would be best friends with the person—but that I'd hear from them from time to time, or see them occasionally, or that it would dwindle down to less frequent meetings, but never really end." He worries that his reluctance to end may give the patient a way out of feeling the sadness of a real termination.

Need for power and control— Dr. Jacobs points to the vulnerability that is entailed in being a psychotherapy patient. "As a man, you're working with some of these attractive young women who are in a position in which you could talk them into almost anything, and it gets into some power and control issues in relationships . . . and yet, it's so inappropriate." When asked how he characteristically deals with such issues as a clinician, he states, "Well, I'd say that this is a theme that I was aware of, and that I've done the most work on trying to change in myself—to try *not* to control people. That I've come to accept over time that I really *don't know* what's best for someone else, and that getting them to be more like me is not necessarily a good thing for them. That they need to go their own way."

Dr. Jacobs explains that he became aware of his conflicts around power and control in the context of sexualized fantasies about certain patients. "At one point it was a little upsetting, when I thought it might mean that I was going to lose control somehow and get myself in trouble. But now I've become more accepting that it doesn't have to mean that at all. That instead of blocking out the fantasies, I ought to allow them and to think about why I'm having these particular kinds of fantasies about a particular patient at a certain time, and what that means about what's going on in the therapy."

When asked to clarify how these sexual fantasies reflected conflicts dealing with power and control, he replies, "Well, in a sexual relationship with a spouse, for instance, one has to be mutual, not just demanding that one's own needs be met, without paying attention to what the other person likes or doesn't like. So the power and control in these fantasies is more like the power and control one would have in a sexual relationship with a prostitute, where you could sort of say 'this is what I want,' and not have to worry about pleasing her."

One could say that Dr. Jacobs learned a great deal of self-control from his father. "I always had the sense with my father that I had to act tough and be strong, and not cry, and not show much feeling." Through his analysis and his analytic training Dr. Jacobs hoped to become more like his first analyst, "to be able to feel more, and to be aware of what was going on inside." Ironically, the role of psychoanalyst may in some ways have reinforced his tendencies to control and inhibit emotion and spontaneity. Dr. Jacobs also points out that the stoic approach to emotions that he learned within his family can color his reactions to clients. "I often have to remind myself that this really *isn't* okay, because there's a part of me that reacts to people complaining about physical pain or something going on at home that wants to tell them 'Shut up! Just be tough and go out there and *do* it.'"

Intimacy— As a child, Dr. Jacobs was "shy, quiet and held back a lot before getting involved in things." He was largely interested in intellectual pursuits, such as reading books about science and nature, playing with his chemistry set, and going to the museum or the planetarium. "Things that I could do myself, because I had to spend a lot of time alone." Although he had some friends, he often felt "like the kid on the outside with his nose pressed against the glass, looking in and wanting to be more a part of the group but feeling that I didn't know how to. . . . There were kids in the neighborhood with whom I was somewhat friendly, but felt like they were more friendly with one another and I was kind of the extra person in the group."

Dr. Jacobs views himself as somewhat driven, in terms of his work hours. When he was largely in private practice, "all of my colleagues would sort of shake their heads and couldn't understand how I could do it—that I'd have days in a row where I would sit in an office by myself for twelve or fourteen hours and see fifteen patients—one every fifty minutes—with barely a break to grab a sandwich, and just be able to do that for endless hours." He concludes, "I'm a bit of a workaholic, like I'm not sure what else to do if I'm not working." In this he is like his father, whom Dr. Jacobs had always admired for being successful at work. His work required little interaction with other people, however, and Dr. Jacobs describes his father as having had a limited capacity for intimacy. "He had friends in his eighties whom he'd known since he was 3 or 4 years old. They kept in contact all that time, yet I doubt that they had ever said a word to one another about a feeling or anything of real significance."

Although his marital relationship is essentially quite positive, Dr. Jacobs states, "I think I'm obsessional, and stay somewhat removed from getting totally involved *with anybody* . . . and always have to think about there being an option to escape from this level of closeness." His closest friends are women. "I have a harder time really getting close to men—I think it's sort of too scary to feel emotionally close to them."

Thus, an important motivation that may have unconsciously influenced Dr. Jacobs's choice of career is the need for greater intimacy and emotional involvement with others. On a conscious level, he was drawn to the intellectual challenge of solving complex puzzles. Unwittingly, however, he may have sensed that the practice of psychotherapy might allow him to develop in those areas that had been relatively neglected—the interpersonal and affective realms. When asked how the work differs from his early expectations, he replies, "It's much more personally, emotionally painful. It takes a lot of personal work *all of the time*. It stirs up painful things about my own life that I'd rather not think about sometimes. I didn't think through the idea that every time I talk to someone about their parent dying—no matter how many times I've done it before—it will bring up feelings again about my own parent dying." Having envisioned the therapeutic process as purely an intellectual enterprise, he experienced a rude awakening: "Guess what? I have feelings too!" On the other hand, his work provides him with relatively intimate contact that "feels safe."

Rescue fantasies and reparation— In general, Dr. Jacobs does not believe that guilt feelings have played much of a role in his life, or in his choice of profession. While reparative wishes do not seem to be in evidence, he acknowledges occasional rescue fantasies. "I sometimes see a desire as a therapist to rescue someone, but that seems to be more tied in to wanting to be seen as special. Especially with female patients, I have this fantasy of making them feel better, of saving them, or even sometimes a fantasy of marrying them. To be idealized for changing their life and having them be eternally grateful to me." These rescue fantasies can be readily viewed as deriving from Dr. Jacobs's childhood experiences as an oedipal victor.

Therapist 3: Tom

Tom is a male doctoral candidate in clinical psychology. He states that he initially became interested in psychology for the following reasons: His father works in the field, he found undergraduate course work of interest, an admired teacher influenced him, and he had an ongoing interest in philosophical questions, such as, "What does it mean to be alive?" As he continued his studies, he realized that he wanted to work with people, so he decided on clinical psychology. "Applying psychology to peoples' lives was the only thing that I could picture myself doing on a career basis and have it be meaningful."

Tom had wanted to become a lawyer as a boy and a pilot as an adolescent; he later considered such areas as sociology, philosophy, and religion, but decided that he did not want to remain in academia. Asked what occupations other than psychology that he now thinks he might find satisfying, he mentioned acting, directing, and being a pilot.

Psychological Disturbances

Tom initially entered into his own treatment during his early twenties. Presenting problems included depression and family conflict. Since that time he has entered therapy twice, for difficulties involving anxiety, panic attacks, and depression.

Family members— His mother had a cancer phobia for many years, beginning when Tom reached adolescence.

Motives Related to Instincts

Reaction formation against aggression— Anger was frowned upon and suppressed in his family, and there were very few fights. "There was strong pressure to be one big happy family." When anger did burst forth, it was in the form of parental arguments or his brother's tantrums. Tom was "always the good boy, a goody-two-shoes. I didn't want to do anything to get anyone mad at me." As an adolescent, Tom had strong fears of parental death, which he views in retrospect as "probably an expression of my anger."

Unresolved oedipal conflict— Tom's mother was the central figure in the family, and everything revolved around her. His father was quite distant and on the periphery. Tom was always closest to his mother. He sided with her when there were parental fights, comforting and taking care of her, and seeing father as cold and cruel. He states, "I probably had a fucked-up oedipal stage, because I never didn't like girls."

Motives Related to Development of the Self

Narcissistic needs— One of the two common motives that Tom attributed to others was that of "narcissistic gratification involved in helping people feel good about themselves. Feeling you're important in someone else's life." Similarly, one of his conscious satisfactions from practicing psychotherapy involves "narcissistic satisfaction—if I've had a good session I feel better about myself."

Parental narcissism— Maternal narcissism can be inferred from Tom's descriptions of his mother as having used him to take care of her emotionally, and to satisfy her needs.

Aggrandized ego-ideal— Although he was the youngest family member, "if there were any sorts of problems, I'd be the one to analyze them and to calm everyone down. I was always calm, cool, and collected." Tom idealized his first therapist and remembers having only positive feelings toward him. "I saw him as omniscient. I thought he saw all and knew all, and just wasn't telling me. . . .

Later on I looked up to him as a role model." A further indication of his having idealized the role of therapist is his report that he had found the practice of psychotherapy more difficult, and at times more boring and less satisfying than he had anticipated. "I had the ideal that it would always be wonderful, dynamic . . . feeling I'm helping people."

Indications of a strong maternal identification can be seen in the material on instinctual motives.

Motives Involving Object Relations

Conflicts concerning dependency— Tom related an early experience of serious illness. Toward the beginning of his second year of life Tom had severe asthma and nearly died. He was hospitalized for two weeks, lying in an oxygen tent and being fed intravenously. "I often wonder about the experience of being so sick and almost dying . . . if that's where I get a lot of my empathy from."

Tom became a parentified child, looking after the needs of older family members. "I served as confidant and interpreter for [my mother] of my sister's adolescent rebellion. I acted as go-between. I was sort of the family psychologist, in that sense, especially for my mother—I took care of her emotionally."

Conflicts concerning separation— When asked how his mother reacted to his moves toward independence, Tom bluntly replied, "She *hated* them. Both my mother and father tried to block them." Tom's father went away on business trips for one and two weeks at a time, and his mother became highly upset over these separations. Tom went away to camp for the first time at age 12, became violently ill, and returned home. He remained very close to his mother throughout adolescence, "and never really went through any rebellion stage. I'm sort of going through that now. Breaking away from her and establishing myself as a separate being who *does* get angry and isn't just there to satisfy all her needs." When he got married Tom's parents became especially "clingy," and tried to hold on to him as the "baby of the family." His father jokingly remarked, "We're going to hold on as hard as we can, kid."

Tom never fully terminated with his first therapist. He left and returned to treatment three times, terminating before it felt complete. "So, usually it wasn't painful. I guess I never really dealt with it a whole lot."

Need for power and control— Tom describes a sense of powerlessness that came with being the youngest child. "I later felt anger at my brother for all the times he beat me up and I felt so helpless." Asked what he finds most frustrating about doing psychotherapy, Tom replies, "The lack of control. Not knowing what the hell I'm doing. Not knowing what the hell is going on in a session or how to respond to it."

Intimacy— One of Tom's conscious gratifications from doing psychotherapy is the "personal satisfaction—if I've really connected with a person on a deeply personal level and communicated at that level." One of the unconscious motives that he ascribes to other therapists involves controlled intimacy. "It's a safe, controlled way to be intimate, which probably appeals to people with intimacy problems. You can get close, but control it—be intimate, but without committing yourself to any real, long-term relationship. So, you can have all this intimate contact, but might not have a friend in the world."

Rescue fantasies and reparation— Tom characteristically took the role of rescuer and savior within his family, especially with his mother, rescuing her from his "cold, cruel" father. This wish to rescue may have stemmed from reparative needs, given his strong guilt concerning his anger and aggression.

Following the interview, Tom had a dream that he felt was related to the material discussed. He reported it as follows:

> *I am in the backyard of my childhood home. Some pigeons fly by and shit on me. I put my hands over my head to protect myself, but it's coming down like rain. I have to go in to take a shower, but the water isn't running. My mother and sister are there—they don't care, or something. Or maybe I'm embarrassed. I feel sort of wet and gross, but I'm not bummed out. I'm not too concerned about this pigeon shit all over me.*

Tom felt that the dream represented his feelings about having been used as a go-between in mediating conflicts between his mother and sister. In retrospect, he felt that they had "dumped their emotional shit" on him, and that he had willingly taken on this role. This martyrlike stance, suggesting masochistic tendencies that had not been so clearly discernible in the interview material, may have contributed to his interest in becoming a psychotherapist.

Therapist 4: Anne

Anne is a female doctoral candidate in clinical psychology. She became interested in the field because of a course she took in college; she had always been introspective, however, and liked movies with psychological themes even as a child. She states that her decision to become a therapist was influenced by her own psychotherapist, whom she viewed as a role model. She feels that her personal therapy gave her the courage to return to school to pursue this goal. "I had been helped so much in therapy myself. I guess I wanted to be a part of that process for others."

Anne was originally a schoolteacher, and has also been a real estate agent and restaurant manager. If she were not a therapist, she would like to practice law.

Psychological Disturbances

Anne entered her own treatment for problems with depression and low self-esteem, as well as marital difficulties. "Initially, I was hell-bent on trying to figure myself out—to see how I ticked. This led to an interest in how other people think, and what makes them do what they do." When asked to name a common unconscious motive of her colleagues, she replied, "the desire to work out their own issues."

Family members— Anne states that all the members of her family, with the exception of one of her three sisters, are prone to depression.

Motives Related to Instincts

Reaction formation against aggression— "With my parents, you really didn't express your opinion, and you certainly didn't express anger at them, or anger at all. But my mother was a big screamer. I remember constant screaming going on, so that really turned me off to screaming."

Unresolved oedipal conflict— Throughout her childhood Anne felt closer to her father and identified more with him. She continues to view herself as more like her father than her mother, in terms of "my manner, my nature, and a lot of my habits." It is unclear, however, whether this identification contributed to her career choice.

Motives Related to Development of the Self

Narcissistic needs— "I was pretty hard on myself, even as a child. The big thing was feeling stupid all the time." Anne's family moved to the United States from Europe when she was 5. Prior to this she had been the "star," reading by age 3, and otherwise precocious. After the move, she had difficulty with the language and fell behind at school.

Anne had continuing problems with self-esteem. "Both of my parents believed that praising their children would only give them a big head, so I received very few positive strokes." As an adolescent, Anne began to feel that she was ugly, and her self-esteem decreased further. In discussing her social history, she jokingly remarked, "I had some boyfriends, which always amazed me."

Parental narcissism— Maternal narcissism can be inferred from a number of statements, such as, "Looking back, I think I was a lot like my mother, and that's what caused her so much difficulty—I think she saw a lot of herself in me." The maternal grandmother was an influential figure in the family, and when she died, Anne's relationship with her mother improved considerably. Anne then realized that much of her mother's behavior had been an attempt to meet her own mother's expectations. Anne felt that she was continually trying to please her mother, and then later her husband, with whom she had a relationship nearly identical to the one with her mother.

Aggrandized ego-ideal— "I felt that I could never meet my mother's expectations. The message was, 'Nothing is ever good enough.'" Anne was the eldest of four daughters, and felt that she had to be her sisters' role model. "I played the role of the 'good child,' until rebelling at age 19 to 24."

Anne states that she initially had a highly idealized picture of her therapist, and believed he was "the greatest thing since sliced bread." She still considers him "terrific—although I now know he's not infallible."

Motives Involving Object Relations

Conflicts concerning dependency— Anne experienced a good deal of deprivation as a young child. There was a shortage of food and often not enough milk, and Anne's baby teeth turned black. One of the important motives that Anne is aware of is her need to take care of others. Anne became a "second mother" to her two youngest siblings. "I treated them how I wished my mother would have treated me. I bought them things, took them places, and gave them a lot of affection—basically, unconditional positive regard." Anne initially worked as a therapist with chronically ill young adults. "I was like their mother. [When I left] it felt like I was abandoning them." She continues to have similar feelings whenever she terminates with a client.

While Anne was in her early twenties, her mother still demanded that she ask her permission to go out. Her mother controlled her bank account and doled out money to her each week. Anne states that she continues to have much difficulty managing her own funds. During her marriage, "the way the relationship was set up, he was the father and I was the little girl."

Conflicts concerning separation—At age 19, Anne began to rebel and had a geat deal of conflict with her mother. "It was hard for both sides. I tried to assert my independence, which she didn't like." Anne moved to her own apartment at age 24. "It was like the end of the world! They'd say 'You hate your family' and I'd say 'Yeah, that's why I'm moving five blocks away.'"

Asked what she had discovered in therapy about her own unconscious motivations for becoming a therapist, Anne replied that "it probably has something to do with the attachments I feel—the bond. Like the feeling I had of abandoning those clients. That might involve a projection of my own fear of being abandoned."

Need for power and control— Anne emphasizes her mother's need to maintain control over her, implying a sense of powerlessness on her part.

One of Anne's satisfactions from doing psychotherapy is "to see people change. The impact one can make in other people's lives." She added that this aspect is frightening as well. "You don't want to feel like you're all-powerful." The enjoyment of a sense of power was also one of the unconscious motivations of which Anne had become aware in her own treatment.

Therapist 5: Dr. Kramer

Dr. Kramer is a clinical psychologist in private practice. He states that it was his father who initially sparked his interest in the field. He remembers his father telling him, as a young boy, about a friend who had suffered a nervous breakdown. His father expressed regret over not having been able to be of more help, and said that he wished he had become a psychoanalyst. When he was in grade school, Dr. Kramer's father took a night course in psychology, further spurring his interest. In high school he was given the nickname of "Freud." In college he initially planned to become a nuclear physicist, until he entered a period of depression in his sophomore year. He was in therapy for three-and-a-half years with an analytically oriented psychologist, with whom he identified strongly. Dr. Kramer remembers looking around his therapist's office during his first session, and asking, "What does it take to do what you do?" Dr. Kramer now believes that he unconsciously carried out his father's covert wish for him to become a psychoanalyst. At the time he thought that he was rebelling, because his father's overt demand was for him to go into the family business.

Psychological Disturbances

At 19, Dr. Kramer became depressed and had difficulties concentrating on his studies. In retrospect, he views this as having involved separation issues, stimulated by his move away from home. Dr. Kramer later entered therapy in graduate school, saw a family therapist for marital problems, and ultimately entered analysis, feeling that he needed "something more intensive and regressive." He comments, "It's a crazy field. You have to listen to people's crazy shit, to hear their misery, day in and day out. I think you have to have a kind of pathology in you—that something's being worked through—or else you couldn't do that."

Dr. Kramer emphasizes that it is through having resolved his own emotional difficulties that he acquired many of the qualities of a proficient psychotherapist: psychological insight, emotional sensitivity, tolerance for clients' pathology, and optimism regarding the therapeutic process.

Family members— Dr. Kramer states that his mother would be diagnosed as a Paranoid Personality Disorder, his father as a Schizotypal Personality Disorder, and his sister as an "overly constricted neurotic."

Motives Related to Instincts

Conflicts concerning aggression— As a child, Dr. Kramer was not allowed to express any anger. "Anger was life-threatening, dangerous. My father would grab his heart, saying 'You're trying to kill me.'" On the other hand, he became a target for the anger of other family members. "I was the only one the whole family could get angry at, and not have fall apart. I'd be strong enough to deal with everyone's anger. . . . That's probably why I can deal with borderline patients, and not get all shook up. I got *that* from my family. It's pathology that becomes a resource, that overt tolerance for hostility."

Dr. Kramer describes himself as having served the function of a "family lightning rod. When they were feeling crazy they dumped it onto me." He elaborates, "I was the family scapegoat—but a *messianic* scapegoat. I was crucified and resurrected again when a new crisis arose and I was needed to complain to and to dump on. . . . They dump, but then they see themselves in you and have to kill you because they can't tolerate what they see. So, being a therapist is really a repetition compulsion. It's like in *The Deer Hunter*, where Christopher Walken goes back and keeps playing Russian roulette—that's what we do. Attempting to form some mastery over that tremendous fear of being killed off."

While this family role may indicate early masochistic trends, Dr. Kramer believes it provided a means to master his fear of being "killed off" by the aggression of others. Within his family, as well as in his professional work, Dr. Kramer feels that he has gradually mastered the ability to withstand being attacked by others without having to become defensive or to respond in kind. This has, by necessity, included his coming to terms with fears regarding his own aggression.

Aggressive impulses are also evident in adolescent wishes for parental death, as well as in the comment that, previous to his analysis, "in intimate relationships I sometimes gave feedback that *seemed* nurturing, but which clobbered the person. The hidden message was, 'You betrayed me, and now you're going to pay.'"

Unresolved oedipal conflict— Given the level of aggression within the family, any full resolution of oedipal conflict would have been difficult. Dr. Kramer states that his mother was at times a "cold, rejecting bitch," and that "you could argue with her, but she was extremely castrating." Furthermore, it was difficult for him to shift his identification to his father during the oedipal phase. He states that, while before the age of 5 he identified with his mother, "after that I *looked* for it with my father, but that wasn't possible, he was so much into his own stuff."

Dr. Kramer states that a primary conflict that he had to resolve in his own analysis concerned competition with his father. Dr. Kramer's father, who had never attended college, encouraged his son to limit his vocational sights to barbering or business. "My father didn't want me to do better than he had done." Meanwhile, he would feign heart attacks whenever his son asserted himself. "Basically, I was afraid I'd kill off my father by succeeding in any way." Dr. Kramer defended against his guilt over the wish to defeat his father by identifying with him as a weak person. Difficulties with assertion and achievement later resulted in academic problems in college, culminating in his entering into psychotherapeutic treatment. Dr. Kramer was only able to pursue his interest in becoming a therapist, a lifelong dream of his father's, after forming a new ego-ideal through his identification with his own therapist.

Motives Related to Development of the Self

Narcissistic needs— When asked what he thinks is the most common unconscious motivation of his average colleague, Dr. Kramer responds that practicing psychotherapy is a safe way to work through one's own issues, vicariously "without the risk of narcissistic injury." He states that such therapists, including himself, eventually are faced with a "great rip-off—they feel they're going to get idealized by their patients, and then encounter negative transferences." Dr. Kramer entered the profession with the fantasized expectations that "my self-esteem deficits would be nourished by idealized patients, that my interpretations would have a magical quality, and that I would be messianic in my power. Very grandiose notions, although I would *never* have admitted them at the time. Now I am very pragmatic."

Parental narcissism— Dr. Kramer states that he was narcissistically used by his parents. "So now when I get a narcissistic transference, it's no big deal—It's what I'm used to!"

Aggrandized ego-ideal— As a young boy, Dr. Kramer idealized his father as a "superman." The grandiosity of his early ego-ideal is seen in his stated role as the "messianic scapegoat . . . crucified and resurrected again."

Dr. Kramer notes that, as a child, his favorite television shows were "The Breaking Point" and "Eleventh Hour." In both of these shows, "the heroes were therapists, and were messianic figures." Dr. Kramer now understands that he was "following a script from my ego-ideal, unconsciously identifying first with my [idealized] father, then with these television heroes, and then with my first therapist."

Motives Involving Object Relations

Conflicts concerning separation— Dr. Kramer states that both of his parents viewed his moves toward independence as threatening and rejecting, and notes that each of them had a parent who had left the family. "My mother had a hard time with separation when I first went to school. She became more distant. . . .Talk about overprotective—I wasn't even allowed to join the Boy Scouts!" As he reached adolescence, such conflict escalated. "As there was more separation and individuation, there was more hostility, since she experienced it as rejection (as she had felt rejected by her father). That's why I got depressed in college—this *horrible* guilt that I'd left my mother."

His father also viewed any moves toward independence—even a difference of opinion—as rebellious and disloyal. This attitude intensified through Dr. Kramer's adolescence, and "it was such an injury for me that I disidentify with it—so when patients separate from *me*, I wish them well and don't hold on to them." As a child, he was so disillusioned by his parents' empathic failures that he "couldn't feel and didn't feel sadness. I would feel it about *animals*—if a pet died I'd grieve tremendously. . . . [Later], with girlfriends, I got physically ill [such as with mononucleosis] when I had to deal with separations." When Dr. Kramer married, he was "unconsciously drawn to someone *exactly* like my mother, in terms of psychodynamics," and now attributes this to his fears of separating from his mother.

Dr. Kramer also recalls having had difficulty separating from his first therapist. "I remember feeling really sad that I was losing my best friend in the world."

Need for power and control— This can be seen in the omnipotent images Dr. Kramer brought to the role of therapist. He says, for example, "that my interpretations would have a magical quality, and that I would be messianic in my power."

Intimacy— As a child he was sorely disappointed in his wishes for intimacy. "I abandoned both of [my parents], and got into my own world of ideas, cathecting something that's abstract in place of something interpersonal." The desired closeness was not fully attained in his first marriage either. In the practice of psychotherapy, Dr. Kramer finds "an intimacy that is mutually fulfilling—although filled with anger and distrust, like any other human relationship— but basically enjoyable. If not, I would have burned out."

Rescue fantasies and reparation— It is likely that both of these motives were underlying factors in Dr. Kramer's willingness to take on the role of family lightning rod and scapegoat. "When they were feeling crazy, they dumped it onto me. I was *groomed* to be a therapist. I almost went crazy—but didn't."

Therapist 6: Julie

Julie is a female doctoral candidate in clinical psychology. She has been interested in psychology since her early teens. Her mother worked with a well-known psychoanalyst. There was a great deal of psychoanalytic literature in the house—and no television—so she read much of it. This interest was supported by her parents, who were highly intellectual, admired Freud's works, and had both been in analysis. By the age of 17, Julie had decided to become an analyst. Her determination was further fueled by the fact that psychoanalysis was considered esoteric and unacceptable to her teachers.

Psychological Disturbances

Julie attended a highly competitive college, feeling pressured into it by her parents. She found herself becoming "desperately unhappy," began drinking, and "slept around something awful." She was "very depressed, but acting it out." Her father suggested to Julie that she needed help. She reacted angrily and became suicidal, but soon entered analysis.

Family members— Julie describes her mother as an hysterical personality and her father as very avoidant, with explosive rage reactions.

Motives Related to Instincts

Voyeurism— One of the common unconscious motives attributed by Julie to her colleagues is that of voyeurism. What she finds the most interesting about practicing psychotherapy is the "sense of discovery." She states that "psychoanalysis has to do with uncovering unknown things. As a child I desperately wanted to know what happened—my father disappearing and reappearing six months later, doors slamming, people crying, and so on." She recalls, "My mother used to take me with her when she went to analysis, and I had to stay in the waiting room. I would wonder what was going on behind the doors. Oedipal stuff, you know. I'd see her come out, having cried, and wondered, 'What's going on with that person she's going to for help?'"

Julie's mother may have unwittingly stimulated voyeurism by inappropriately confiding in her daughter. "She used to tell me things I didn't even want to hear about her relationship with my father—sexual things."

At age 15, Julie decided that she wanted to be a spy, and went so far as to make inquiries at the State Department. She later played with the idea of becoming a model, a desire that she now views as having stemmed from exhibitionistic and voyeuristic tendencies.

Unresolved oedipal conflict— Julie mentions a strong and continuing identification with her father, noting that she was very interested in studying economics, her father's field. Becoming a therapist was one way in which she felt that she could surpass him. "My father is an eminent economist—he's a genius. But he couldn't deal with emotions. It was always . . . everything I could do he could do better. But dealing with emotions was something I could do better."

Julie often felt caught between her parents in a way that could not have been conducive to a full resolution of oedipal issues. "My mother confided in me, and that put me in a difficult position. I felt torn, and that was rough. I'd think, 'What can I say? I can't win whatever I say.'" The level of hostility that was frequently present may also have been an interfering factor. Julie describes her parents' relationship as "very stormy. They both had temper tantrums . . . arguments with shouting, doors slamming, and things like that." At times there was physical violence as well. At age 6, in the midst of the oedipal period, Julie's father had an affair and left the family for six months.

Julie's father's extreme possessiveness made it difficult for her to shift her attachment to another male. "He was very possessive of me sexually. On my wedding day he wouldn't say a word to my husband. . . . He was sad that his daughter was getting married— that he wasn't the number-one man in my life—so he got angry."

Motives Related to Development of the Self

Narcissistic needs/Parental narcissism— Intense maternal narcissism is apparent. Julie states that her mother is a difficult person to disagree with, or to oppose. "If you argue a different viewpoint, she takes it as a personal rejection." In many ways, her mother looked to Julie to fulfill her own needs, and had difficulty recognizing and responding to those of her daughter. Her mother worried when Julie went into analysis, telling her, "I know you're saying bad things about me in there." In recent years, "she has been grasping at me, as if to say, 'Come back! I need you to confirm my sense of self.'"

Paternal narcissism is also apparent in her father's jealously clinging attitude. "He has great possessiveness of me as *his* daughter."

Aggrandized ego-ideal— "As the only child, I felt that I had to be everything to my mother." Julie states that her mother is highly insecure, and that "in some ways I'm like a role model for what a woman can do. I have really encouraged her to go out and build her own career. . . . I'm the parent to my parents in some ways, I know."

Motives Involving Object Relations

Conflicts concerning dependency— When she was younger, Julie wished to be a veterinarian. She kept many pets, "possibly because I was an only child and rather lonely." A sense of emotional deprivation is conveyed in many of her family anecdotes.

Julie was highly aware of her mother's dependency needs. She states that when she was a baby, things were easier for her mother. "*She* paints a rosy picture, anyway. It's because she needs me so much. She's a very fragile person. So when I was relying on her more, it was better for her. As I became more of an individual it became increasingly difficult. . . . As I grow older, I've become aware of her being very needy of me. A year ago she was calling up all the time—things were terrible, and she needed to lean on me."

Julie had a recent dream in which her father appeared very old and infirm. She worries about her parents becoming "sick and dependent on me. It's awful, really awful."

Conflicts concerning separation— Julie was separated from her father at age 6, when he left home for half a year. Separations have generally been quite difficult for Julie, and she is highly sensitized to her parents' anxieties concerning separation. Speaking of her mother, Julie states, "If I try to keep my distance, she gets very hurt and experiences it as a rejection." When Julie informed her mother that she was engaged, "she said 'What? You can't do this!' She seemed to think I was asking permission."

In retrospect, Julie views her depression during her college years as largely "due to leaving my family, although at the time I wouldn't have admitted it. I was making believe I was very independent and mature." Julie sees herself as having denied the loss, as she did when she moved to go to graduate school. "If I looked too much at their reaction, it would be too hard to extricate myself."

When asked what it was like to terminate her own therapeutic treatment, Julie replies, "Awful. [Laughs]. I laugh because it wasn't as if I were *devastated*. . . . My throat seized up and everything. I didn't feel ready to end. It was like forced ejection into the cold world of reality."

Rescue fantasies and reparation— Julie asserts that a common unconscious motive of her average colleague involves the "wish to make reparation." It appears that she experienced a strong need to rescue and "repair" both internal and external objects. Sitting outside the office of her mother's analyst, Julie recalls thinking, "*I* want to help my mother, and be in that position." Back at home, she remembers musing, "'If I could only make things better—say the right thing and it would all be alright.' And, of course, that relates to being a therapist." In discussing the satisfactions she derives from practicing psychotherapy, Julie states, "If you really help somebody and they get back on their feet—that's incredibly exciting."

On the night following her interview, Julie had a dream that she believed was related to the material discussed:

> It took place in our old house in San Francisco, where I lived between the ages of 2 to 9. I was with a group of people, including one woman with long, filthy hair which stank. The two locks on the front door could easily be forced open. I was looking around for a chair and padlock to lock it properly when suddenly a helicopter came overhead and started to let rip with machine-gun fire. Everyone dropped to the ground and tried to take shelter. I wriggled from one hiding place to another, trying to get into the basement, which eventually I did. Down there, there were lots of people I know, including my husband and my old friend Katie (whom I'd spoken to on the phone before going to bed last night). Everyone was terrified by the helicopter, which continued to bombard the house and then began even to drop bombs. There was a little girl, aged about 2, who looked terrified, and I gathered her up in my arms and I ran with her to the part of the basement which was reinforced with concrete.

Katie was there and I was very relieved to see that she was un-harmed. The bombs were exploding around us and we knew if there was a direct hit, we'd all be killed. But then suddenly, the noise stopped and the helicopter went away. Joyfully, my husband and I danced out of the shelter together.

Julie had the sense that this dream was clearly about her own childhood. She comments, "My feeling is that the machine-gun fire is like my mother, and the bombs like my father. The little 2-year-old child is myself, whom I rescue. And the end of the dream is perhaps an expression of feeling that, by marrying, I've broken out of the parental home." The dream appears to illustrate the intense fear and sense of danger experienced by Julie in her warlike family environment. Rescue fantasies as well as concerns over separation are readily apparent.

Therapist 7: Dr. Glaser

Dr. Glaser is a clinical psychologist employed in an outpatient clinic. Although she initially wished to go into medicine, she lacked the academic prerequisites; she decided on psychology after receiving vocational counseling. She had done volunteer work with the disabled, and "had a strong feeling of wanting to do good." Aside from medicine, Dr. Glaser had thought about working as a teacher or as a writer, and greatly enjoyed acting when she was in school. If she were not a therapist, Dr. Glaser believes that she would enjoy being a high school teacher.

Psychological Disturbances

When Dr. Glaser first entered into her own treatment she "felt quite empty." She states, "In retrospect, I think I had a severe narcissistic personality disorder, and I was very depressed."

Dr. Glaser expresses disappointment regarding the persistence of her emotional problems. "I had a great metaphor for it of 'closing the book'—you work through some issues and that's it! But that wasn't the case. My issues will always be with me, and they return." She also did not anticipate that her work as a psychotherapist might heighten her awareness of her own difficulties. "I didn't expect that other people's problems could be so painful because they bring up my own. I thought it would just be an intellectual process."

Family members— Dr. Glaser's father was an alcoholic and was prone to physical violence. Her mother was "severely depressed all of her life." Dr. Glaser has recently begun to recall frightening early memories, "such as the image of my mother with a knife in her hand, and I've begun to think there might have been some psychosis." She has a younger brother who has been in and out of psychiatric hospitals. He is an alcoholic, has been divorced three times, and "is incapable of working or having relationships."

Motives Related to Instincts

Voyeurism— Dr. Glaser cites curiosity as the most common unconscious motivation of her average colleague. "We get to see how other people live. It's voyeurism, really. We have the license to be exposed, to ask questions and elicit very secret and intimate details."

Exhibitionism— In grade school, Dr. Glaser liked to perform in class plays, to read poetry, and to do "other things having to do with making a show, presenting." When asked about her use of the phrase "to be exposed," which could indicate exhibitionistic tendencies, she explains, "I expose myself to other people's intimate details. I actively look for it."

Conflicts concerning aggression— As a child, Dr. Glaser describes herself as having been very stubborn. "I had a bad temper, and a lot of difficulty modulating anger." She was confronted with familial violence. "My father became ugly and violent when he got drunk. And, at least in my mind, my mother protected us from his violence. At least, that's what she said." Dr. Glaser also participated at times in the arguments and fights, and "screamed louder than everybody." She also sees herself as having gratified her mother's masochism. "I gave my mother a chance to suffer a lot, and she loved to suffer. I did so many things she disapproved of, and she used them to show how ungrateful I was."

Dr. Glaser continues to harbor a great deal of anger toward the memory of her parents. Only half in jest, she declares, "I'm glad they're dead because, if not, I might murder them."

Regarding her therapeutic technique, Dr. Glaser states that "my interpretations are too fast, and I have poor timing," possibly reflecting unconscious aggression toward her clients.

Unresolved oedipal conflict— As a young child, Dr. Glaser was intensely involved with her father, whom she describes as "an extremely handsome, gorgeous looking man." During her oedipal period, Dr. Glaser's brother was born, and her relationship with her father was seriously disrupted. "Up until the age of 6—when my ratty brother showed up—I was the princess. My father was extremely proud of me. I had lovely curls and was very beautiful. Then my brother appeared and I became second-class, which ruined the good ol' oedipal."

As she reached adolescence, and sexual maturity, her father became highly protective of her. Both father and brother clearly had difficulties relinquishing their oedipal fantasies. "He became my ally, my protector. I wasn't allowed to go to dances by myself, but my father came along. There was a real sort of flirtatious relationship. He liked my beauty. We danced, and of course no 16- or 17-year-old boy could compare with my father on the dance floor. So . . . I think I was in love."

Motives Related to Development of the Self

Narcissistic needs— As a young girl, Dr. Glaser basked in the admiration of her parents, and her brother's birth represented an intense narcissistic injury. "I was most severely dethroned, and have always resented it. I was extremely jealous of him all my life, and as an adult I'm delighted that he is amounting to nothing."

On the day of her last scheduled session with her first therapist, Dr. Glaser was informed that he had suffered a heart attack and was in the hospital. A sense of omnipotence was triggered. "What a sense of power! I leave my therapist and he gets a heart attack. . . . The fantasy was that my absence was such a shock to him that he'd almost died."

As a therapist, Dr. Glaser initially felt that she was "invincible." One of the satisfactions she derives from doing therapy is "being brilliant," and she finds she has difficulty "holding myself back and letting them do the work."

Parental narcissism— Both as a child and as an adult, Dr. Glaser's parents responded to her as a narcissistic extension of their own selves. "I was the one who was successful and was held up to be admired. I went to college, moved to the city, married—all this reflected on the health and success of the family. Both of my parents made a big fuss when I got a new degree. They had it put in the newspaper. This always angered me because I felt that I'd succeeded *in spite of them,* and they would go and make it their own."

Diffuse identity— Shortly before entering her own treatment, Dr. Glaser recalls sitting in the cafeteria at school, feeling depressed. "I remember a friend came by and asked how I was doing. I said, 'I don't know, all the pieces are on the floor.' There was a real sense of fragmentation, like there was nothing that was holding my self together."

Motives Involving Object Relations

Conflicts concerning dependency— Dr. Glaser notes, "As a child I had an extremely dependent relationship with my mother. She didn't want me to play with other children. She was terrified that I would get sick, get dirty—that *something* would happen to me. So I hung around her a lot."

The following vignette illustrates the sense of deprivation that she experienced as a young child: "I remember going to the theatre to see a children's play with Snow White, and when I got home somebody had come and had taken away my pacifier. So I cried a lot. . . . The whole thing was a trick so that when I came back they could say 'you can't have it any more.'"

As an adolescent, she "did the expected flip-flop, and became fiercely, fiercely independent." This, however, meant incurring a great deal of guilt. "In our family, independence is not something that is encouraged. It means that you leave them. So when you *do* move away—which I did, and which meant putting an entire continent between us—you pay for it with heavy guilt."

As an adult, Dr. Glaser's dependency needs remained strong.

She was married for some time to a man "who was very much like my mother. He was somebody who also didn't want me to be independent. I needed him tremendously in order to get through my program, and we were both very dependent on one another."

Conflicts concerning separation— Separation difficulties contributed to her ambivalence regarding academic and professional achievement. "I cried and cried when I got the scholarship. Success meant that I would leave them. I came to the East Coast, but soon returned, I felt so damned guilty. How could you leave your parents and go into the big world?"

Dr. Glaser felt responsible for her mother's death: ". . . That if I'd been around, it would have been easier for her to deal with my father's death." Similarly, on a fantasy level, she felt responsible when she heard that her therapist had a heart attack just as she was leaving treatment.

Need for power and control— Regarding her interest in psychotherapy and the satisfactions she derives from practicing it, Dr. Glaser states, "I like to fix things and to make order out of chaos. . . . I get a real kick out of it when something I've suggested works, and I get very mad when it doesn't—the famous 'plop intervention,' where you hear it fall to the floor and die a quiet death."

Her initial experiences with clinical work proved frustrating. "I felt powerless to deal with their misery. . . . I lost my voice from screaming. I was very frustrated—people wouldn't do what I'd say." She later elaborates, "Well, I was a real good-deed doer. People lived such shitty lives. I thought I knew the answers, and that if I just told them, they'd get better. I think I was a very arrogant young woman who had a misunderstanding of how you help people. I had a real bulldozer technique—just move in and, by God, you'd better get well. I just felt I was invincible. Knowing so much psychology—it was great power. I think I was on a power trip and terribly frustrated when it didn't work."

When asked what she finds most difficult about practicing psychotherapy, Dr. Glaser replies, "Holding myself back. Giving the client the autonomy he or she deserves, but which is also necessary for any change to occur. My inclination is to take control, take charge, so I'm very good in crisis intervention. But the day-to-day plodding is the hardest, where it's *their* work, not mine, that's important."

Intimacy— Conflicts concerning intimacy are evident. "When I get close to people," she states, "I fear losing myself. I'm afraid they'll suck me in and I'll die. My parents were very devouring people—they never let go."

When Dr. Glaser returned to clinical practice after working in administration for several years, it was, in part, because she "became quite lonely. There was something missing—the richness of contact with others."

Need for reparation— There are indications in a number of Dr. Glaser's comments of strong reparative needs. She says, for example, "Oh, I have felt very heavy guilt. I was not a good daughter. . . . A good daughter would have stayed in the hometown, just around the block. She'd have become a secretary, married early, and had lots of kids. So when my mother died, I felt very bad. That if I'd been a good daughter she might not have died then. That if I'd been around it would've been easier for her to deal with my father's death. There wouldn't have been that emptiness."

The same theme emerges when she discusses what it was like to terminate with her first therapist. "Oh, it was terrible, just terrible. It ended with a big bang. I had my last session with him, and I'd brought some flowers. But the office was closed. I found out that he'd had a heart attack the night before, although it turned out not to be a real one. The last time I saw him was in the hospital, and it brought up the issue of having felt responsible for the death of my mother. And while I was there he was on a monitor, and his pulse kept going lower and lower. So I was really afraid of my destructiveness."

The need for reparation is also evident in Dr. Glaser's comment regarding the satisfactions she derives from practicing psychotherapy. "I like to repair things, or at least to give people the tools to repair what is broken, or twisted, or warped."

Therapist 8: Dr. Lucas

Dr. Lucas is a university-based clinical psychologist. He states that his first conscious interest in psychology developed while he was in the service, when he worked as a nurse in a psychiatric setting. Dealing with soldiers suffering from combat fatigue, Dr. Lucas became "fascinated with people's strange behaviors, and impressed that there could be such changes in an individual." His interest in psychotherapy derived from a mentor relationship with a psychiatrist, who also persuaded him to enter into analysis. This soon awakened "all the feelings, fears, and curiosities stirred up by my experience in the service, which had been put on hold and buried."

Dr. Lucas recalls that, in his childhood environment, "there were always some people around who were likable but 'crazy'—probably ambulatory schizophrenics." He remembers wondering about them as a child. "In hindsight, I went into psychology because I never satisfied my curiosity about those crazy individuals I came into contact with as a youngster, as well as the year-and-a-half I spent working as a nurse with psychotics."

Dr. Lucas had also seriously considered becoming a journalist; he thought briefly about medicine and, in particular, psychiatry. Currently, if he were not a psychologist, he feels that he might like to be a writer, a television commentator, or an historian.

Psychological Disturbances

While in his twenties, Dr. Lucas developed a mild phobia that disappeared after a brief course of treatment. Dr. Lucas also states that one of his unconscious motivations for entering the profession, which he discovered in his own analysis, was the "fear of going crazy." Over the years he has experienced "a definite blurring of the boundaries between what's normal and abnormal."

Family members— "Nothing in the sense of severe pathology— borderline at worst. My mother was a very needy, narcissistic person. My father was probably too passive for his own good."

Motives Related to Instincts

Conflicts concerning aggression— As a child, Dr. Lucas was confronted with a considerable amount of overt familial conflict, from which he typically withdrew. "Everybody screamed at everybody.

If it got too hot, somebody usually left. But I can remember a couple of times when a cop car showed up and took my parents away. . . . I generally kept out of it, unless it directly affected me. I never dared get involved in their fighting. I was almost, you know, under the table."

Given his father's basic passivity, Dr. Lucas lacked a strong model of well-modulated male aggression. It was his mother who made all of the decisions. "My father's role was to bring home the bacon. Everything else was in the hands of my mother." When they had fights, it was "usually my mother doing most of the yelling, and my father pretty much taking it." By the time he was 8 or 9, Dr. Lucas's father had "pretty much moved out of my life."

Motives Related to Development of the Self

Narcissistic needs— Omnipotent strivings are seen in Dr. Lucas's early expectations regarding the practice of psychotherapy. "I thought that it would be much more mysterious and magical. I thought that people were crazier than they really are, and I thought that they were curable more quickly."

One of the satisfactions that Dr. Lucas derives from doing therapy is "to feel that I am somebody very important to the patient." His own sense of self-esteem very much enters into the therapeutic process. When asked what he finds most difficult about practicing psychotherapy, he describes "a frequently felt sense of impotence, of inadequacy, when I can't make the connections, or when I make them and it doesn't help. I'm probably affected too negatively when progress doesn't occur."

Aggrandized ego-ideal— As a boy, Dr. Lucas held a special place in his family, but was constantly having to prove his worth. His mother called him her *goldena siegala* (golden triumph) and regarded him as the "center of the universe." Dr. Lucas states, "She *did* focus a lot of attention on me, but with a definite stipulation— that I *produce*. . . . I was the achiever, and was considered the brightest. This brought a certain amount of respect and admiration, but also a good deal of envy. From my mother, the best was expected of me, and nothing but the best was accepted. If I brought home ninety-nine A's and one B, I got yelled at for the B."

Parental narcissism— Dr. Lucas describes his mother as "a very narcissistic person. When I was a child she was basically a smothering but rejecting mother whose expectations I could never live up to." As an adult, he has a warm relationship with his mother, "because I no longer have to please her."

Maternal identification— Dr. Lucas was closest to his mother throughout his childhood, and tends to identify more with her than with his father. "I am much more like my mother, in terms of being more narcissistic, more desirous of being liked, and not nearly as passive or able to be so tolerant as my father."

Motives Involving Object Relations

Conflicts concerning dependency— Before the age of 3, Dr. Lucas contracted a series of infectious illnesses, resulting in approximately six months of hospitalization.

Dr. Lucas cites the "wish to feel needed" as the most common unconscious motivation of his colleagues. In regard to his own satisfactions in practicing psychotherapy, he states that "what I really enjoy—and I guess this is part of feeling needed—is seeing patients get better." Referring to potential difficulties this can create, he says, "I think I tend to have more difficulty than most analysts with countertransference. I tend to get too emotionally involved with patients."

Conflict concerning separation— Early maternal interference with separation and individuation can be inferred from the following comment: "From what I reconstructed in my analysis . . . my mother had a difficult time letting go of me as a kid. She was a very smothering person. But, by adolescence it was really a matter of my doing what I wanted. For all intents and purposes I had moved out of the house."

Concerning his father's reactions to his steps toward autonomy, Dr. Lucas states that "he couldn't have cared less." As an adolescent, Dr. Lucas "very quickly emancipated myself—although not psychologically. I had very little to do with home, and joined the service at 17. After that I had very little connection with my mother and avoided being home."

As a psychotherapist, Dr. Lucas terminates with clients "with difficulty." In order to deal with these difficulties, he has "almost developed a system—a somewhat rigid way of ending," in which he gradually phases out the visits. He comments, "But, paradoxically, once I stop seeing patients regularly, I really *do* put them out of my mind. Maybe that's why I do the six-month follow-up. It's as if I know I can only put them out of mind if I know they're coming back." Dr. Lucas states that he frequently calls to check up on patients whom he has not seen for years and views this as a part of his own countertransference.

Rescue fantasies and reparation— Guilt feelings toward his mother may reflect reparative needs that find fulfillment in the practice of psychotherapy. Dr. Lucas states, "I have felt guilt over how I treated my mother—when I just cut myself off from her, turned her off, and did things that were at least in part rebellious."

Rescue fantasies may have played a part in Dr. Lucas's decision to specialize in an area of clinical psychology that is directly related to an actual deficit of his father's.

Therapist 9: Dr. Moore

Dr. Moore is a psychiatrist in private practice. In college he was a biology major, with minors in English and philosophy. In medical school, Dr. Moore found that the psychiatry teachers were the best around, and he liked that "they weren't too medically oriented." Aside from psychiatry, he considered specializing in pathology and in internal medicine. He ruled the former out because he did not wish to do research, and he lost interest in the latter. Dr. Moore found that psychiatry provided a "nice wedding" of his various interests. Nevertheless, during his first ten years of practice, he repeatedly had the desire to return to pathology. Within the field of psychiatry, Dr. Moore found psychotherapy "more interesting than the biological stuff."

Psychological Disturbances

The most common unconscious motivation that Dr. Moore attributes to his colleagues is the wish "to solve their own problems," a motive that he feels he shares with most other therapists.

During his first year of medical school, Dr. Moore experienced "an outburst of obsessional symptoms and moderately severe depression." He felt that his violent temper was endangering his marriage. In retrospect, he views himself as "reenacting my father's narcissism—repeating his psychopathology."

Family members— When asked the question, "Who made up your family of origin?" Dr. Moore replied, while maintaining a straight face, "Probably Strindberg." Dr. Moore describes his mother as highly narcissistic and his father as openly sadistic. One of his earliest memories is of when he was 5 or 6, being "the only kid crying *on the way home* from camp." He states that his was "one of the most fucked-up families I've ever seen. That's why I can't do family therapy—it's too frightening. I just burrow under the seats."

Motives Related to Instincts

Conflicts concerning aggression— As an adolescent, Dr. Moore took his "enormous hatred" and "sublimated it into the idea of being a hit man." This became somewhat of an obsession at times. "I wanted to be a hit man for the Mafia—if I could have pulled it off I would have been a private killer. I just couldn't figure out how I'd get paid without getting knocked off. . . . This was a fantasy, but at times a preoccupation."

Within his family, Dr. Moore felt that he took the brunt of his father's violent temper. "I was the punching bag, the abuse bag for my father." When asked whether he had experienced fears of parental death, he replied, "very little of *parental* death. In fact, I would have enjoyed being a *party* to it." As an adult he continued to struggle with his own flare-ups of rage.

During adolescence Dr. Moore experienced strong desires to kill himself as well. Even as an adult he "finds the idea reassuring. I *will* commit suicide one day."

Reaction formation against aggression— Through reaction formations, some of Dr. Moore's anger and aggression was fended off and manifested as a fear of hurting others. Explaining his attraction to pathology as a medical specialty, Dr. Moore states, "The corpse was dead, and therefore not capable of being hurt or injured. I was extremely uncomfortable causing pain. Killing is one thing, causing pain is another. . . . I was always comfortable with dead bodies because you couldn't hurt them, and because they were so beautiful inside. This accounts for some of my interest in psychic structure."

Dr. Moore also learned to use his sense of humor to defuse aggression, and at one point considered becoming a stand-up comedian. Speaking of a humorous uncle, he notes, "I take after him. He was the negotiator between my parents. He used humor to keep them from killing each other—so do I."

Unresolved oedipal conflict— A family atmosphere in which the father is perceived as "very sadistic, cruel, physically violent, verbally abusive, and strangely masochistic in his submission to my mother," and the mother is seen as a "rapacious, overwhelming bitch," is unlikely to allow for a full resolution of oedipal concerns. Dr. Moore likens his early interactions with his father to a jousting match. "You carry her handkerchief into battle, and kill your father or sister or anyone who's her enemy. Then, forty years later, you realize that it was a mission impossible, and that she was sending you into battle against your friends."

During his twenties, guilt feelings and a fear of success interfered with Dr. Moore's academic progress. Through psychoanalysis, he states, he was able to resolve a great deal of his castration anxiety.

As a psychotherapist, Dr. Moore views himself as a "kind of antihero in action," perhaps reflecting enduring oedipal concerns.

Motives Related to Development of the Self

Narcissistic needs/Parental narcissism— Dr. Moore notes his family's emphasis upon appearances, which he feels was falsely maintained at all costs. "Inside the house it was monstrous. But everyone saw their *outside* selves, in which they projected the image of being capable and responsible. It was all a fraud. And so, later, I became interested in such existential concepts as 'bad faith' and 'betrayal of the self.'"

While both of Dr. Moore's parents are described as immature and self-serving, it is his mother who is presented as a portrait of narcissism. "She was highly neurotic and self-centered, and always threatening suicide in a grand style. I can't tell you what she was like in relation to *me* because she never really related to me. . . . My compassion decreased as the years went on. She was not mean, just extremely narcissistic."

Unlike many of the mothers of the therapists in the sample, Dr. Moore's mother apparently did not interfere with his attempts to gain autonomy. "My mother supported them, because she had no interest in me. . . . She didn't oppose it because she wasn't *with* me. She didn't want to be in my life. She wanted me to be with her in those rare cases that she needed to vomit *her* stuff up."

Aggrandized ego-ideal— "I was assigned the role of problem-solver and savior. I was to carry my mother's colors."

Motives Involving Object Relations

Conflicts concerning dependency— Dr. Moore's descriptions of his childhood history convey a strong sense of emotional deprivation. For instance, in reference to his mother, Dr. Moore states that "she was never a mother. She was *his wife*—that was clear. But I didn't feel much about her as a mother. . . . I have few memories of her. I'm not repressing—they're just *not there!*" He later states, "I wasn't a child; I was an adult. . . . I could either raise her or I could leave the house. I was the parent. When she was senile she actually called me 'daddy.' You could say it was senility, but that's what I was."

Dr. Moore's father had, as a child, been deserted by his own father, and, according to Dr. Moore, displaced his anger over this onto his son. As Dr. Moore took steps toward his own autonomy, "my father told me that if I *didn't* become independent, that was tough shit because he wasn't paying for anything." During his last year in high school, his father suffered a heart attack, largely breaking up the family unit.

Conflicts concerning separation— Dr. Moore contends that the biggest problem therapists have in terminating with clients is that "therapists were always parents in their family of origin. They struggle with terminations because they could never leave their *parents*." Concerning his own difficulties in this area, he states,

"Endings were always the hardest part of therapy for me—it appeared to me as *impossible*. I didn't know what constituted ending, and this had to do with boundary difficulties. . . . When I left my wife—that is, my mother—endings became easy and natural. I can say goodbye to people because I don't need them. I found that you *can* leave, can end with someone."

Need for power and control— One comment of Dr. Moore's conveys the sense of vulnerability and powerlessness that he experienced as a child. Referring to his mother, he states that "she wasn't intrusive, she was *invasive*."

Intimacy— In discussing his initial motivations for becoming a psychotherapist, Dr. Moore states that the profession provides "a format in which you could have a certain amount of emotional intimacy with people in a safe way."

Dr. Moore experienced little intimacy with his parents, and states that his marriage became a "substitute intimacy for my childhood." Certainly his parents' marriage failed to provide an adequate model of intimacy. Dr. Moore describes it as "stormy, violent, sadomasochistic—the 'Fifty-Five Years' War!'"

Rescue fantasies and reparation— Dr. Moore views the role he played in his family as that of "negotiator and mother-rescuer." His mother, who dramatically threatened to kill herself on numerous occasions, often burdened her young son with her own emotional difficulties. "As a child, I very much worried about and was taken with her problems. I kind of adored her."

Dr. Moore very literally envisions his professional activity as "rescue work." "I like the idea of helping people to find themselves, since most of the influences around them are toward destruction and not finding. Sometimes I think, romantically, that I'm kind of an antihero in action, saving people from their establishment burials. I feel like I'm in rescue work, saving corpses. As if I'm their last chance of stopping the perpetual burial of themselves."

Dr. Moore clearly links these motives and attitudes with his prototypical life role within his family of origin. "I help make people more comfortable with their insides—less anxious, less hurt. That's related to my 'assignment' in childhood to help save my mother, who was supposedly my father's victim—although, I learned only later, it was the other way around. So I think my motive is in part a reaction to having been a total failure in saving my mother. You could say I've always been a therapist, although unpaid for the first twenty years [laughs]." This passage also illustrates how closely related are rescue fantasies and reparative needs.

CONCLUSION

Because of the methodological weaknesses of this study, any conclusions to be drawn must be regarded as tentative in nature. The sample size was small, and no attempt was made to ensure that it is representative of the psychotherapy profession as a whole. Furthermore, it is not known whether therapists who volunteer to participate in such a study differ significantly from those who choose not to. Finally, as is true of nearly all of the studies reviewed, there are no control groups to which the subjects can be compared.

With these limitations acknowledged, the interview results nevertheless appear to be consistent with much of the literature that has been reviewed. The interview material provides additional support for the general hypothesis that an important determinant of the desire to practice psychotherapy involves the attempt to come to terms with one's own psychological conflicts. Furthermore, there are indications that nearly all of the specific unconscious motivations addressed in the literature review are present, to a greater or lesser degree, in this small sample of therapists. Finally, the results suggest that these unconscious motives might best be understood within the historical context of each therapist's early development and family dynamics.

8

CONCLUSIONS AND FURTHER REFLECTIONS

This volume presents a summary of the various unconscious factors that may contribute to the decision to become a psychotherapist. A review of the relevant literature reveals a broad consensus that, regardless of primary discipline, a major determinant of this career choice involves the wish to resolve one's own emotional problems. Those individuals who choose to become therapists typically manifest significant psychological conflicts of their own. When adequately understood and mastered, however, such difficulties may ultimately allow therapists to be of greater help to their clients. Those who have experienced and borne the scars of emotional pain appear to have an enhanced capacity to understand and to empathize with it in others.

Mental health professionals have been somewhat reluctant to acknowledge and to explore the satisfactions and gratifications that they derive from the clinical situation. A fuller understanding of the therapeutic process, however, requires that the psychodynamics of both participants be taken into account. The therapist's motivations and gratifications can be likened to the client's presenting problems. These are what initially impel each participant to engage in the therapeutic interaction.

Therapists' motives have been approached from vantage points that correspond to the predominant psychoanalytic models: Drive Theory, Self Theory, and Object Relations Theory.[1] There is clearly a good deal of overlap among these models. Nevertheless, they provide a means of dealing systematically with a complex question. In the brief summary that follows, the numerous citations that can be found in the body of the text are omitted.

First are those motives related to instinctual aims, both libidinal and aggressive. Libidinal strivings may be seen in voyeuristic and exhibitionistic tendencies, as well as in more direct attempts at sexual gratification. In the extreme, when fully desublimated, the latter may culminate in actual sexual relations between therapist and client. Aggressive strivings include sadistic and masochistic tendencies in the therapist. Sadistic impulses are typically transformed, via reaction formations, into a desire to heal and nurture. When particularly strong, this may result in an overzealous need to cure and to rescue clients. Sadistic impulses may also be expressed more or less directly in the therapeutic relationship, manifesting as conscious or unconscious attempts to deprive, frustrate, frighten, humiliate, punish, reject, or abandon clients, or to otherwise hinder their progress. Masochistic tendencies may also be involved in the choice of a vocation that can exert a high emotional toll on the practitioner. Just as some sadistic tendencies may be necessary in order for therapists to help their clients confront painful realities, a degree of masochism may allow therapists to function by making bearable the punishing aspects of their work.

In that the practice of psychotherapy requires intuition, empathy, nurturance, passivity, and other personal characteristics generally regarded in our culture as largely feminine, it may be that males who become therapists have not completely resolved their childhood oedipal conflicts. For some men, the role of psychotherapist appears to represent a continuing maternal identification, as well as a way of dealing with unconscious anxiety and guilt regarding aggressive and libidinal impulses. For female clinicians who have oedipally based conflicts concerning gender identification, the

---

[1] Aspects of Ego Psychology, a fourth theoretical framework, have been incorporated into these discussions.

practice of psychotherapy may offer a way to integrate masculine and feminine tendencies.

The second category includes motives stemming from the early development of the self. Strong narcissistic needs and wishes for magical omniscience and omnipotence can contribute to the desire to be a therapist. Clients' transferential love and admiration, as well as the therapist's position of authority and power, can provide potent narcissistic gratifications. Practitioners can make use of their clients as both mirroring and idealized selfobjects.

When parental narcissism is excessive, children may be burdened with unrealistically high expectations and ambitions. Such individuals develop inflated ego-ideals and may be drawn to a profession that allows for fantasies of perfection, omnipotence, and grandiosity. The narcissistically cathected child develops an exquisite sensitivity to the unconscious needs of others, providing the necessary empathic capacities for the practice of psychotherapy. The development of empathy may also be furthered by such factors as a strong maternal identification and an ego-identity that remains relatively diffuse. There is some evidence that each of these factors is rather common among psychotherapists.

The third category includes motives involving object relations. These motivations stem from conflicts regarding emotional relatedness. Therapists with strong dependency needs may form dependent relationships with their clients, or may gratify such wishes vicariously by providing clients with the care and nurturance that they themselves crave. Individuals with conflicts concerning psychological separation from love objects may derive from clinical work continuing opportunities to deal with the issues of symbiosis and differentiation. Yet others, with conflicts concerning intimacy, may view the therapeutic situation as providing them with human contact in a uniquely controlled and nonthreatening fashion.

The wish to exercise power and to control others can also contribute to the decision to become a therapist. Individuals who were excessively dominated by their parents may compensate for feelings of powerlessness by dominating and controlling their clients. Other therapists, misusing the therapeutic situation to re-create their own pathogenic pasts, may unconsciously attempt to drive their clients crazy. Unconscious rescue fantasies, frequently involving a depressive mother, may lead to the desire to come to the aid of those who are psychologically distressed. Finally, strong unconscious guilt feelings concerning aggression directed at love objects can result in reparative needs. Here the healing of others represents a symbolic attempt at restitution and atonement.

In defending his attempt to apply psychoanalytic concepts to an understanding of the personality of a genius, such as Leonardo da Vinci, Freud (1910a) writes that "there is no one so great as to be disgraced by being subject to the laws which govern both normal and pathological activity with equal cogency" (p. 63). The same can be said regarding the psychological functioning of the psychotherapist. It is by becoming aware of their unconscious motivations that therapists may overcome potential handicaps, and even transform them into therapeutic assets. As Freud (1910b) states elsewhere, "We have noticed that no psychoanalyst goes further than his own complexes and internal resistances permit" (p. 145). An encouraging aspect of the interview material presented in Chapter 7 is the degree to which these therapists appear to have become cognizant of motivations that were previously unconscious.

In conclusion, the decision to become a psychotherapist must be seen as involving the interplay of a multitude of factors. Each individual therapist presents a unique combination of underlying dynamics contributing to the desire to practice psychotherapy. Some determinants are healthy and promote the therapeutic process, while others are neurotic (or psychotic) and are potentially destructive of that process. These motives and personality patterns appear to be deeply rooted in the therapist's developmental past and the dynamics of the family of origin.

DANGERS OF DEFICIENT
SELF-KNOWLEDGE

It has perhaps been too readily assumed that when psychotherapy is not beneficial, it is nonetheless benign (Meares and Hobson 1977). The literature reviewed in Chapter 2 indicates that many individuals enter the field with moderate, and even severe, degrees of emotional disturbance, and that these difficulties may actually supply a good deal of the impetus for becoming a therapist. Many are apparently able, through personal treatment, to understand and resolve their own conflicts adequately. Logic would dictate, however, that others are not so fortunate.

A significant proportion of ordinary psychotherapy patients fails to make substantial progress in treatment—why should the success rate be appreciably higher when therapists are the patients? In fact, a review of the empirical literature on personal therapy in training found that between 15 and 40 percent of trainees report unsatisfactory outcomes or negative effects, a figure that is significantly higher than comparable estimates for ordinary psychotherapy patients (Macaskill 1988). In one study, therapists who had treated psychotherapy trainees were found to agree that the students' knowledge of psychology tended to increase resistance and thereby impede, rather than promote, treatment (Kaslow and Friedman 1984). Overall, one can only conclude that a significant number of therapists remain insufficiently aware of their own psychological functioning.

As Hammer (1972) notes, when psychotherapists remain overly defended against objectionable parts of themselves, including their motivations for practice, this insensitivity and unawareness tends to carry over into their relationships with clients. When this occurs, therapeutic progress may be hindered or even reversed. Indeed, in a review of studies relating therapists' levels of adjustment to treatment outcome, Fisher and Greenberg (1977) found consistent support for the notion that emotional disturbance in the therapist is antitherapeutic and potentially damaging to clients. This potential for harm is further extended when one takes into account that the very practice of psychotherapy and psychoanalysis may aggravate the emotional conflicts of some practitioners (Freudenberger and Robbins 1979, Wheelis 1959).

Maeder (1989) suggests that, for certain individuals, professional training provides a means of *avoiding* personal problems: "The wounded healer who might have healed himself and become better as a result, may take the route of the encapsulated wound, where his ultimate aim is to protect himself, and where his wounds grow forever invulnerable to cure" (p. 257). Through training, Maeder notes, such individuals may acquire an arsenal of defensive techniques and rationalizations for deflecting criticism and shifting blame, insulating them from underlying conflicts.

Therapists who have not come to terms with their own narcissism and grandiosity may fail to refer clients to other practitioners when that would be appropriate. Taking a one-answer-to-many-questions approach, they believe that their own brand of therapy is the treatment of choice for everyone who enters the office. When therapists discover and understand their motives for practice, they decrease the likelihood of choosing techniques and modalities on the basis of their own underlying needs, rather than in the best interests of their clients.

BURNOUT IN THERAPISTS

There are hidden dangers for therapists, as well as clients, when their motives remain unexplored. One of these potential hazards is that practitioners may be at greater risk for becoming burned out. The term *burnout* refers to the physical and emotional depletion, lowered performance, and indifferent attitude that can result from excessive job-related demands and stressors. Freudenberger (1974) is generally credited with being the first to apply this drug-culture term to health care professionals.

In his review of the literature on the topic, Guy (1987) cites a wide range of symptoms that have been associated with the burnout syndrome. Affective symptoms include anxiety, depression and despondency, loneliness, fearfulness, emotional exhaustion, helplessness, anger and irritability, feelings of guilt and self-doubt, as well as decreased concern for clients, emotional detachment, and a desire to withdraw from both clients and colleagues. Cognitive aspects can include attitudes of intolerance, inflexibility, closed-mindedness, defensiveness, cynicism, pessimism, depersonalization, boredom, omnipotence, suspicion, and even blatant paranoia. Behavioral features include decreased productivity, increased distractibility, aimlessness, and aggressive or contentious behaviors. Also noted are an increase in addictive and risk-taking behaviors, as well as proneness to accidents. Physical symptoms may include fatigue, exhaustion, sleep disturbance, muscle tension, and lowered resistance to disease. Problems with headaches, lower back pain, high blood pressure, asthma, allergies, weight gain, and gastrointestinal disturbances may develop or recur. Interpersonal conflicts, impaired capacity to communicate, and increasing social withdrawal are also common in professionals who are experiencing burnout.

There have been few studies concerning the incidence of burnout among psychotherapists. Reported results have ranged from approximately 6 percent (Farber 1985) to more than 32 percent (Wood et al. 1985), although the latter figure included therapists who acknowledged having experienced burnout *or depression* serious enough to interfere with work performance. Research on career dissatisfaction among therapists is also sparse and methodologically questionable. The figures reported, however, are quite consistent and must be considered rather alarming. Kelly and colleagues (1978) found, for example, that after twenty five years in the field, 46 percent of those surveyed expressed dissatisfaction with their careers in psychotherapy by indicating that they would not enter the field if they were to live their lives over again. Similar surveys by Prochaska and Norcross (1983) and by Walfish and colleagues (1985) produced virtually the same percentages. In addition, there exists a growing body of research indicating that clinical practice exerts a negative toll on the practitioner, particularly in the form of excessive anxiety, moderate depression, and emotional underinvolvement with family members (Bermak 1977, Cray and Cray 1977, Farber 1983, Looney et al. 1980).

What are the factors that contribute to dissatisfaction and burnout among clinicians? A profusion of determinants has been put forward in the literature. Farber (1983), for instance, suggests that burnout results when unrelenting stress and aversive features of clinical work overwhelm an individual's personal resources. Edelwich (1980) proposes that those in the helping professions are particularly vulnerable to burnout because of the following: high initial enthusiasm and aspirations, lack of criteria for measuring accomplishments, low pay, sexism (for females), inadequate funding and institutional support, inefficient use of resources, and high public visibility coupled with popular misunderstanding and suspicion. Roeske (1986) points to the inevitable conflict between the demands of the professional role and the need for personal gratification. Similarly, one study (Farber and Heifetz 1982) revealed that a majority of those psychotherapists who were interviewed attributed the occurrence of burnout to "non-reciprocated attentiveness, giving and responsibility demanded of the therapeutic relationship" (p. 295).

Certain attitudes within the profession itself help to create a climate in which burnout is more likely to occur. Jaffe (1986) addresses a number of these:

> First, the health professional is taught that his/her needs have no place in health work and that a competent health professional has learned to submerge all needs except an abstract desire to be helpful. Second, the professional's feelings are also considered not relevant and, when they erupt, are considered to get in the way of effective treatment. . . . Even among colleagues, the sharing of feelings or the presence of personal needs is taboo. Cynical detachment is the expectation. . . . The final nail on the coffin of the healer's feelings is the disinterest of colleagues and institutions in these processes and the lack of social support and validation for looking at these pressures. [pp. 196–197]

Unlike traditional shamans, modern-day healers are expected to be psychologically strong, robust, and stoical; those who become openly depressed or anxious are liable to be viewed by colleagues as somehow inferior or weak (Gilbert et al. 1989). As incongruous as it may seem, the profession that aims to assist people in accepting and coming to terms with their feelings and needs often fails to tolerate or to even acknowledge such human concerns in its practitioners.

While many of the factors contributing to the phenomenon of burnout derive from the nature of the profession and the cultural setting, the psychology of the individual practitioner also comes into play. Indeed, many of the unconscious motivations surveyed in the previous chapters can contribute to the development of the burnout syndrome when left unexamined and unrestrained. For example, therapists who use the clinical situation to obtain sexual gratification directly or indirectly are likely to experience guilt and lowered self-esteem (quite appropriately so, when such impulses have been acted upon), and to depersonalize clients. When unchecked, masochistic tendencies and reaction formations against aggression can leave the practitioner overextended and drained, and make the practice of psychotherapy more demanding and onerous than it need be. Excessive *expressions* of aggressive impulses, on the other hand, can also instill guilt feelings, and can produce an adversarial climate that takes its toll on both participants in the treatment process.

Extending this list to those motives involving the development of the self, therapists who base their personal or professional self-esteem upon clients' admiration, gratitude, or therapeutic progress will be subject to frequent and intense mood swings. Both as mirroring and idealized selfobjects, psychotherapy clients (or anyone else, for that matter) are likely to bestow repeated disappointments. Practitioners' hopes for realizing an aggrandized ego-ideal via the role of psychotherapist are doomed from the start: they can never be wise, loving, or powerful enough, and the illusion of a perfected self will be continually tarnished by negative transferences as well as the actual limitations of clinical technique. In short, the unrealistically high expectations of the internalized parents can never be successfully met, leading to a Sisyphean struggle that, left unanalyzed, can end only in depression or self-delusion. Excessive identity diffusion can also contribute to professional burnout. Empathy can only be therapeutically applied when the requisite loosening of ego-boundaries is *partial* and *transient*. Those individuals who overidentify with their clients will be less effective practitioners and will be more likely to become overwhelmed by the emotional pain they encounter on a daily basis, resulting in what Chessick (1978) refers to as a "full-blown case of anguish of the soul" (p. 6).

To complete this brief recapitulation, let us look at those motives involving object relations. Clinicians with reaction formations against dependent strivings, who are driven by the need to give to others, tend to do too much for their clients and do not attend sufficiently to their own needs. Moreover, they may undermine the treatment process by making their clients overly dependent on them, resulting in a low success rate. Similarly, therapists with excessive separation anxieties may unwittingly interfere with their clients' growth and individuation. In order to manage eventual separation, their clients may be forced to terminate in an abrupt or hostile manner, making a difficult aspect of the work even more painful, and perhaps exacerbating the therapist's fears of separation.

Practitioners who are excessively concerned with issues of power and control may find it increasingly difficult to be patient and accepting of clients, or to see things from the client's point of view. Unable to force total compliance, such therapists can become ever more frustrated and resentful. Socially isolated or inept individuals, who become therapists in search of intimacy, are also likely to be disappointed and unhappy. The clinical situation only provides one-way intimacy, and chronic exposure to this form of relating may further diminish the therapist's capacity for closeness with family members and friends. Finally, therapists who harbor unanalyzed rescue fantasies and reparative needs are also likely to feel that they can never do enough for their clients. Faced with the harsh realities of clinical work, their therapeutic zeal may sour and turn to cynicism and despair. Those clients whose difficulties persist or worsen will furnish unending sources of guilt and self-reproach.

Just *listing* this litany of therapeutic hazards and burnout-producing psychodynamics is almost enough to produce a degree of cynicism and despair. There are, however, preventive measures that may significantly decrease the risks and negative fallout associated with clinical practice. The remainder of this chapter shall focus on these various safeguards.

SELECTION OF TRAINEES

Storr (1980) makes the following comment about those individuals who are drawn to the practice of psychotherapy:

> I once had a conversation with the director of a monastery. "Everyone who comes to us," he said, "does so for the wrong reasons." The same is generally true of people who become psychotherapists. It is

> sometimes possible to persuade people to become psychotherapists who have not chosen the profession for their own personal reasons; but, for the most part, we have to put up with what we can get; namely, ourselves. [p. 165]

There clearly appears to be a selective process, operating on a largely unconscious basis, that determines who decides to enter the field. As Bugental (1964) notes, this fact can neither be viewed as altogether good, nor as altogether bad. It can only be accepted and worked with.

Although the pool of applicants to training programs is not subject to control, selection committees do have the opportunity to screen and to choose students from among those who apply. A full exploration of the personality characteristics that are desirable or undesirable in prospective therapists is beyond the scope of this book. In regard to the degree of acceptable psychopathology, it appears that individuals who are either overcome by personal problems, or else are totally unaware of possessing any, will be unsuitable for clinical practice. But as Ackerman (1949) warns, not everyone who has suffered and can identify with emotional suffering in others will be an effective therapist. These characteristics must be coupled with the following features: the capacity to control such identifications; the experience of having *learned* from one's own suffering, and thereby having matured; and the capacity for synthesizing pleasurable, as well as painful, life experiences. Extensive interviewing is clearly required in order to investigate such matters and to reach an adequate understanding of an applicant's motives for becoming a therapist. Psychological testing could prove invaluable to the selection process; it raises questions of validity and fairness, however, and may be seen by applicants as overly intrusive.

Selection committees can, of course, make mistakes. These errors are not irrevocable and should be faced as promptly and as tactfully as possible. It is certainly not fair to students to wait until they are years into a training program before informing them that they are unfit for clinical practice. It is unethical and irresponsible, on the other hand, to allow such individuals to obtain their degrees and become practitioners. A final point is that prospective trainees ought to be fully informed of the potential risks associated with training and practice in the field of psychotherapy.

PROFESSIONAL TRAINING

Most training programs do a fine job of teaching psychological theory and clinical skills. When it comes to the more personal and subjective aspects of psychotherapeutic work, however, they are typically lacking. As Basch (1980) declares:

> Our only instrument is our personality; and to pretend that we do not react as human beings while engaged in a task that embodies so many of our hopes, fears, wishes, and ambitions is to make the development of that personality into an effective instrument more difficult than it needs to be. [p. 5]

Training programs do little to encourage students to be open about their emotional struggles as trainees and as novice clinicians. Many of them recommend, or even require, that students engage in personal treatment. This is certainly an important part of training, but fails to provide the opportunity to share with, and to gain support from, peers and colleagues. By limiting self-disclosure to students' own individual therapy, we perpetuate a professional culture in which clinicians do not feel free to expose their vulnerabilities, doubts, or emotions. Support groups in which students can air feelings and share experiences could help humanize the training process.

Course work and class discussions tend to focus on such areas as clinical theory and technique, diagnosis, psychopathology, professional ethics, and so on. Only rarely do instructors broach topics related to the needs and motivations of practitioners or to the satisfactions and frustrations of clinical work. This omission appears to be a result of the institutionalization of the profession's "dedicated," "selfless" stance. Although it may spring from the best of intentions, there is no question that it does harm—both to trainees and, ultimately, to the clients who seek their help.

It is essential that trainees receive adequate exposure to the concepts of transference and countertransference. Even practitioners who are behaviorally, cognitively, or biologically oriented need to be aware of how these phenomena can shape and distort their interactions with clients. Clinical seminars should also include frank discussions of treatment failures. As Pfifferling (1986) notes, students can benefit from the willingness of faculty members to disclose their clinical errors, thereby modeling personal and professional humility.

It is also of great importance that training programs begin to address adequately the issue of therapist–patient sexual relations. The mental health professions can no longer afford to avoid this painful topic, suppressing it as incestuous families conceal their shameful secret. Students would do well to become familiar with Epstein and Simon's (1990) "Exploitation Index," a self-assessment questionnaire that is designed as an early-warning indicator of boundary violations in psychotherapy. Unfortunately, published research studies have yet to demonstrate that either education or personal therapy effectively reduces the incidence of sexual abuse of patients. Pope (1990), in fact, cites several studies in which these preventive measures were found to be *positively* correlated with tendencies to abuse. Nevertheless, informed practitioners are more likely to be alert to this issue and to support legislation aimed at criminalization of the act (as several states have already passed) or prohibiting perpetrators from continuing or resuming clinical practice.

In a paper entitled "Suicide and Psychiatric Education," Kelly (1973) makes a number of recommendations for reducing the number of breakdowns and suicides among psychiatry residents. In addition to some of the measures already addressed, he suggests: early and explicit discussion of suicidal thoughts and other stress reactions that may be experienced; periodic assessment of emotional status during training; participation in an intensive personal group; selective assignment to stressful clinical duties; prompt referral for treatment, preferably without financial burden to the trainee; and "anticipatory exploration of the heavy demands and relative isolation of private practice" (p. 467).

Finally, it may be useful to invite professionals who have suffered and overcome experiences of burnout to talk with trainees about this subject. When clinicians begin to falter under the strains of clinical practice, their colleagues and employing institutions too often recoil in fear and aversion, rather than provide the support and understanding that might help avert further impairment. It may be possible to alter such professionwide attitudes by familiarizing students with the issue early on in their training.

CLINICAL SUPERVISION

Supervisors are in a position to have enormous influence on how their trainees come to view clinical practice. Even more crucial than what is imparted didactically are the *attitudes* conveyed. Does the supervisor create a climate in which trainees feel safe enough to explore and to expose their motives, feelings, anxieties, and vulnerabilities? Does the supervisor convey expectations of compliance and of perfection, or does he encourage students to be active learners and to benefit from candid inquiry into difficulties and mistakes? Does the supervisor acknowledge that *therapists* have needs, and assist supervisees in determining which ones are acceptable and which may be detrimental to the treatment process? These and other attitudes, both explicit and covert, will contribute to the professional self-images that supervisees eventually acquire.

Supervisors can model an approach to the therapeutic interaction that values, rather than ignores, the therapist's subjective reactions. Reid (1977) delineates some key questions that therapists need to pose for themselves in handling countertransference issues:

> What am I feeling inside when I am with this person? Is the client doing something to activate these feelings? If I were to unleash my most impulsive response to this person, what would it be? Does this person resemble someone in my life? What role do I find myself playing with this person? [p. 606]

Students should be encouraged to discuss feelings that are uncomfortable or "forbidden," and supervisors ought to raise issues of sexual feelings and exploitation when appropriate (Averill et al.

1989). Trainees need to learn that they can treat neither clients they strongly dislike, nor those whom they like too much (Cooper 1986).

It is also important that trainees gain an understanding of their dispositional tendencies as helpers, and to learn how to compensate for these proclivities. Gilbert and colleagues (1989), for example, differentiate between two types of therapists: *facilitators* and *regulators*. Facilitators focus on affect and the inner life of patients, are oriented toward insight and exploration, and emphasize "being with" patients. In contrast, regulators focus on symptoms and problem-solving, and are oriented toward educating, modifying, and "doing to" patients. The authors insist that both of these styles are valid, and that problems emerge only when therapists adhere too rigidly to one model.

> Extreme facilitators run the risk of becoming "contaminated" by patients and thus being unable to maintain a helpful therapeutic distance. They may have difficulty in setting limits and are prone to overidentification with patients. Extreme regulators, however, do not make enough contact with patients and are prone to fail to provide a sufficiently trusting environment which will allow patients with deep shame-based disturbances of the self to express and work through these feelings. [p. 11]

Supervisors can help their students to recognize where they lie on such a spectrum and to make any necessary adjustments.

As is true of good psychotherapy, effective supervision creates a holding environment in which trainees can come to terms with their narcissistic injuries and gradually establish more secure and realistic self-images. As Lackie (1983) states, "Professional education requires a kind of loss of innocence, a giving up of goodness. We are not as good as we look; but forgiveness comes when we discover that we are not as bad as we feel" (p. 319). A degree of depression and narcissistic deflation is inevitable when beginning therapists are confronted with negative transferences, resistances, and hostile or indifferent patients who reject what they have to offer. Supervisors can promote growth and mastery by providing a context in which trainees can mourn the loss of their idealized professional aspirations.

As Brightman (1984-1985) argues, such a process can be disrupted when supervisors have not come to terms with their own grandiosity, and present themselves as all-knowing or lacking in the capacity for uncertainty. Indeed, the unconscious agenda of the *supervisor* is an important topic in its own right, and one that has been largely neglected. Langs (1979) notes the dearth of literature on the supervisor's countertransferences and expressions of psychopathology within the supervisory process. Teitlebaum (1990) also points to the reluctance on the part of many supervisors to look beyond the therapist's learning problems, and to consider their own teaching problems and the emotional sources from which they spring.

On an even more fundamental level, training programs need to reassess the ways in which supervision is provided. Clinical supervision is modeled on the traditional apprenticeship. Just as the young artist allies himself with a master painter, so the neophyte therapist attempts to learn the craft from a more experienced clinician. Yet, one wonders what sort of instruction the student of painting might receive were his apprenticeship subject to the same set of constraints with which psychotherapy trainees must struggle. He would get no glimpse of the master's artworks. Nor could he display his own paintings. All the young artist could do would be to describe the work-in-progress. He may report, for instance, "So then I added some indigo along the edge of the lake and highlighted it with cobalt." To which the master might reply: "Cobalt? What you need is *turquoise!*" Under such conditions, one would hardly be surprised to find many aspiring artists resorting to paint-by-numbers or even "wild sketching."

In short, new approaches to supervision need to be implemented, whereby students can more reliably demonstrate their work and view that of their supervisors. Family therapists seem to have taken the lead in this area, making wide use of such methods as role-playing, audio and video tape-recording, one-way mirrors, and live supervision. Group supervision can also be valuable, especially when risk-taking is promoted. Too often we are cowardly, holding back from the frank exploration and emotional honesty we expect of our patients. It may also be helpful if, early in training, students received instruction on how to make optimal use of supervision.

PERSONAL THERAPY

Although there is disagreement as to where supervisors should draw the line between supervision and therapy, all concur that this line must be drawn. Supervision is not the appropriate place for clinicians to become absorbed in deep and protracted explorations of their own psychodynamics. In order for trainees to deal adequately with their personal difficulties, as well as their motivations for practice, it is essential that they become involved in psychotherapeutic treatment. Personal therapy enables practitioners to identify and come to terms with their "ego-horror" (Reik 1948, p. 147) as well as their ego-ideal. It can help therapists develop greater flexibility of character and improve their capacity to tolerate ambivalence and uncertainty, all necessary attributes of effective practitioners. Moreover, as Roth (1987) notes, personal therapy furnishes the clinician with the conviction that the treatment works, providing "a deep well of faith and hope in an endeavor that is characterized by ongoing uncertainty, doubt, and self-questioning" (p. 6).

This notion, that personal treatment enhances the professional functioning of therapists, is not backed up by rigorous empirical research. The existing studies linking personal therapy with treatment outcome are inconclusive (Greenberg and Staller 1981). Nevertheless, surveys of psychotherapists consistently find that the majority report having received considerable personal and professional benefits from their treatment (Buckley et al. 1981, Norcross and Prochaska 1986, Norcross et al. 1988, Shapiro 1976). Further support also comes from single case reports, such as the following one from Felton's (1986) article, "The Psychotherapist as the Interminable Patient." She presents the case of a training and supervising analyst who had sought treatment at two critical junctures of her life: during her training because of conflicts in integrating her career with her marriage, and after several years of successful professional practice when self-analysis failed to resolve her headaches, depression, insomnia, and sexual dysfunction. The author writes:

She recognized this time that she had become depressed, in part, because of an overinvolvement and overidentifcation with her patients' problems. She discovered a gnawing sense of inadequacy from strong and overdetermined wishes to rescue them from their pain. Formal treatment enabled her to clarify her own attributes and conflicts. She became more conscious of how her own childhood and fantasy life had affected her motivations to become a psychotherapist and teacher. [p. 104]

Thus, for this therapist, personal treatment served both to diminish her own unconscious conflicts and to facilitate her work with clients.

As noted above, most training programs in psychotherapy and psychoanalysis require or strongly encourage trainees to enter into their own treatment. It is ironic that this prerequisite, if successfully carried out, could potentially alleviate the trainee's inner need to practice psychotherapy. Nielson (1954) alludes to this point when he makes the statement that the wish to be an analyst is actually a *resistance* in the training analysis. He explains, "If we were able to analyze it thoroughly, would that not make an end of further training? . . . Is it not very daring to contend that the result of a thorough analysis must be an analyst? Might not the opposite be the truth?" (p. 248).

Will therapists lose interest in the practice of psychotherapy if they fully resolve the unconscious conflicts that fuel that interest? Searles (1966) maintains that becoming aware of unconscious dynamics does not necessarily dissipate their motivating power. He suggests, for example, that it is pointless to attempt to rid oneself of omnipotent strivings. "Rather, we need to become more freely *aware* of our omnipotent strivings, which are never 'resolved' throughout life and which remain, indeed, our most priceless wellsprings of energy" (p. 322).

The possibility of the emergence of new motives must also be kept in mind. Whitaker and Malone (1953) suggest that therapists' professional experiences with clients and colleagues alter their original motivations and allow new motivations to develop, promoting the continuation of practice. They state: "Whatever the needs which originate the decision to become a psychotherapist, the process of development as a therapist carries him beyond them" (p. 145).

FINDING A BALANCE

As many authors have noted, the demands and strains of clinical practice make it imperative that therapists achieve some sort of balance in their lives. There are few individuals who are suited to spending all of their working hours in the practice of psychotherapy. Most therapists (and their clients) will benefit from a more varied approach, which may include other professional activities, such as teaching and supervision, writing, research, consultation, and administration, or other forms of clinical practice, such as biological treatments, biofeedback, and psychological testing.

Vaillant and colleagues (1972) astutely proclaim that "the care of other people rather than oneself is a superb form of adaptation—but only if the self is also cared for" (p. 375). It may appear rudimentary to state that therapists need to pay adequate attention to their personal lives. There is a great deal of evidence, however, that many practitioners consistently ignore this truism. The physical inactivity, relative passivity, and emotional deprivation that characterize the work of psychotherapists must be counterbalanced in their outside activities and involvements. It is essential that therapists enjoy a reasonable degree of interpersonal intimacy in their everyday lives, otherwise they will be more likely to seek it inappropriately in the clinical setting. In the words of Guggenbuhl-Craig (1971), "The important thing is the involvement, the joy and sorrow, the disappointment and surprise, which flows back and forth between people who love one another" (p. 151). Lack of time should not be an acceptable excuse for neglecting one's private life. As Gabbard and Menninger (1988) write in regard to physicians' marital difficulties:

> The demands of practice are a convenient rationalization. Physicians work long hours to deny dependency; to eradicate any trace of aggression or destructiveness that they fear others may suspect; to win the unconditional love and approval of colleagues, patients, and community; to maintain complete control; and to conquer the terror of death. It is not the demands of practice but the physician's compulsive character that wreaks havoc in the marriage. [p. 35]

Immersion in some form of creative activity may also be a vital factor in replenishing spirits and preventing burnout. In reference to traditional healers, Lommel (1967) writes: "Again and again the shaman has to free himself from a deep depression by a creative act. By action he has to bind the disintegrating elements of his psyche into a unity by means of a synthesis, a mysterious psychic activity" (p. 13). Involvement in such pursuits as music, poetry, dance, drawing, painting, photography, woodwork, and sculpture may help keep therapists sane and at peace with themselves.

Let us not forget that the practice of psychotherapy can itself be a creative endeavor, and one in which practitioners can grow and transform themselves. Menninger is one of the few psychoanalytic authors to suggest that the motivations for becoming a healer do not all derive from negative, conflictual sources. He writes:

> To assume that the positive is only a reaction to the negative is one of our professional psychiatric fallacies. There are positive motivations in the human spirit not born of fear and guilt and hate, but of life and love. . . . Healing is more than repairing, more than not destroying; it is creating. [1959, p. 495]

A balanced perspective is one in which both the positive and negative, the constructive and destructive are acknowledged.

BEYOND NOSTALGIA

The psychology of the psychotherapist is a rich and compelling topic, fraught with implications for the therapeutic process. The exploration of this subject, however, is not a purely intellectual enterprise. Indeed, it involves introspection of a sort that can be quite painful and disturbing. Most therapists possess a high degree of emotional investment in tending to the needs of others. Consequently, it can be narcissistically wounding to discover and to acknowledge the various ways in which their therapeutic efforts serve their own needs and hidden agendas. Not only does such inquiry raise doubts about the meaning and purpose of one's professional activity; it challenges core aspects of one's very personality and world view.

The therapeutic process typically subjects clients to a good deal of pain and anguish. Cherished illusions, untruths, and self-deceptions are successively cast off as the need for their protection subsides. Therapists have long been aware of the many ways in which their clients resist this process of change. Unfortunately, the ways in which therapists obstruct it are too often ignored or denied. Such concepts as objectivity, neutrality, and transference can enable clinicians to avoid the discomfort inherent in a mutually engaging and affectively charged therapeutic relationship.

Freud's metaphors of the analyst as blank screen, mirror, or surgeon provided useful guidelines for practitioners who were just learning to acknowledge and to appreciate intrapsychic phenomena. Today these analogies seem quaint and naive. Therapists may be forgiven if at times they look back wistfully on the days when the clinical focus was squarely on the client, and the psychodynamics of the therapist were largely overlooked. The clinical and conceptual simplicity of the one-person model of psychotherapy has long since vanished. For better or worse, the introduction of the concept of countertransference eventually opened up a Pandora's box that has irrevocably altered the face of psychoanalytic theory and technique.

Nostalgia aside, those of us who choose to practice psychotherapy can no longer afford not to explore our own motivations to heal. Our opening question to clients—"What brings you here?"— must be posed to ourselves as well. Granted, this does not come easily. And that is why it is best that the role of psychotherapist remain a calling, and not just a vocation.

APPENDIX

INTERVIEW QUESTIONS[1]

Vocational Choice

1. When and how did you first become interested in the field of psychology/psychiatry?
   a. Were there any particular people who stimulated this interest?
   b. Were there any particular experiences that stimulated this interest?
2. When and how did you first decide to become a psychotherapist?
   a. Were there any particular people who influenced this decision?
   b. Were there any particular experiences that influenced this decision?
3. What do you recall were your reasons at the time for wanting to become a therapist?

---

[1]Approximately one-half of the questions were derived from Henry and colleagues (1971/1973). The rest were constructed by this author.

4. What would you say now as you look back about what your motivations were?
5. What would you guess might be the most common unconscious motivation of your average colleague?
6. What alternative vocations had you considered entering?
7. What other occupations do you think you might find satisfying?

Experience as Therapist

8. How long have you practiced as a psychotherapist?
9. How would you characterize your theoretical orientation?
10. What do you find the most interesting about practicing psychotherapy?
11. What satisfactions do you derive from practicing psychotherapy?
12. What do you find the most difficult about practicing psychotherapy?
13. How do you experience the process of terminating with a patient?
14. How does the practice of psychotherapy differ from what you had envisioned it to be prior to entering the profession?

Experience as Patient

15. When and for what reason did you first enter your own therapeutic treatment?
16. Were you satisfied with the results?
17. How did you feel about your therapist?
18. What was it like to terminate treatment?
19. Were you aware of any continuing identification with your therapist?
20. Discuss any subsequent treatments along these dimensions.
21. What have you discovered in therapy or self-analysis concerning your unconscious motivations for becoming a therapist?

Family Background

22. Who made up your family of origin?
23. What are/were your parents' occupations?

24. Which parent played the more dominant role in the family?
25. How would you characterize your relationship with your mother/father:
    a. as a child?
    b. as an adolescent?
    c. as an adult?
26. How did your mother/father react to your moves toward independence?
27. What was the nature of your parents' relationship as you were growing up?
28. How were emotions dealt with in your family?
29. How well were you able to deal with family arguments and tensions?
30. Which parent were you closest to?
31. Which parent were you the most like?
32. How would you describe your relationships with your siblings during childhood, adolescence, and adulthood?
33. Were there any family disruptions due to:
    a. illness or death of family member?
    b. separation from parents?
34. Describe any psychological disturbances among family members.
35. What role(s) do you see yourself as having played within your family?

Personal Development

36. What are your earliest memories?
37. Do you have any childhood memories that you would consider relevant to your eventual choice of vocation?
38. What were you like as a child?
39. How would you characterize your relationships with same sex and opposite sex peers during childhood?
40. What were you like as an adolescent?
41. Describe your relationships as an adolescent.
42. What are your religious background and present beliefs?
43. As you were growing up, to what degree did you experience a fear of death? Of parental death?
44. To what extent have feelings of guilt played a part in your life?

Current Personal Life

45. Are you currently married or intimate with someone?
    a. How would you describe your spouse/lover?
    b. How would you characterize your relationship?
46. If you have children, discuss your relationships with them.
47. Describe your social life and the nature of your current friend-ships.
48. Describe any interests and hobbies.

REFERENCES

Ackerman, N. W. (1949). The training of case workers in psychotherapy. *American Journal of Orthopsychiatry* 19:14-24.

Adler, G. (1972). Helplessness in the helpers. *British Journal of Medical Psychology* 45:315-326.

—— (1985). *Borderline Psychopathology and Its Treatment*. New York: Jason Aronson.

Apfel, R. J., and Simon, B. (1986). Sexualized therapy: causes and consequences. In *Sexual Exploitation of Patients by Health Professionals*, ed. A. W. Burgess and C. R. Hartman, pp. 143-151. New York: Praeger.

Averill, S. C., Beale, D., Benfer, B., Collins, D. T., Kennedy, L., Meyers, J., Pope, D., Rosen, I., and Zoble, E. (1989). Preventing staff-patient sexual relationships. *Bulletin of the Menninger Clinic* 53:384-393.

Azorin, L. A. (1957). The analyst's personal equation. *American Journal of Psychoanalysis* 17:34-38.

Bandura, A., Lipner, D. H., and Miller, P. E. (1960). Psychotherapists' approach-avoidance reaction to patients' expressions of hostility. *Journal of Consulting Psychology* 24:1-8.

Barnes, M., and Berke, J. (1971). *Mary Barnes: Two Accounts of a Journey Through Madness*. New York: Ballantine Books.

Basch, M. F. (1980). *Doing Psychotherapy*. New York: Basic Books.

Bates, C. M., and Brodsky, A. M. (1989). *Sex in the Therapy Hour: A Case of Professional Incest*. New York: Guilford.

Beattie, J. (1978). Observations on post-natal depression, and a suggestion for its prevention. *International Journal of Social Psychiatry* 24:247–249.

Berger, L. (1974). *From Instinct to Identity*. Englewood Cliffs, NJ: Prentice-Hall.

Bermak, G. E. (1977). Do psychiatrists have special emotional problems? *American Journal of Psychoanalysis* 37:141–146.

Bion, W. (1962). *Learning from Experience*. New York: Basic Books.

Blumenstein, H. (1986). Maintaining a family focus: underlying issues and challenges. *Clinical Social Work Journal* 14:238–249.

Borys, D. S., and Pope, K. S. (1989). Dual relationships between therapist and client: a national survey of psychologists, psychiatrists, and social workers. *Professional Psychology: Research and Practice* 20:283–293.

Boswell, J. (1791). *Life of Johnson*. New York: Doubleday, 1946.

Bouhoutsos, J., Holroyd, J., Lerman, H., Forer, B., and Greenberg, M. (1983). Sexual intimacy between psychotherapists and patients. *Professional Psychology* 14:185–196.

Bowen, M. (1976). Theory in the practice of psychotherapy. In *Family Therapy: Theory and Practice*, ed. P. J. Guerin, pp. 41–90. New York: Gardner Press.

Boxley, R., Drew, C. R., and Rangel, D. M. (1986). Clinical trainee impairment in APA approved internship programs. *Clinical Psychologist* 39:49–52.

Brenner, C. (1974). *An elementary textbook of psychoanalysis*. Rev. ed. New York: Anchor Books.

Brightman, B. K. (1984–1985). Narcissistic issues in the training of the psychotherapist. *International Journal of Psychoanalytic Psychotherapy* 10:293–317.

Brodsky, A. M. (1989). Sex between patient and therapist: psychology's data and response. In *Sexual Exploitation in Professional Relationships*, ed. G. O. Gabbard, pp. 35–37. Washington, DC: American Psychiatric Press.

Bucher, B., and Lovaas, O. I. (1968). Use of aversive stimulation in behavior modification. In *Miami Symposium on the Prediction of Behavior, 1967: Aversive Stimulation*, ed. M. R. Jones, pp. 77–145. Coral Gables, FL: University of Miami Press.

Buckley, P., Karasu, T. B., and Charles, E. (1981). Psychotherapists view their personal therapy. *Psychotherapy: Theory, Research and Practice* 18:299–305.

Bugental, J. (1964). The person who is the therapist. *Journal of Consulting Psychology* 28:272–277.

Buie, D. H. (1982-1983). The abandoned therapist. *International Journal of Psychoanalytic Psychotherapy* 9:227-231.

Burnside, M. (1986). Fee practices of male and female therapists. In *The Last Taboo: Money as Symbol and Reality in Psychotherapy*, ed. D. Kruger, pp. 48-54. New York: Brunner/Mazel.

Burton, A. (1970). The adoration of the patient and its disillusionment. *American Journal of Psychoanalysis* 29:194-204.

———, ed. (1972). *Twelve Therapists*. San Francisco: Jossey-Bass.

——— (1975). Therapist satisfaction. *American Journal of Psychoanalysis* 35:115-122.

Butler, S., and Zelen, S. L. (1977). Sexual intimacies between therapists and patients. *Psychotherapy: Theory, Research and Practice* 14:139-145.

Carey, A. (1977). Relationships of psychotherapists' personality and therapy methods. *Dissertation Abstracts International* 38:1392-1393.

Chaplin, J. (1989). Rhythm and blues. In *On Becoming a Psychotherapist*, ed. W. Dryden and L. Spurling, pp. 169-188. New York: Tavistock/Routledge.

Chessick, R. D. (1978). The sad soul of the psychiatrist. *Bulletin of the Menninger Clinic* 42:1-9.

Chodorow, N. (1978). *The Reproduction of Mothering: Psychoanalysis and the Sociology of Gender*. Berkeley, CA: University of California Press.

Christie, R., and Geis, F. L., eds. (1970). *Studies in Machiavellianism*. New York: Academic Press.

Chwast, J. (1978). Personality and opportunity in psychotherapist's choice of theoretical orientation or practice. *Psychotherapy: Theory, Research and Practice* 15:375-381.

Claman, J. M. (1987). Mirror hunger in the psychodynamics of sexually abusing therapists. *American Journal of Psychoanalysis* 47:35-40.

Collins, D. T. (1989). Sexual involvement between psychiatric hospital staff and their patients. In *Sexual Exploitation in Professional Relationships*, ed. G. O. Gabbard, pp. 151-162. Washington, DC: American Psychiatric Press.

Condit, P. (1987). The analyst as parent. *Current Issues in Psychoanalytic Practice* 4:67-74.

Cooper, A. (1986). Some limitations on therapeutic effectiveness: the "burnout syndrome" in psychoanalysis. *Psychoanalytic Quarterly* 55:576-598.

Cooper, D. (1967). *Psychiatry and Anti-Psychiatry*. London: Tavistock Publications.

Cray, C., and Cray, M. (1977). Stresses and rewards within the psychiatrist's family. *American Journal of Psychoanalysis* 37:337–341.

Cunningham, S. (1985). Rollo May: the case for love, beauty and the humanities. *APA Monitor* 16:17.

D'Addario, L. (1977). *Sexual relations between female clients and male therapists.* Unpublished doctoral dissertation. Los Angeles: California School of Professional Psychology.

Dahlberg, C. C. (1970). Sexual contact between patient and therapist. *Contemporary Psychoanalysis* 6:107–124.

Darley, J. M., Glucksberg, S., and Kinchla, R. A. (1981). *Psychology.* Englewood Cliffs, NJ: Prentice-Hall.

Deutsch, C. J. (1984). Self-reported sources of stress among psychotherapists. *Professional Psychology: Research & Practice* 15:833–845.

—— (1985). A survey of therapists' personal problems and treatment. *Professional Psychology: Research & Practice* 16:305–315.

Donnay-Richelle, J. (1971). The personality of the psychiatrist and its importance in his choice of profession. *Feuillets Psychiatriques de Liege* 4:551–575.

Donnay-Richelle, J., Timsit, M., and Dongier, M. (1972). Study of the deep motivations of vocational choice in psychiatry candidates and students in psychology. *Acta Psychiatrica Belgica* 72:345–365.

Dryden, W., and Spurling, L., eds. (1989). *On Becoming a Psychotherapist.* London: Routledge.

Eagle, P. F., and Marcos, L. R. (1980). Factors in medical students' choice of psychiatry. *American Journal of Psychiatry* 137:423–427.

Eber, M., and Kunz, L. B. (1984). The desire to help others. *Bulletin of the Menninger Clinic* 48:125–140.

Edelwich, J. (1980). *Burn-Out: Stages of Disillusionment in the Helping Professions.* New York: Human Sciences Press.

Eidelberg, L. (1968). *Encyclopedia of Psychoanalysis.* New York: Free Press.

Eisendorfer, A. (1959). The selection of candidates applying for psychoanalytic training. *Psychoanalytic Quarterly* 28:374–378.

Eissler, K. R. (1952). Remarks on the psychoanalysis of schizophrenics. In *Psychotherapy with Schizophrenics,* ed. E. B. Brody and F. C. Redlich, pp. 130–167. New York: International Universities Press.

Eliade, M. (1964). *Shamanism, Archaic Techniques of Ecstasy.* Princeton, NJ: Bollingen Series.

Elliot, G. P. (1974). Buried envy. *Harper's,* July, pp. 12, 14–18.

Ellis, A. (1972). Psychotherapy without tears. In *Twelve Therapists,* ed. A. Burton, pp. 103–126. San Francisco: Jossey-Bass.

—— (1978). Personality characteristics of rational-emotive therapists and other kinds of therapists. *Psychotherapy: Theory, Research and Practice* 15:329–332.

English, F. (1977). What is a good therapist? *Transactional Analysis Journal* 7:149–155.

Ephross, P. H. (1983). Giving up martyrdom. *Public Welfare* 41:27–33.

Epstein, L. (1983). The therapeutic function of hate in the countertransference. In *Countertransference: The Therapist's Contribution to the Therapeutic Situation*, ed. L. Epstein and A. H. Ferner, pp. 213–234. New York: Jason Aronson.

Epstein, R. S., and Simon, R. I. (1990). The exploitation index: an early warning indicator of boundary violations in psychotherapy. *Bulletin of the Menninger Clinic* 54:450–465.

Farber, B. A. (1983). Dysfunctional aspects of the psychotherapeutic role. In *Stress and Burnout in the Human Service Professions*, ed. B. A. Farber, pp. 97–118. New York: Pergamon.

—— (1985). Clinical psychologists' perceptions of psychotherapeutic work. *Clinical Psychologist* 38:10–13.

Farber, B. A., and Heifetz, L. J. (1981). The satisfactions and stresses of psychotherapeutic work: a factor analytic study. *Professional Psychology* 12:221–230.

—— (1982). The process and dimensions of burnout in psychotherapists. *Professional Psychology* 13:293–301.

Farber, L. H. (1966). *The Ways of the Will.* New York: Basic Books.

Feldman, M. J. (1955). The use of obscene words in the therapeutic relationship. *American Journal of Psychoanalysis* 15:45–48.

Feldman-Summers, S., and Jones, G. (1984). Psychological impacts of sexual contact between therapists or other health care practitioners and their clients. *Journal of Consulting and Clinical Psychology* 52:1054–1061.

Felton, J. R. (1986). The psychotherapist as the interminable patient. *Psychotherapy Patient* 3:101–110.

Fenichel, O. (1980). Theoretical implications of the didactic analysis. *Annals of Psychoanalysis* 8:21–34.

Ferenczi, S. (1988). *The Clinical Diary of Sandor Ferenczi.* Trans. J. Dupont. Cambridge, MA: Harvard University Press.

Fieldsteel, N. D. (1989). Analysts' expressed attitudes toward dealing with death and illness. *Contemporary Psychoanalysis* 25:427–432.

Fine, R. (1983). *Psychoanalytic Psychology.* New York: Jason Aronson.

Finell, J. S. (1985). Narcissistic problems in analysts. *International Journal of Psycho-Analysis* 66:433–445.

Fisher, K. A. (1969). Motivation of the therapist. *Voices* 5:88–98.

Fisher, S., and Greenberg, R. P. (1987). *The Scientific Credibility of Freud's Theory and Therapy*. New York: Basic Books.

Ford, E. S. C. (1963). Being and becoming a psychotherapist: the search for identity. *American Journal of Psychotherapy* 17:472–482.

Frank, H., and Paris, J. (1987). Psychological factors in the choice of psychiatry as a career. *Canadian Journal of Psychiatry* 32:118–122.

Frederickson, J. (1990). Hate in the countertransference as an empathic position. *Contemporary Psychoanalysis* 26:479–496.

Freud, S. (1900). *The Interpretation of Dreams. Standard Edition* 4/5.

—— (1901). The psychopathology of everyday life. *Standard Edition* 6:1–296.

—— (1905a). Fragment of an analysis of a case of hysteria. *Standard Edition* 7:1–122.

—— (1905b). On psychotherapy. *Standard Edition* 7:257–268.

—— (1910a). Leonardo da Vinci and a memory of his childhood. *Standard Edition* 11:59–137.

—— (1910b). The future prospects of psychoanalytic therapy. *Standard Edition* 11:141–151.

—— (1912). Recommendations to physicians practicing psychoanalysis. *Standard Edition* 12:111–120.

—— (1914). On narcissism. *Standard Edition* 14:67–102.

—— (1918). Lines of advance in psycho-analytic therapy. *Standard Edition* 17:157–168.

—— (1920). Beyond the pleasure principle. *Standard Edition* 18:27–143.

—— (1924). The dissolution of the Oedipus complex. *Standard Edition* 21:223–243.

—— (1926). The question of lay analysis. *Standard Edition* 20:179–258.

—— (1930). Civilization and its discontents. *Standard Edition* 21:64–145.

—— (1933). New introductory lectures on psycho-analysis. *Standard Edition* 22:1–182.

—— (1937). Analysis terminable and interminable. *Standard Edition* 23:209–253.

—— (1938). An outline of psychoanalysis. *Standard Edition* 23:139–207.

Freudenberger, H. J. (1974). Staff burnout. *Journal of Social Issues* 30:159–165.

Freudenberger, H. J., and Robbins, A. (1979). The hazards of being a psychoanalyst. *Psychoanalytic Review* 66:275–296.

Gabbard, G. O., ed. (1989). *Sexual Exploitation in Professional Relationships*. Washington, DC: American Psychiatric Press.

————— (1991). The psychodynamics of sexual boundary violations. *Psychiatric Annals*.

Gabbard, G. O., and Menninger, R. W., eds. (1988). *Medical Marriages*. Washington, DC: American Psychiatric Press.

Galinsky, M. D. (1962). Personality development and vocational choice of clinical psychologists and physicists. *Journal of Counseling Psychology* 9:299–305.

Garetz, F. K., Raths, O. N., and Morse, R. H. (1976). The disturbed and the disturbing psychiatric resident. *Archives of General Psychiatry* 33:446–447.

Garfinkel, P. E., and Waring, E. M. (1981). Personality, interests, and emotional disturbance in psychiatric residents. *American Journal of Psychiatry* 138:51–55.

Gartrell, N., Herman, J., Olarte, J., et al. (1986). Psychiatrist–patient sexual contact: results of a national survey. *American Journal of Psychiatry* 143:1126–1131.

Gechtman, L. (1989). Sexual contact between social workers and their clients. In *Sexual Exploitation in Professional Relationships*, ed. G. O. Gabbard, pp. 27–38. Washington, DC: American Psychiatric Press.

Gechtman, L., and Bouhoutsos, J. C. (1985). *Social workers' attitudes and practices regarding erotic and nonerotic physical contact with their clients*. Paper presented at the annual conference of the California Society for Clinical Social Work, Universal City, CA, October.

Gilberg, A. L. (1977). Reflections on being a psychoanalyst. *American Journal of Psychoanalysis* 37:83–84.

Gilbert, P., Hughes, W., and Dryden, W. (1989). The therapist as a crucial variable in psychotherapy. In *On Becoming a Psychotherapist*, ed. W. Dryden and L. Spurling, pp. 3–13. London: Routledge.

Gill, M. M. (1982). *Analysis of Transference*. Vol. 1. New York: International Universities Press.

Gill, M. M., and Brenman, M. (1959). *Hypnosis and Related States*. New York: International Universities Press.

Gitelson, M. (1952). The emotional position of the analyst in the psychoanalytic situation. *International Journal of Psycho-Analysis* 9:1–16.

————— (1973). *Psychoanalysis: Science and Profession*. New York: International Universities Press.

Glauber, I. P. (1953). A deterrent in the study and practice of medicine. *Psychoanalytic Quarterly* 22:381–412.

Glover, E. (1929). The psychology of the psychotherapist. *British Journal of Medical Psychology* 9:1–16.

Goldberg, C. (1986). *On Being a Psychotherapist: The Journey of the Healer*. New York: Gardner Press.

Greben, S. E. (1975). Some difficulties and satisfactions inherent in the practice of psychoanalysis. *International Journal of Psycho-Analysis* 56:427–434.

Greenacre, P. (1961). A critical digest of the literature on selection of candidates for psychoanalytic training. *Psychoanalytic Quarterly* 30:28–55.

Greenberg, J. R., and Mitchell, S. A. (1983). *Object Relations in Psychoanalytic Theory*. Cambridge, MA: Harvard University Press.

Greenberg, R. P., and Staller, J. (1981). Personal therapy for therapists. *American Journal of Psychiatry* 138:1467–1471.

Greenson, R. R. (1962). That "impossible" profession. *Journal of the American Psychoanalytic Association* 14:9–27.

—— (1967). *The Technique and Practice of Psychoanalysis*. New York: International Universities Press.

Greenwald, D. (1976). Personality characteristics of clinical psychology applicants and graduate students. *Dissertation Abstracts International* 37:3074–3075.

Greif, A. C. (1985). Masochism in the therapist. *Psychoanalytic Review* 72:491–501.

Grey, A. L. (1988). Work role and private self. *Contemporary Psychoanalysis* 24:484–497.

Groddeck, G. (1928). Some fundamental thoughts on psychotherapy. In *The Meaning of Illness*, vol. 2, ed. G. Groddeck, pp. 211–221. New York: International Universities Press, 1977.

Groesbeck, C. J., and Taylor, B. (1977). The psychiatrist as wounded physician. *American Journal of Psychoanalysis* 37:131–139.

Guggenbuhl-Craig, A. (1971). *Power in the Helping Professions*. Irving, TX: Spring Publications.

Guntrip, H. (1975). My experience of analysis with Fairbairn and Winnicott. *International Journal of Psycho-Analysis* 2:145–156.

Gutheil, T. G. (1989). Borderline personality disorder, boundary violations, and patient–therapist sex: medicolegal pitfalls. *American Journal of Psychiatry* 146:597–602.

Guy, J. D. (1987). *The Personal Life of the Psychotherapist*. New York: Wiley & Sons.

Guy, J. D., and Liaboe, G. P. (1985). Suicide among psychotherapists: review and discussion. *Professional Psychology: Research & Practice* 16:470–472.

Hafner, J. L., and Fakouri, M. E. (1984a). Early recollections and vocational choice. *Individual Psychology: Journal of Adlerian Theory, Research, and Practice* 40:54–60.

—— (1984b). Early recollections of individuals preparing for careers in clinical psychology, dentistry, and law. *Journal of Vocational Behavior* 24:236–241.

Hammer, M. (1972). *The Theory and Practice of Psychotherapy with Specific Disorders.* Springfield, IL: Charles C Thomas.

Harris, B. M. (1976). Recalled childhood experiences of effective child psychotherapists. *Dissertation Abstracts International* 36:3607.

Hawke, C. C. (1950). Castration and sex crimes. *American Journal of Mental Deficiency* 55:220–226.

Heimann, P. (1950). Dynamics of transference interpretation. *International Journal of Psycho-Analysis* 37:303–310.

Henry, W. E. (1966). Some observations on the lives of healers. *Human Development* 9:47–56.

Henry, W. E., Sims, J. H., and Spray, S. L. (1971). *The Fifth Profession: Becoming a Psychotherapist.* San Francisco: Jossey-Bass.

—— (1973). *Public and Private Lives of Psychotherapists.* San Francisco: Jossey-Bass.

Hiatt, H. (1965). The problem of termination of psychotherapy. *American Journal of Psychotherapy* 19:607–615.

Hinze, E. (1987). Transference and countertransference in the psychoanalytic treatment of older patients. *International Review of Psycho-Analysis* 14:465–474.

Holroyd, J. C., and Brodsky, A. M. (1977). Psychologists' attitudes and practices regarding erotic and nonerotic physical contact with patients. *American Psychologist* 32:843–849.

—— (1980). Does touching patients lead to sexual intercourse? *Professional Psychology* 11:807–811.

Holt, R. R., ed. (1971). *New Horizons for Psychotherapy.* New York: International Universities Press.

Holt, R. R., and Luborsky, L. (1958a). *Personality Patterns of Psychiatrists: A Study of Methods for Selecting Residents.* Vol. 1. New York: Basic Books.

—— (1958b). *Personality Patterns of Psychiatrists: A Study of Methods for Selecting Residents.* Vol. 2. New York: Basic Books.

Horner, A. J. (1990). From idealization to ideal—from attachment to identification: the female analyst and the female patient. *Journal of the American Academy of Psychoanalysis* 18:223–232.

Imber, R. R. (1990). The avoidance of countertransference awareness in a pregnant analyst. *Contemporary Psychoanalysis* 26:223–236.

Issacharoff, A. (1983). Barriers to knowing. In *Countertransference: The Therapist's Contribution to the Therapeutic Situation*, ed. L. Epstein and A. H. Feiner, pp. 27–44. New York: Jason Aronson.

Issacharoff, A., and Hunt, W. (1983). Beyond countertransference. In *Countertransference: The Therapist's Contribution to the Therapeutic Situation*, ed. L. Epstein and A. H. Feiner, pp. 147–168. New York: Jason Aronson.

Jaffe, D. S. (1986). Empathy, counteridentification, countertransference: a review with some personal perspectives on the "analytic instrument." *Psychoanalytic Quarterly* 55:215–243.

Jaffe, D. T. (1986). The inner strains of healing work: therapy and self-renewal for health professionals. In *Heal Thyself: The Health of Health Care Professionals*, ed. C. D. Scott and J. Hawk, pp. 194–205. New York: Brunner/Mazel.

Jones, E. (1913). The God Complex. In *Essays in Applied Psychoanalysis* 2:244–265. London: Hogarth Press, 1951.

—— (1957). *The Life and Work of Sigmund Freud*. New York: Basic Books.

Jung, C. G. (1934). Civilization in transition: The state of psychotherapy today. In *Collected Works*, vol. 10, pp. 157–173. Princeton, NJ: Princeton University Press, 1964.

—— (1946). The psychology of the transference. In *Collected Works*, vol. 16 ed., pp. 163–323. Princeton, NJ: Princeton University Press, 1966.

Kafka, H. (1989). Keeping the passion in a long-term analysis. *Contemporary Psychoanalysis* 25:283–309.

Kagan, J. (1984). Acquisition and significance of sex-typing and sex-role identity. In *Review of Child Development Research*, vol. 1, ed. M. L. Hoffman and I. W. Hoffman, pp. 137–168. New York: Russell Sage Foundation.

Kaplan, A. G. (1979). Toward an analysis of sex-role related issues in the therapeutic relationship. *Psychiatry* 42:112–120.

Kardener, S. H. (1974). Sex and the physician–patient relationship. *American Journal of Psychiatry* 131:1134–1136.

Kardener, S. H., Fuller, M., and Mensh, I. (1973). A survey of physicians' attitudes and practices regarding erotic and nonerotic physical contact with patients. *American Journal of Psychiatry* 130:1077–1081.

Kaslow, N. J., and Friedman, D. (1984). The interface of personal treatment and clinical training for psychotherapist trainees. In *Psychotherapy with Psychotherapists*, ed. F. W. Kaslow, pp. 33–57. New York: Haworth Press.

Kasper, A. M. (1959). The doctor and death. In *The Meaning of Death*, ed. H. Feifel, pp. 259–270. New York: McGraw-Hill.

Kauff, P. F. (1977). The termination process: its relationship to the separation–individuation phase of development. *The International Journal of Group Psychotherapy* 28:3–18.

Keller, U., and Schneider, R. (1976). Specific problems in the initial phase of psychoanalytic training. *Dynamische Psychiatrie* 9:12–39.

Kelly, E. L., and Fiske, D. W. (1950). The prediction of success in the VA training program in clinical psychology. *American Psychologist* 5:395–406.

Kelly, E. L., Goldberg, L. R., Fiske, D. W., and Kilkowski, J. M. (1978). Twenty-five years later: a follow-up study of graduate students in clinical psychology assessed in the VA selection research project. *American Psychologist* 33:746–755.

Kelly, W. A. (1973). Suicide and psychiatric education. *American Journal of Psychiatry* 130:463–468.

Kernberg, O. K. (1967). Borderline personality organization. *Journal of the American Psychoanalytic Association* 15:641–685.

—— (1975). *Borderline Conditions and Pathological Narcissism*. New York: Jason Aronson.

—— (1980). *Internal World and External Reality*. New York: Jason Aronson.

Khan, M. M. R. (1974). *The Privacy of the Self*. New York: International Universities Press.

Klauber, J. (1976). Some little-discussed elements of the psychoanalytic relationship and their therapeutic implications. *International Review of Psycho-Analysis* 3:283–290.

—— (1983). The identity of the psychoanalyst. In *The Identity of the Psychoanalyst*, ed. E. D. Joseph and D. Widlocher, pp. 41–50. New York: International Universities Press.

Klein, H. R. (1965). *Psychoanalysts in Training: Selection and Evaluation*. New York: Columbia College of Physicians and Surgeons.

Kohut, H. (1971). *The Analysis of the Self*. New York: International Universities Press.

—— (1977). *The Restoration of the Self*. New York: International Universities Press.

Kohut, H., and Wolf, E. S. (1978). The disorders of the self and their treatment. *International Journal of Psycho-Analysis* 59:413–425.

Kottler, J. A. (1986). *On Being a Therapist*. San Francisco: Jossey-Bass.

Kramer, E. (1987). The analyst's resolution of revenge resulting from the treatment of his parents. *Modern Psychoanalysis* 12:207–219.

Lackie, B. (1983). The families of origin of social workers. *Clinical Social Work Journal* 11:309-322.

—— (1984). Learned responsibility and order of birth: a study of 1,577 social workers. *Smith College Studies in Social Work* 54:117-138.

Laing, R. D. (1960). *The Divided Self*. London: Tavistock Publications.

Lampl-de Groot, J. (1954). Problems of psycho-analytic training. *International Journal of Psycho-Analysis* 35:184-187.

—— (1976). Personal experience with the psychoanalytic technique and theory during the last half century. *Psychoanalytic Study of the Child* 31:283-296. New Haven: Yale University Press.

Langs, R. (1973). *The Technique of Psychoanalytic Psychotherapy*. Vol. 1. New York: Jason Aronson.

—— (1976). *The Bipersonal Field*. New York: Jason Aronson.

—— (1979). *The Supervisory Experience*. New York: Jason Aronson.

—— (1980). *Interactions: The Realm of Transference and Countertransference*. New York: Jason Aronson.

—— (1983). The interactional dimension of countertransference. In *Countertransference: The Therapist's Contribution to the Therapeutic Situation*, ed. L. Epstein and A. H. Feiner, pp. 71-104. New York: Jason Aronson.

Langs, R., and Searles, H. F. (1980). *Intrapsychic and Interpersonal Dimensions of Treatment: A Clinical Dialogue*. New York: Jason Aronson.

Laschet, U. (1973). Antiandrogen in the treatment of sex offenders: mode of action and therapeutic outcome. In *Contemporary Sexual Behavior: Critical Issues in the 1970s*, ed. J. Zubin and J. Money, pp. 297-318. Baltimore: Johns Hopkins University Press.

Lester, E. P. (1990). Gender and identity issues in the analytic process. *International Journal of Psycho-Analysis* 71:435-444.

Levenson, E. (1983). *The Ambiguity of Change*. New York: Basic Books.

Levine, S. P., Barzansky, B., and Blumberg, P. (1983). Can psychiatrists be recruited in medical school? *Journal of Psychiatric Education* 7:240-248.

Levinson, H. L. (1977). Termination of psychotherapy: some salient issues. *Social Casework* 58:480-489.

Levis, D. J., and Hare, N. (1977). A review of the theoretical rationale and empirical support for the extinction approach of implosive (flooding) therapy. In *Progress in Behavior Modification*, vol. 4, ed. M. Herson, R. M. Eisler, and P. M. Miller, pp. 300-376. New York: Academic Press.

Lewin, B. D. (1946). Counter-transference in the technique of medical practice. *Psychosomatic Medicine* 8:195-199.

Lewin, B. D., and Ross, H. (1960). *Psychoanalytic Education in the United States*. New York: Norton.

Lindner, H. (1978). Therapists and theories: I choose me. *Psychotherapy: Theory, Research, and Practice* 15:405–408.

Little, M. (1951). Countertransference and the patient's response to it. *International Journal of Psycho-Analysis* 32:32–40.

––––– (1981). *Transference Neurosis and Transference Psychosis*. New York: Jason Aronson.

Lommel, A. (1967). *Shamanism: The Beginnings of Art*. New York: McGraw-Hill.

Looney, J. G., Harding, R. K., Blotcky, M. J., and Barnhart, F. D. (1980). Psychiatrists' transition from training to career: stress and mastery. *American Journal of Psychiatry* 137:32–35.

Macaskill, N. D. (1988). Personal therapy in the training of the psychotherapist: is it effective? *British Journal of Psychotherapy* 4:219–226.

Maeder, T. (1989). *Children of Psychiatrists and Other Psychotherapists*. New York: Harper & Row.

Mahler, M., Pine, F., and Bergman, A. (1975). *The Psychological Birth of the Human Infant*. New York: Basic Books.

Main, T. F. (1957). The ailment. *British Journal of Medical Psychology* 30:425–431.

Malcolm, J. (1981). *Psychoanalysis: The Impossible Profession*. New York: Alfred Knopf.

Maltsberger, J. T., and Buie, D. H. (1974). Countertransference hate in the treatment of suicidal patients. *Archives of General Psychiatry* 30:625–633.

Marks, M. J. (1978). Conscious/unconscious selection of the psychotherapist's theoretical orientation. *Psychotherapy: Theory, Research, and Practice* 15:354–358.

Marmor, J. (1953). The feeling of superiority: an occupational hazard in the practice of psychotherapy. *American Journal of Psychiatry* 110:370–376.

––––– (1972). Sexual acting-out in psychotherapy. *American Journal of Psychoanalysis* 32:3–8.

––––– (1976). Some psychodynamic aspects of the seduction of patients in psychotherapy. *American Journal of Psychoanalysis* 36:319–323.

Maroda, K. J. (1991). *The Power of Countertransference*. New York: Wiley & Sons.

Marsh, S. R. (1988). Antecedents to choice of a helping career: social work vs. business majors. *Smith College Studies in Social Work* 58:85–100.

Marston, A. R. (1984). What makes therapists run? A model for analysis of motivational styles. *Psychotherapy* 21:456–459.

Martin, E. S., and Schurtman, R. (1985). Termination anxiety as it affects the therapist. *Psychotherapy* 22:92–96.

Masters, W. H., and Johnson, V. E. (1970). *Human Sexual Inadequacy.* Boston: Little, Brown.

McCartney, J. I. (1966). Overt transference. *Journal of Sex Research* 2:227–237.

McLaughlin, J. T. (1961). The analyst and the Hippocratic Oath. *Journal of the American Psychoanalytic Association* 9:106–123.

―――― (1981). Transference, psychic reality, and countertransference. *Psychoanalytic Quarterly* 50:639–664.

McWilliams, N. (1987). The grandiose self and the interminable analysis. *Current Issues in Psychoanalytic Practice* 4:93–107.

Meares, R. A., and Hobson, R. F. (1977). The persecutory therapist. *British Journal of Medical Psychology* 50:349–359.

Meier, C. A. (1967). *Ancient Incubation and Modern Psychotherapy.* Evanston, IL: Northwestern University Press.

Menninger, K. (1957a). Psychological factors in the choice of medicine as a profession. *Bulletin of the Menninger Clinic* 21:51–58.

―――― (1957b). Psychological factors in the choice of medicine as a profession, II. *Bulletin of the Menninger Clinic* 21:99–106.

Miller, A. (1981). *The Drama of the Gifted Child.* New York: Basic Books.

Milner, M. (1950). A note on the ending of an analysis. *International Journal of Psycho-Analysis* 31:191–193.

Milrod, D. (1982). The wished-for self image. *Psychoanalytic Study of the Child* 37:95–120. New Haven: Yale University Press.

Mintz, E. (1969). Time-extended marathon groups. *Psychotherapy: Theory, Research, and Practice* 6:232–234.

Money-Kyrle, R. E. (1959). Normal countertransference and some of its deviations. *International Journal of Psycho-Analysis* 37:360–366.

Moore, A. C. (1982). Well-being and the woman psychiatrist. *Journal of Psychiatric Treatment and Evaluation* 4:437–439.

Moore, B. E., and Fine, B. D., eds. (1968). *A Glossary of Psychoanalytic Terms and Concepts.* 2nd ed. New York: The American Psychoanalytic Association.

Morse, J. J., and Young, D. F. (1973). Personality development and task choices: a systems view. *Human Relations* 26:307–324.

Moyer, K. E. (1971). The physiology of aggression and the implications for aggression control. In *Control of Aggression and Violence: Cognitive and Physiological Factors,* ed. J. L. Singer, pp. 61–92. New York: Academic Press.

Mullan, H., and Sangiuliano, I. (1964). *The Therapist's Contribution to the Treatment Process.* Springfield, IL: Charles C Thomas.

Nachman, B. (1960). Childhood experience and vocational choice in law, dentistry and social work. *Journal of Counseling Psychology* 7:243–250.

Namnum, A. (1980). Trends in the selection of candidates for psychoanalytic training. *Journal of the American Psychoanalytic Association* 28:419–438.

Natterson, J. (1991). *Beyond Countertransference*. Northvale, NJ: Jason Aronson.

Nemiah, J. C. (1961). *Foundations of Psychopathology*. New York: Oxford University Press.

Nielson, N. (1954). The dynamics of the training analysis. *International Journal of Psycho-Analysis* 35:247–249.

Norcross, J. C., and Prochaska, J. O. (1986). Psychotherapist heal thyself—I: The psychological distress and self-change of psychologists, counselors, and laypersons. *Psychotherapy* 23:102–114.

Norcross, J. C., Strausser-Kirtland, D., and Missar, D. C. (1988). The process and outcome of psychotherapists' personal treatment experiences. *Psychotherapy* 25:36–43.

Norwood, R. (1985). *Women Who Love Too Much*. New York: Simon and Schuster.

Nunberg, H. (1938). Psychological interrelations between physician and patient. *Psychoanalytic Review* 25:297–308.

Olinick, S. L. (1980). *The Psychotherapeutic Instrument*. New York: Jason Aronson.

Pardell, S. S. (1950). Psychology of the hypnotist. *Psychiatric Quarterly* 24:483–491.

Pederson, F. A., and Bell, R. Q. (1970). Sex differences in preschool children without histories of complications of pregnancy and delivery. *Developmental Psychology* 3:10–15.

Perlman, G. (1972). Change in self and ideal self-concept congruence of beginning psychotherapists. *Journal of Clinical Psychology* 28:404–408.

Pfifferling, J. H. (1986). Cultural antecedents promoting professional impairment. In *Heal Thyself: The Health of Health Care Professionals*, ed. C. D. Scott and J. Hawk, pp. 3–18. New York: Brunner/Mazel.

Poal, P., and Weisz, J. R. (1989). Therapists' own childhood problems as predictors of their effectiveness in child psychotherapy. *Journal of Clinical Child Psychology* 18:202–205.

Pollak, O. (1976). *Human Behavior and the Helping Professions*. New York: Spectrum.

Pope, K. S. (1989). Therapist–patient sex syndrome: a guide for attorneys and subsequent therapists to assessing damage. In *Sexual Exploitation in Professional Relationships*, ed. G. O. Gabbard, pp. 39–55. Washington, DC: American Psychiatric Press.

——— (1990). Therapist–patient sex as sex abuse: six scientific, professional, and practical dilemmas in addressing victimization and rehabilitation. *Professional Psychology: Research and Practice* 21:227–239.

Pope, K. S., Keith-Spiegel, P., and Tabachnick, B. G. (1986). Sexual attraction to clients: the human therapist and the (sometimes) inhuman training system. *American Psychologist* 41:147–158.

Pope, K. S., Levenson, H., and Schover, L. (1979). Sexual intimacy between patients and psychotherapists. *American Psychologist* 34:682–689.

Pope, K. S., Tabachnick, B. G., and Keith-Spiegel, P. (1987). Ethics of practice: the beliefs and behaviors of psychologists as therapists. *American Psychologist* 42:993–1006.

Prochaska, J. O., and Norcross, J. C. (1983). Contemporary psychotherapists: a national survey of characteristics, practices, orientations, and attitudes. *Psychotherapy: Theory, Research, & Practice* 20:161–173.

Racker, H. (1953a). A contribution to the problem of countertransference. *International Journal of Psycho-Analysis* 34:313–324.

——— (1953b). The meaning and uses of countertransference. *Psychoanalytic Quarterly* 26:303–357.

——— (1958). Psychoanalytic technique and the analyst's unconscious masochism. *Psychoanalytic Quarterly* 27:555–562.

——— (1968). *Transference and Countertransference*. London: Hogarth Press.

Racusin, G. R., Abramowitz, S. I., and Winter, W. D. (1981). Becoming a therapist: family dynamics and career choice. *Professional Psychology* 12:271–279.

Reich, G. V. (1984). The family of origin's influence on the professional activities of counselors and therapists. *Praxis der Kinderpsychologie und Kinderpsychiatrie* 33:61–69.

Reid, K. E. (1977). Nonrational dynamics of the client–worker interaction. *Social Casework* 58:600–606.

Reik, T. (1948). *Listening with the Third Ear*. New York: Farrar, Straus and Co.

Rich, C. L., and Pitts, F. N. (1980). Suicide by psychiatrists: a study of medical specialists among 18,730 consecutive physician deaths during a 5-year period, 1967–72. *Journal of Clinical Psychiatry* 41:261–263.

Riemann, F. (1968). The personality structure of the analyst and its influence on the course of treatment. *American Journal of Psychoanalysis* 28:69–79.

Robertiello, R. C. (1986). *A Psychoanalyst's Quest*. New York: St. Martin's/ Marek.

Roe, A. (1956). *The Psychology of Occupations*. New York: Wiley & Sons.

Roe, A., and Siegleman, M. (1964). *The Origins of Interests*. Washington, DC: American Personnel and Guidance Association.

Roeske, N. C. (1986). Risk factors: predictable hazards of a health care career. In *Heal Thyself: The Health of Health Care Professionals*, ed. C. D. Scott and J. Hawk, pp. 56–70. New York: Brunner/Mazel.

Rogers, C. (1951). *Client-Centered Therapy*. Boston: Houghton Mifflin.

Rogow, A. A. (1970). *The Psychiatrists*. New York: G. P. Putnam's Sons.

Rosenbaum, M. (1963). Psychological effects on the child raised by an older sibling. *American Journal of Orthopsychiatry* 33:515–520.

Roth, S. (1987). *Psychotherapy: The Art of Wooing Nature*. Northvale, NJ: Jason Aronson.

Ruderman, E. B. (1986). Gender-related themes of women psychotherapists in their treatment of women patients: the creative and separative use of countertransference as a mutual growth experience. *Clinical Social Work Journal* 14:103–126.

Russell, A. T., Pasnau, R. O., and Taintor, Z. C. (1975). Emotional problems of residents in psychiatry. *American Journal of Psychiatry* 132:263–267.

Sachs, H. (1947). Observations of a training analyst. *Psychoanalytic Quarterly* 16:157–169.

Salzman, L. (1968). *The Obsessive Personality*. New York: Jason Aronson.

Saul, L. J. (1962). The erotic transference. *Psychoanalytic Quarterly* 31:54–61.

Schachtel, Z. (1986). The "impossible profession" considered from a gender perspective. In *Psychoanalysis and Women: Contemporary Reappraisals*, ed. J. L. Alpert, pp. 237–255. Hillsdale, NJ: Analytic Press.

Schafer, R. (1954). *Psychoanalytic Interpretation in Rorschach Testing*. New York: Grune & Stratton.

——— (1983). *The Analytic Attitude*. New York: Basic Books.

Schechter, N. (1978). Therapist typologies and their developmental and motivational correlates. *Dissertation Abstracts International* 39:3006.

Schwing, G. (1954). *A Way to the Soul of the Mentally Ill*. New York: International Universities Press.

Searles, H. F. (1959). The effort to drive the other person crazy: an element in the other aetiology and psychotherapy of schizophrenia. *British Journal of Medical Psychology* 32:1–18.

——— (1965). *Collected Papers on Schizophrenia*. New York: International Universities Press.

——— (1966). Feelings of guilt in the psychoanalyst. *Psychiatry* 29:319–323.

——— (1967). The "dedicated physician" in the field of psychotherapy and psychoanalysis. In *Countertransference and Related Subjects*, ed. H. F. Searles, pp. 71–88. New York: International Universities Press, 1979.

—— (1979). *Countertransference and Related Subjects*. New York: International Universities Press.

Segal, H. (1981). *The Work of Hanna Segal: A Kleinian Approach to Clinical Practice*. New York: Jason Aronson.

Segal, S. J. (1961). A psychoanalytic analysis of personality factors in vocational choice. *Journal of Counseling Psychology* 8:202–210.

Serban, G. (1981). Sexual activity in therapy: legal and ethical issues. *American Journal of Psychotherapy* 35:76–85.

Shapiro, D. (1976). The analyst's own analysis. *Journal of the American Psychoanalytic Association* 24:5–42.

Shapiro, E. R. (1982–1983). The holding environment and family therapy with acting out adolescents. *International Journal of Psychoanalytic Psychotherapy* 9:227–231.

Sharaf, M. R., and Levinson, D. J. (1964). The quest for omnipotence in professional training. *Psychiatry* 27:135–149.

Sharpe, E. F. (1930). The technique of psycho-analysis. In *Collected Papers on Psycho-Analysis*, ed. E. F. Sharpe, pp. 9–106. London: Hogarth Press, 1950.

—— (1947). The psychoanalyst. *International Journal of Psycho-Analysis* 28:1–6.

Shepard, M. (1971). *The Love Treatment: Sexual Intimacy Between Patients and Psychotherapists*. New York: Wyden.

Shepard, M., and Lee, M. (1970). *Games Analysts Play*. New York: G. P. Putnam's Sons.

Simmel, E. (1926). The "doctor-game," illness and the profession of medicine. *International Journal of Psycho-Analysis* 7:470–481.

Simon, R. I. (1989). Sexual exploitation of patients: how it begins before it happens. *Psychiatric Annals* 19:104–112.

Singer, E. (1971). The patient aids the analyst: some clinical and theoretical observations. In *In the Name of Life: Essays in Honor of Erich Fromm*, ed. B. Landis and E. S. Tauber, pp. 56–68. New York: Holt, Rinehart, & Winston.

Slocum, S. (1975). Woman the gatherer: male bias in anthropology. In *Toward an Anthropology of Women*, ed. R. R. Reiter, pp. 36–50. New York: Monthly Review Press.

Smith, S. (1984). The sexually abused patient and the abusing therapist. *Psychoanalytic Psychology* 1:89–98.

—— (1989). The seduction of the female patient. In *Sexual Exploitation in Professional Relationships*, ed. G. O. Gabbard, pp. 57–69. Washington, DC: American Psychiatric Press.

Sonne, J., Meyer, C. B., Borys, D., et al. (1985). Clients' reactions to sexual intimacy in therapy. *American Journal of Orthopsychiatry* 55:183–189.

Steppacher, R. C., and Mausner, J. S. (1973). Suicide in professionals: a study of male and female psychologists. *American Journal of Epidemiology* 98:436–445.

Stierlin, H. (1972). Self-actualization and philosophical awareness. In *Twelve Therapists*, ed. A. Burton, pp. 127–142. San Francisco: Jossey-Bass.

Stolorow, R. D. (1986). Critical reflections on the theory of self psychology: an inside view. *Psychoanalytic Inquiry* 6:387–402.

Stolorow, R. D., and Atwood, G. E. (1979). *Faces in a Cloud: Subjectivity in Personality Theory*. New York: Jason Aronson.

Stone, A. A. (1976). The legal implications of sexual activity between psychiatrist and patient. *American Journal of Psychiatry* 133:1138–1141.

—— (1984). *Law, Psychiatry, and Morality: Essays and Analysis*. Washington, DC: American Psychiatric Press.

Stone, L. (1961). *The Psychoanalytic Situation*. New York: International Universities Press.

Storr, A. (1980). *The Art of Psychotherapy*. New York: Methuen.

Strean, H. S. (1988). *Behind the Couch: Revelations of a Psychoanalyst*. New York: Wiley.

Strupp, H. H. (1958). The psychotherapist's contribution to the treatment process. *Behavioral Science* 3:34–67.

—— (1959). Toward an analysis of the therapist's contribution to the treatment process. *Psychiatry* 22:349–362.

Sussman, M. B. (1987). *Unconscious motivations for becoming a psychotherapist*. Unpublished doctoral dissertation. Philadelphia: Hahnemann University.

Suzuki, R. (1989). Adolescents drop out from individual psychotherapy—is it true? *Journal of Adolescence* 12:197–205.

Szasz, T. S. (1956). On the experiences of the analyst in the psychoanalytic situation. *Journal of the American Psychoanalytic Association* 4:197–223.

Tarachow, S. (1962). Interpretation and reality in psychotherapy. *International Journal of Psycho-Analysis* 43:377–387.

Teitlebaum, S. H. (1990). Supertransference: the role of the supervisor's blind spots. *Psychoanalytic Psychology* 7:243–258.

Templer, D. I. (1971). Analyzing the psychotherapist. *Mental Hygiene* 55:234–236.

Tiger, L., and Fox, R. (1971). *The Imperial Animal.* New York: Holt, Rinehart, and Winston.

Tower, L. (1956). Countertransference. *Journal of the American Psychoanalytic Association* 4:256–265.

Twemlow, S. W., and Gabbard, G. O. (1989). The lovesick therapist. In *Sexual Exploitation in Professional Relationships*, ed. G. O. Gabbard, pp. 71–87. Washington, DC: American Psychiatric Press.

Usandivaras, R. J. (1982). Iatrogenicity in psychoanalytic psychotherapy. *Revista de Psicoanalisis* 39:695–706.

Vaillant, G. E., Sobowale, N. C., and McArthur, C. (1972). Some psychological vulnerabilities of physicians. *New England Journal of Medicine* 287:372–375.

Valenstein, A. F. (1980). The concept of "classical" psychoanalysis. In *Psychoanalytic Explorations of Technique*, ed. H. P. Blum, pp. 113–136. New York: International Universities Press.

Van Raalte, P. (1984). *The impact of death of the psychoanalyst on the patient.* Unpublished doctoral dissertation. New Brunswick, NJ: Rutgers University.

Walfish, S., Polifka, J. A., and Stenmark, D. E. (1985). Career satisfaction in clinical psychology: a survey of recent graduates. *Professional Psychology: Research & Practice* 16:576–580.

Walker, E., and Young, P. D. (1986). *A Killing Cure.* New York: Holt, Rinehart, & Winston.

Wallerstein, R. S. (1983). Reflections. In *The Identity of the Psychoanalyst*, ed. E. D. Joseph and D. Widlocher, pp. 265–276. New York: International Universities Press.

Washburn, S., and Lancaster, C. (1968). The evolution of hunting. In *Man the Hunter*, ed. R. B. Lee and I. DeVore, pp. 293–303. Chicago: Aldine.

Weddington, W. W., and Cavenar, J. O. (1979). Termination initiated by the therapist: a countertransference storm. *American Journal of Psychiatry* 136:1302–1305.

Weigert, E. (1954). Counter-transference and self analysis of the psychoanalyst. *International Journal of Psycho-Analysis* 35:242–246.

Weinberg, G. (1984). *The Heart of Psychotherapy.* New York: St. Martin's Press.

Wheelis, A. (1959). The vocational hazards of psychoanalysis. *International Journal of Psycho-Analysis* 37:171–184.

—— (1987). *The Doctor of Desire.* New York: W. W. Norton.

Whitaker, C. A., and Malone, T. P. (1953). *The Roots of Psychotherapy*. New York: Brunner/Mazel.

Whitman, R. M., and Bloch, E. L. (1990). Therapist envy. *Bulletin of the Menninger Clinic* 54:478–487.

Willi, J. (1983). Higher incidence of physical and mental ailments in future psychiatrists as compared with future surgeons and internal medical specialists at military conscription. *Social Psychiatry* 16:305–315.

Williams, J. (1977). *Psychology of Women*. New York: W. W. Norton.

Winnicott, D. W. (1949). Hate in the counter-transference. *International Journal of Psycho-Analysis* 30:69–74.

—— (1965). *The Maturational Processes and the Facilitating Environment*. London: Hogarth Press.

—— (1986). *Home Is Where We Start From*. New York: W. W. Norton.

Wishnie, H. (1977). *The Impulsive Personality*. New York: Plenum.

Wohlberg, J. (1990). *The psychology of therapist sexual misconduct: a victim's perspective*. Paper presented at scientific meeting on psychological aspects of therapist sexual abuse, Boston Psychoanalytic Institute, February.

Wolstein, B. (1959). *Countertransference*. London: Grune & Stratton.

Wood, B., Klein, S., Cross, H. J., et al. (1985). Impaired practitioners: psychologists' opinions about prevalence, and proposals for intervention. *Professional Psychology: Research & Practice* 16:843–850.

Wylie, M. S. (1989). The mother knot. *Networker*, Sept./Oct., pp. 43–51.

Yalom, I. D. (1989). *Love's Executioner*. New York: Basic Books.

Yulis, S. A., and Kiesler, D. J. (1968). Countertransference response as a function of the therapist anxiety and content of patient talk. *Journal of Consulting and Clinical Psychology* 32:413–419.

Zabarenko, R. N., Zabarenko, L., and Pittenger, R. A. (1970). The psychodynamics of physicianhood. *Psychiatry* 33:102–118.

Zetzel, E. R. (1956). Current concepts of transference. *International Journal of Psycho-Analysis* 37:369–376.

INDEX

Ackerman, N. W.
  on masochistic tendencies, 89
  on trainees, selection of, 249
Adler, G.
  on idealized selfobject, use of, 102
  on inferiority complex, 6
  on overzealousness, 171–172
  on sibling rivalry, 6
Aggression
  definition of, 51
  expressions of
    Aversion Therapy and, 79
    Bioenergetics Therapy and, 79
    Bucher and Lovaas on, 79
    Bugental on, 79, 82
    Elliott on, 82n
    Feldman on, 79
    Freud on, 77
    Glover on, 79, 81
    Greenson on, 78
    Guggenbuhl-Craig on, 81
    Guy on, 80
    Hammer on, 80
    Jaffe on, 78
    Klauber on, 82
    Langs and Searles on, 82n
    Levis and Hare on, 79
    Main on, 80–81

Primal Therapy and, 79
    Rolfing, 79
    sadistic therapist and, 81
    Searles on, 80, 82n
    Tarachow on, 77–78
    Whitman and Bloch on, 82
  reaction formation against
    Beattie on, 74
    definition of, 73
    Frederickson on, 74
    Henry on, 74
    Maltsberger and Buie on, 76
    Menninger on, 73
    Reich on, 74
    Rosenbaum on, 73–74
    Schafer on, 74
    Searles on, 77
    Winnicott on, 74
  testosterone levels, 89
Aggressive impulses, burnout and, 247
Aggressive strivings
  Berger on, 71–72
  Greenson on, 72–73
  human work and, 72
  hunting and, 71n
  Menninger on, 72
  sadomasochism and, 72–73
  Simmel on, 72